UNDEFEATED
SCORED ON ONCE

ATTY. ALFRED CATALFO, JR.

DEDICATION

GAIL (VARNEY) CATALFO

This book is dedicated to my fabulous, talented, devoted wife, Gail. We met in April of 1971, were engaged in 1977, and married in 1988. I have been in love with her from day one. We have spent forty three years together.

To my three wonderful children who became two lawyers and a college professor. My four grandchildren. Jay and Donna, their full names have been excluded to protect their privacy. My deepest love to all of them.

The Author

Forward

In the face of impossible odds, I was born into poverty. My parents were without an education and did not have any special trade. I was condemned from the moment I took my first breath to live a life of a common laborer or even worse.

As a first generation Italian and being the oldest of six living children, the only language we spoke at home was Italian. This handicapped us with speaking the English language. We learned street English and very little in grammar school. My parents worked long hours in the cotton factory and earned very little money.

We lived among Italian families who spoke Italian. My last year in grammar school was in a French-Canadian Catholic School where we learned even less English during the year. I graduated from Ecole St. Joseph in 1932 and shortly after I got a job on the second shift in a cotton factory, the Pacific Mills in Dover, New Hampshire. I earned $14.40 a week. I gave my father all of my pay except forty cents. A year later I was allowed to keep a dollar and a half a week. At the time I was told it was my duty to help support La Familia and I believed it.

As I grew older I entertained ambitions of going to high school, to college, to law school and becoming a lawyer. When I talked about my plan I was made fun of by many. At the time, I spoke broken English. I also was without support of this ambition from my parents.

I was surrounded by people who discouraged or attempted to discourage me from attempting that road. Some would ask me, "Do you realize how old you will be when you graduate from high school?" My answer was, "Of course, I will be 23 ½ years old." I would pause and then add, "You know I am going to be 23 ½ years old in 4 years, with or without a high school education."

In the late spring of 1936, I joined the military then known as the Civilian Military Training Program. I was so limited in English that I had some young lady working in the First Aid Medical station in the mill help me in filling my application. I believe she was the only person in the mill with a high school education.

I enjoyed serving in the military at Fort McKinley in Portland, Maine that summer and when I returned home I matriculated Berwick Academy at South Berwick, Maine. I had no intention of going back to work. I was greeted with hostility at home. I did not expect such a negative response. It was not my responsibility to support my father's and mother's family.

In a short while I learned to speak English better than most of my classmates. I learned every word in the Webster Dictionary. I was elected as editor in chief of our class paper, "The Tattler" and later editor in chief of the school paper, "The Academy Quill" and I also made the debating team as well.

Upon graduation I had scholarships in six separate colleges, but I went to the University of Alabama. The next year I transferred to the University of New Hampshire and then Pearl Harbor was attacked. My two brothers and I joined the Navy.

I was badly injured when our plane, on takeoff, suffered engine failure and crashed I ended up being hospitalized for 9 months in an arm and body cast with a broken back, broken left upper arm in three places, a cornea cut of my right eye and a damaged hip.

And that is just the beginning of this autobiography. I graduated from college and from law school and became a lawyer – a good lawyer.

One of the nicest things that was said of me as a lawyer was by Fred "Fritz" Wetherbee on February 2006, he sent me a copy of a book he wrote and delivered to me by my son and wrote the following:

"To Freddie – the best damned lawyer the State of New Hampshire ever had."

Enjoy this autobiography, I am sure you will find it interesting.

Enjoy life
Fred Catalfo

CONTENTS

Dedication..i

Forward..ii

Chapter 1:   No Way Out.......................................1

Chapter 2:   My Story Begins...............................5

Chapter 3:   The Ugly Years................................37

Chapter 4:   Berwick Academy............................49

Chapter 5:   A Dream Comes True-College.............73

Chapter 6:   The War Comes Home.....................89

Chapter 7:   The End of a Goal - Now What?..........111

Chapter 8:   The Beginning of a New Life...............129

Chapter 9:   A Dream Come True.........................145

Chapter 10:   Me - Attorney at Law........................155

Chapter 11:   Success...189

Chapter 12:   A New Generation...........................217

Chapter 13:   Life, Politics and JFK......................235

Chapter 14:   Changes...259

Chapter 15:   Gone..279

Chapter 16:   Love Returns...................................309

Chapter 17:   My Philosohy..................................317

Acknowledgements..327

Chapter 1:

No Way Out

Imagine spending your entire life being told that you were nothing. That your life was destined to be no more than a series of endless days spent toiling at a dead end job that you hated with every breath that you took.

A job where there was no way out.

Imagine living in the land of your birth and yet not speaking the language. Being thought a foreigner on your own home soil and being ridiculed for the tongue you were taught from the cradle.

Imagine, my friends, that you had no future.

This is the life that I faced from the moment I took my first breath. My parents, God rest their souls, had my entire future planned for me right down to the type of girl that I would marry and the second that I would work my first shift at the factory.

But I can't blame them. Some might, you might even, but I do not.

Why?

Because they were doing what they felt was right. In their eyes, you worked hard and you lived. This was what life was about, and it was enough for them. They did not understand why it might not be enough for their children. Part of it was an aversion to change, and part was simply their inability to see that someone might want, and even strive for a life different from the one they had been given.

This, however, is a truth they should have understood better then most. For they were the ones who had chosen to leave behind their homeland, their families and their entire lives to move to America. To literally turn their backs on everything they had ever known to grasp at the straws of a better life.

In Italy, my parents were landowners. They had their little home and their acreage given to them upon their marriage. In America, they were nothing. Yet they fought and clawed their way up the ladder until they found their footing and created a new life.

I only wanted the same for myself. I wanted the chance to build my life on *my* terms and to create the life that I dreamed of.

I wanted to be a lawyer.

It was a desire that began to burn in my heart from a very young age. These were the men who lived life on their own terms. Who fought for what was right and stood for those who were unable to stand for themselves.

They stood for people like my mother.

My mother who faced criminal charges for selling alcohol in brown paper bags as a way to scrape together enough money to put food on the table.

Standing in that courtroom I knew right then and there that this was what my life was meant to be. In my mind, being a lawyer was a gateway to a better life. It was the bridge between who I was, and the person that I wanted to be.

Growing up, we had nothing. We lived hand to mouth, and sometimes we did not even manage to do that. And when you grow up with nothing, you notice quickly that not everyone lives as you do.

For as long as I can remember I was aware that some of my friends and schoolmates enjoyed a higher standard of living than what my parents provided for my siblings and myself. They dressed better, they spoke better, and they did not have that hungry look in their eye on any given day. In short, they lived better.

What I wanted to know......was why?

I mean, I could quickly tell that these children were not smarter than I was. They did not hold some significant and mysterious mental advantage over me. I noticed that they could speak English better than I could, but then I could speak Italian better than they could.

The real difference, as I soon came to understand, was in our parents. My parents spoke no English and they were very limited in what they could do for us as a family. Remember, I do not blame my parents for this. Right, wrong or indifferent, this was our reality, and I was not willing to wait on them or someone else to waltz in and change it.

I knew then and I know now that if I wanted a better life, then it would be up to me to build it for myself.

The path was clear. If I wanted to be a lawyer, then I would need an education. Four years of high school, four years of college, and three years of law school before I could even sit for the bar exam.

I shared my dream and everyone laughed. Here I was, this almost 20 year old first generation immigrant who could barely speak English saying that not only do I want to go to high school, but I want to go even further and get an advanced law degree.

I can still hear them now.

"Do you know how old you will be when you finish? IF you finish? Look at all the time you will have wasted!"

Yes, I would think. I will be 11 years older. But you know what? School or no school, I will still be 11 years older when that day comes and look at all the time I will have wasted if I do not go.

I was not afraid of my path. In fact, that was one thing that I had on my side from day one. I was never afraid. If anything, the only fear that I held in my heart was of being forced to live a life that I hated, one that was chosen for me rather than by me. This was the reality that drove me to work harder with each passing day.

My path was not an easy one, but then the most worthwhile things in life rarely are. The point was that it was my life, and therefore, come hell or high water; *it was going to be my choice.*

Chapter 2:

My Story Begins

My Story Begins....

My story begins. Those are powerful words, words that have meaning. Especially to the person charged with the telling of the tale. But the questions always begs.....where do I begin?

Do I begin by telling you that I am a first generation American? That my parents immigrated here from Sicily, Italy as lawful immigrants and that I spent my formative years in Rollinsford, New Hampshire?

Well, that may be going a bit too far back.

So in my case I think that we will start at the beginning. The very beginning. My story begins on in Lawrence, Massachusetts on January 31st, 1917. It begins here, because this is the day that I was born.

It was on this day that I was condemned from the moment I took my first breath to live the life of a common laborer or worse. No matter how you looked at it, odds were stacked against me. In fact, they were practically impossible. My parents had no formal education, they were not acquainted with any special skill or trade, and we lived our lives day by day in extreme poverty.

Curious about what led them to this point? I thought you might be.

My parents grew up in Biancavilla, Sicily, a beautiful city seeped in both culture and family history. When I was smaller, I can remember asking my father about how he met my mother and those bright early days of their courtship.

My father told me that he saw his future wife coming out of a Sunday morning Catholic Mass at the Church of Santa Maria di Elemosina. It was love at first sight. As she walked down the stairs with her father and stepmother, she looked to him like a beautiful angel. And, she would always say that he appeared courageous, adventurous and handsome. She was only 18 years old at the time.

My father? He was 25!

Over the next several months their attraction for each other grew through tentative glances and distant signals. And during that time, my father did not miss a single Sunday Mass at the Church of Santa di Elemozia! Soon, my father began to inquire as to who she was and where she lived. The next step was to make his intentions known to both his parents and hers.

Now, keep in mind that we are talking about a courtship that happened roughly 100 years ago in Italy. Things were different then. Softer, slower in some ways. My parents did not "date" as a young couple would today. Not even close! Once their families met and brought about La Familia, approval and preparation of a marriage, they were allowed to spend time together at family gatherings, but were never alone.

But that does not mean that their love did not begin to blossom and thrive during this time.

My father often told the story of the night before their wedding. He wanted to do something special for my mother. Something that would prove his love for her and make her anticipate their wedding day. So he hired the services of a six-piece string musical group. The musicians serenaded my mother for hours from below her bedroom window. The music filled the warm sultry evening with familiar Italian love melodies, favorites of both of my parents, and was truly a romantic gesture that lived with them the rest of their lives. My father's favorite part of the tale was sharing with us that my mother had danced in her bed for as long as the music continued to play.

The following day my parents were wed at the Church of Santa Maria di Elemozina, the largest of the 20 Catholic churches in Biancavilla. The reception that followed was an affair to remember that lasted well into the night. It was a colorful affair attended by members of both families and friends with plenty of food and sweets, wine and music. The date was June 28th, 1912.

In those days when a woman entered Holy Matrimony, she did so with a dowry. In my mother's case, this consisted of a five-acre piece of property some three miles outside the village of Biancavilla, which was affectionately called "chiusopera" or pear enclosure. Four high walls composed of lava rock deposits from Mount Etna surround land rich with groves of almond, olive, orange and lemon trees as well as grape vines, wheat and other produce. There was also a five-room home included in the dowry located as Via Pinpo in Biancavilla.

This marriage marked the first steps of an adventure into life. Two fiercely romantic, devout Catholics; two beautiful youthful Italians ready to enjoy their love for each other and to confront the challenges ahead.

Sounds fantastically romantic doesn't it? Two star-crossed lovers joining their lives together as they scrape out their own piece of history on 5 beautiful acres of the Italian countryside? But you know that there has to be more to it than that. After all, if there wasn't, I would not be a first generation immigrant, and the bulk of this story would take place in Italy rather than New Hampshire.

The first real turning point in this story happened when my father's best friend, Placido Bonomo, talked him into immigrating to America not long after he and my mother had been married.

Why, you ask?

Well the answer is both fantastically complicated and amazingly simple all at the same time. First, you have to understand that my father suffered no political oppression and did not entertain any political agenda. He was already a free man. But the problem was that he was a peasant. And as a peasant, even a land owning peasant, there was no future for him in Italy. There truly was no other place for him to go, and no other way for him to live his life. In his mind, his only choice was to pick up his family and immigrate to either Argentina or America.

So he did.

In the spring of 1914, my parents, their young son and their friends, the Bonomos, made the decision to immigrate to America. This was not an easy task, and was much easier said than done for several reasons. First, the Italian government campaigned to discourage immigration. Additionally, it was necessary to go through miles of Italian bureaucratic red tape. They needed to obtain a permit to leave the country called "nulla ostra", which required them to travel to Catania. They had to have a police clearance, a certificate that their military obligation had been completed or excused, and school records, as well as birth and health certificates. Just obtaining all of this complex documentation was a difficult task for uneducated peasants such as my parents. Much less the courage that it took to leave "La familia" and their way of life to start a new life in a strange and foreign land.

On July 12, 1914, my father, Alfio, my mother, Vincenza, and their 10 month old son, Guiseppe embarked on their long journey to America. To mark the beginning of their passage, a special Catholic Mass was given specifically for my parents in order to ask God to watch over them and see them safely to their new home. Looking back on this turbulent time, I can't even imagine the emotions my parents must have faced. To leave everything that they had ever known behind them and step into an unknown future took a strength that I admire to this day.

Their goodbye could not have been an easy one. Tears would have flowed like rain as they hugged loved ones closely, many for the last and final time as they said their goodbyes.

On that day they left Biancavilla, and on that day they forever changed the course of their lives.

Two weeks later on July 27, 1914, the SS Santa Anna sailed through the narrow straits between Brooklyn and Staten Island after a dreadful two-week journey. As the frightened passengers crowded the decks, each straining for their first glimpse of their new home, they were greeted by Lady Liberty herself, and finally "L' America!"

Now, in today's world there are many paths that a new immigrant can take into the United States, and most of them end in the form of airport customs of some sort.

I can promise you that this was not the case in 1914. In those days there was a single main route into the country and it took you to Ellis Island. History books show Ellis Island as the gateway to the new world, my parents spoke of it as a torture chamber.

Each passenger was forced to wait in endless lines to be examined by uniformed officers. They were subjected to a rigid physical examination and eye examination that in today's world would be considered inhumane as they were separated and fenced like cattle. Men, Women and Children were checked for any sign of cough, slowness of speech, limp or any other visible limitation that could cause the immigrant to be rejected and sent back to their home country. How those officers failed to notice my sick brother is difficult for me to understand.

Now that they had finally reached their destination, it was time for my mother and father to begin their new life. This meant first finding shelter. Shelter that they could both afford and that offered them a small taste of the home they had left behind.

My father and my mother took up residence in the Italian quarters and occupied an apartment at 38 Common Street in Lawrence, Massachusetts. My father started to work in the Pacific Mills located along the Merrimac River getting paid just $1.00 a day for 12 hours of work.

Even though life was hard, my parents were hopeful. They felt that America held new promise for them that could not be found in Italy. It was this hope, and their unwavering faith, that helped them to stand strong through the first of many tragedies that marked their young lives.

Tragedy struck on September 10, 1914, when my brother, Guiseppe Catalfo, died from pulmonary tuberculosis at just two days short of his first birthday. He had been in L'America for only one and one-half months. As I sit here now, later in my life with children of my own, it is hard for me to even imagine how my parents found the strength to move forward. Losing a child is every parent's worst fear, and a loss that I do not believe could ever truly be overcome.

But life continues on, and time, as always moves forward. Therefore it is somewhat fitting that shortly after this traumatic event, my parents were encouraged to obtain employment at the Salmon Falls Manufacturing Company in Rollinsford, New Hampshire. At this time, many Italian immigrants found employment here and lived in the village.

While in Rollinsford, New Hampshire, my second brother was born on July 7, 1915. He was also named Guiseppe (Joseph) Catalfo and died of pneumonia in Rollinsford on March 9, 1916 at the age of eight months. After the death of their second son, my parents left Rollinsford and returned to Lawrence, Massachusetts to work in the Pacific Mills.

Their new apartment was a small, dingy, dark apartment on the second floor at 43 Essex Street, Lawrence, Massachusetts, located directly above a Chinese laundry and about 100 yards from the Holy Rosary Catholic Church. At this point in their lives, my parents were factory workers. They were immigrants who worked hard, yet had very little money to show for it. This meant that when I was born there was no money for a doctor, and my mother had to settle for a home birth assisted by a midwife. An Italian midwife with no formal education and whose only credentials were the nurses uniform that she wore. I still wonder how I managed to survive my birth.

January 31st, 1917. We are back to the beginning again. Only this time you know how we got there and you also know that it was by luck and the grace of God that I was born normal.

Now, while I am the oldest of my surviving siblings, I was not my parent's first child. But, as each of their first two sons were named Guiseppe (Joseph) and each had died before reaching the age of one, my parents decided that I should have a different name. They were slightly superstitiously and felt that this was a bad omen. Therefore I was named Alfio Catalfo, after my father's own name. I was not named Alfred, or Fred or Freddie. I was not named after Alfred the Great. I was named as my own father was, after the patron saint, Saint 'Alfio of Trecastagni, Sicily.

On February 23rd, 1917 I was baptized at the Holy Rosary Roman Catholic Church, Lawrence, Massachusetts, by Father P. A. Paglina. My godfather and godmother were Placido and Francesca Bonomo. I was born Alfio and I was baptized Alfio. But as you can tell by the name on the front of this book, I am not known as Alfio.

How did this happen? It happened when I attended the first grade. My teacher, Miss Mabel Golden, who probably thought my parents could not spell my name properly changed the spelling of my name. It is a direct result of her decision, not my parents, that I have gone through life with the name of Alfred rather than Alfio.

As I look back on stories of my childhood, I am often reminded that this was more than a completely different time that my parents lived in, it was also a completely different world. One of the most elaborate examples of this observation took place in May of 1918.

12

I was about 15 months old and very very ill. A doctor (and this time it was a real medical doctor) told my parents that I was suffering from pneumonia and that there was nothing that he could do. I was going to die, and my parents were going to be forced to bury yet another child.

It was more than they could bare.

In desperation they sought help from an extremely unlikely source, a "stregoneria" or Italian witch. She was precise and brutal in her instructions as she told my father to go to the poultry shop and purchase a live black chicken. He did exactly as she asked. He went to Common Street where there was a poultry shop and he returned shortly after with a large black-feathered chicken.

The ritual started with a blanket placed on the dinner table. My clothing was removed and I was laid on my stomach on the blanket. Then this Italian stregoneria took the butcher knife and split the live chicken in half with a single devastating strike. The animal cried out violently and was placed, still shrieking and flapping, directly onto my naked back.

My mother claims that I was screaming while the chicken was pressed against my body and, adding to the confusion, loud Christ-like prayers filled the room and in charge of it all was this crazy Italian witch. The blood from the chicken flowed from my back onto the blanket and table to the floor.

After a few minutes, the stregoneria instructed my mother to clean and dress me in fresh clothes, then put me back to bed. This curious ceremony was now complete. Within hours I was smiling. The fever had vanished and I appeared the picture of perfect health. Against all odds the crisis was over and I had made a full recovery.

Now, obviously I was not old enough at the time to remember any of this, but I can remember the matching looks of disbelief that my parents wore each time they recounted the tale. They had a hard time believing what they had seen even though they witnessed it with their own eyes!

They told me, and now I am telling you.

On July 23rd, 1918 our little family grew by one. It was on that day that "Guiseppe" Catalfo was born and I became a big brother for the first time. An interesting fact to note here that the name Guiseppe represents the Italian name for "Joseph."

With Guiseppe's birth my parents decided to return to the village of Salmon Falls within the Town of Rollinsford, New Hampshire. They left the Italian community of Lawrence, Massachusetts to this smaller Italian community and to renew their work as mill hands at the Salmon Falls Manufacturing Company. At the time, there existed an Italian community within the village. Everything was Italian - food, customs, the Catholic religion, language, and even the closeness of the family - "la familia." The truth was that my parents missed their home, and Rollinsford, New Hampshire was the closest they could get without crossing an ocean.

On December 24th, 1919 my mother gave birth to her 5th son, Salvatore Cataflo. Salvatore was the name of our savior Lord Jesus, but my brother was simply known as "Sammy." Now, even though he might have something different to say about it, the only thing that my brother, Salvatore, had that my brother, Guiseppe and I did not have is that he was delivered by Frank Ross, M.D., a real medical doctor who practiced across the Salmon Falls River in South Berwick, Maine. Meaning that he did not have to suffer the rituals of an Italian midwife that his two older brothers managed to live through.

The sixth boy, Antonio, was also born in Rollinsford, New Hampshire on October 20, 1921 and he also got the luxury of being delivered at home by Dr. Frank Ross. At the time, we were residing at the intersection of Foundry and Main Streets in the Village of Salmon Falls within the Town of Rollinsford, New Hampshire. It was here that I lived through one of the most terrifying experiences of my young life.

Shortly after Antonio's birth, when I was nearly five years of age; my brother, Guiseppe three and a half years old; my brother, Salvatore, age two; and our newest addition, Antonio, was two months old, our family suffered another disaster.

Luckily no one died this time, but we were all very nearly consumed by a fire.

On Wednesday evening, December 21, 1921, we were in the midst of a severe cold snap that crashed through town accompanied by heavy gusts of wind and blowing, drifting snow. It was cold, it was nasty, and it was also the season to be merry. It was buon natale.

Our next-door neighbor was a man named Guiseppe Franco. Guiseppe lived alone and had a reputation of both making and selling intoxicating liquor. This particular evening Guiseppe had left his coal stove on with the draft open and headed out to the Italian convenience store located on Second Street at the foot of Short Street. His plan was to purchase a few key necessities to help see himself through the storm, but he got involved in an Italian poker game being held in the back room of the store. While he watched and/or participated in the game, his stove overheated and set fire to the apartment. In no time the entire building was ablaze.

The flames grew quickly out of control, and in a very short time, the blaze lit up part of the street. It was a stroke of sheer luck that the engineer of a passing freight train happened to notice the glow of fire and stopped his train. He began to repeatedly blast the train whistle in an effort to arouse the neighborhood. Time was of the essence as heavy winds blasted the street and fanned the flames into a roaring frenzy.

Between the heat of the fire and the incessant call of the train whistle, our neighbors began to wake. The first to respond was Frank Cincotta who lived directly across the street from my family. He raced to our home and began to loudly pound against the heavy wooden door, hoping to wake us before it was too late.

At first, my father thought the banging was caused by the wind slamming the door of the outhouse open and closed behind the building. Suddenly, both he and my mother realized that they were faced with real and immediate danger - heavy smoke filled the room and flames pressed against one of the walls.

My father grabbed my brother, Guiseppe, and me, while my mother, took Salvatore and Antonio as we started toward the only exit, a narrow staircase leading downstairs and then to freedom.

As young as I was, I remember this horrible night. I was just a month from reaching the age of five. The house was filling with smoke and the wall of the staircase was already ablaze as we hurried to safety. I could hear men outside the house screaming in Italian "fuoco - fuoco - fuoco" and my mother screaming with fear. I can still remember the feel of my brother Guiseppe's hand in mine as my father raced us to safety.

When it was all over, nothing was saved except for the blankets from the beds that covered us - all else was lost, except our lives.

And Guiseppe Franco? The man who started it all? While we were racing to safety, he raced back to his own side of the flaming house. With the help of several volunteer fireman, he fought through the flames and entered the burning building.

Led by a blasting fire hose, Guiseppe was able to save the $900.00 that he had kept in one of his bureau drawers. This act of heroism/stupidity led to a false rumor that it was my father who was able to save the $900.00. Keep in mind, $900 in 1921 was very different from $900.00 in today's world. In fact, this sum is equivalent to roughly $10,341.00 in purchasing power in the year 2007.

Within a day or two, the Salmon Falls Manufacturing Company provided my parents with a new apartment to live in on Second Street; a first floor dwelling in a brick building only several hundred yards from the Salmon Falls Manufacturing Company industrial building.

As a result of the bad weather during the fire, my youngest brother, Antonio, came down with a severe case of pneumonia. To this day I can remember the sound as he cried and cried as well as the candle that was lit and placed next to his ear. I was only 5 at the time, but I could tell that my parents did not know what to do for him. And there was no money to call for a doctor.

As Antonio's condition deteriorated the rumor of my father rescuing $900 from the fire continued to grow. It thrived and spread until it took on a life of its own and brought the attention of some very unsavory characters onto my family. The reality was that these men had him confused with

Guiseppe Franco. But reality did not matter to them. What mattered was the thought of having $900.00 cold hard cash in their own greedy hands.

On the night that they came to the house, I was in bed with my brothers. I remember the noises that they made, eerie scratches and scrapes down the side of the house, and the fear that I felt. It was like the monster that children imagine to live in their closet, only this monster was real and it was right behind the shade of our bedroom window.

My father took out his 38 revolver and calmly loaded it, shell after shell. He told me to watch over my three brothers and not to be afraid. He then walked out the front door and then locked it, leaving all four of us in the same bed and alone in the house.

Now, this sounds much worse that it actually was. Remember that there were no telephones in those days, and no way to call the police. He left us in order to quickly run to the mill and bring my mother home to sit with us.

With the family together we were ready, united. I was only five, but I could feel the tension in the air and the resolve in my parents. We were ready, and it was time.

Okay you bastards, let's go to war.

Suddenly the sound of gunshots cut through the air. At the time, all I knew what that sharp sound screaming through the dark of night. My father filled me in on the details much later in life.

He told me that he found one of the men holding another on the windowsill and two others were standing by. The gunshots, fired into the air, startled the criminals and caused

18

them to change tactics. The four criminals moved towards my father seeking to overpower him and take the money they believed that he had.

But my father was ready for them. He fired twice more, this time at their feet. The tactic worked, and the misfits ran.

At this point I can tell you that they were lucky that they dealt with my father that night and not the adult version of his son. Had it been me, I would have happily blown them out of existence and never looked back.

As an immigrant, my father had no license to own or carry a revolver and he faced deportation just for firing one at another person. Even if that other person was in the act of breaking into his home with the intent to harm his family. So, before the State Police arrived, the gun belonging to my father was removed by some of his paesano friends and disposed of, never to be seen again.

When the police arrived they asked about the gunshots, these same friends convinced the troopers that those shots came from those criminal intruders. My father won the battle that night, but at great cost. With the tragedies in his life mounting and the health of my youngest brother continually deteriorating, my father could not continue to keep shouldering these types of devastating blows.

He became ill.

He became so ill that it was feared that he would never recover. Several of my parents friends suggested that my father be taken back to the old country so that he might have a chance to heal and put the past, and his trauma behind him once and for all.

So we left.

In July of 1922 my mother gathered her husband and her four sons and began the journey back to Italy on the SS Conte di Savoia - Italian flotte riuntt and we arrived in Naples. Looking back now, much of the trip is nothing more than a blur of days, one bleeding into another. Yet, there is one memory that stands sharply from the rest. I remember being on the ship, and how each day the cook would bring around a large pot and bang on it, yelling "Pasta di Bambini!" Meaning spaghetti for the children. They would give each child a small bowl of soup. It is strange to me how on a trip packed with moments I swore I would never forget, this one stands out from all the rest.

From there it was a taxi, a train and several more days before we finally made our way back to Biancavilla, Sicily.

To my parents, it was home. To us boys, it was a grand adventure. We were now at my mother's home. The house that she was given by her father on the day that she and my father were married. The house was small, only 5 rooms, but larger than what we were use to back in America.

Plus, the weather was amazing. My parents were finally back in the arms of "la familia", and as infants, we were being further exposed to the Sicilian culture of our ancestors. We were showed off to new relatives that we had never known and showered with love and attention. The trip was so pleasant that my father began thinking of staying in Sicily. Yet it was my mother, Vincenza, who was the decision maker in these types of situations and she treated the trip as a vacation rather than a permanent move.

I can remember the time spent in Sicily as an exciting adventure where each day was more magical and enjoyable than the day before. We enjoyed the warm climate, the

20

friendly relatives, the excitement of several religious celebrations, and were even able to attend the wedding of one of our relatives. There always seemed to be music in the air and children to play with, who were not only our own ages, but they also spoke our language.

It was like living on a permanent holiday.

Alas, all good things must come to an end. And my grand Italian adventure ended the first week of November, 1922. While in Italy, my brothers and I were able to put the unpleasant details of our past behind us. We were so loved by our new extended family that the realities of my father's condition and the extended sickness of my youngest brother seemed to fade into the background.

We simply acted as if they did not exist.

But they did.

My father entered the hospital in Catania. His condition had reached the point where he needed a high level of care if he was ever to recover. While he was gone, my youngest brother, Antonio, began to deteriorate. His condition worsened until November 8, 1922.

On that day, my brother died, and on that day my parents lost yet another son.

My mother was devastated. My father had no idea that this sad event had even taken place.

With all that was going on, one event blends over into the next until the only thing that I can clearly remember is the wake. It was held in our home and the vigilance was night and day. Friends and relatives flooded the house and spent hours showering our family with both love and support. The priest of the Catholic Church became a near constant visitor.

The funeral was a surreal experience that hovered between a nightmare and a dream. Antonio's casket was draped with white lace and carried by four young men who were dressed as altar boys. The casket was so small it took them no effort at all to lift and carry it on their shoulders. A Catholic priest led the procession and others, mostly dressed in black, followed first to the Catholic Church, Santa Maria of Elemosina, and then all the way to the cemetery about a mile out of town. Relatives and friends followed the casket on foot. Many tears were shed; even by little me at the age of five and a half.

When my father returned home from the hospital, my mother was forced to face the fact that he did not know the fate of his son. At first, when he would inquire as to Antonio's whereabouts, my mother would deceive him by saying that he was at one relative's place or another. But finally, two days later, he demanded to see his son. My mother was forced to tell him the truth.

I was there for that moment, and in that moment I saw my own father cry like a child. Both of my parents held each other as they wept and it was as if the grief of the passing months flowed out of us with their tears.

Even at the tender age of five, I was not sure that I wanted any part of this life.

This was a defining moment in my young life. It is a moment that I have managed to put behind me, but one that I have never forgotten.

Through the sheer strength of my mother's will we were able to finally return to America in January of 1923. I can remember this trip and thinking about how the Atlantic Ocean always seemed to be angry about something. It tossed our little ship around like a matchstick in a pond. Huge waves slammed into the vessel, practically engulfing the deck and making me fear that I would never see dry land again. I certainly never thought that I would be happy to be back in Rollinsford, New Hampshire, living in one of the four-tenements on Main Street.

It was not until our return from Italy that I began my formal education. I started grammar school at the local Town Hall on Main Street in February of 1923. My first day of school I wore a bright red shirt homemade created just for me by my talented mother. I can't even imagine what I must have looked like, but she thought I looked cute and that was all that really mattered.

The class consisted of about 40 first graders. Keep in mind that at this point in my life I was six years of age, pure Italian, and unable to speak even a word of English. About half of the students in my class were Italian and most of us did not speak English at all. We caught on fast that our teacher, Miss Mabel Golden, was as handicapped linguistically as we were, maybe a lot worse. She could not speak Italian. Occasionally we would nudge each other and say in Italian, "questra maestra e stupida - non sape una parola Italiana". (This teacher is stupid - she does not know a word in Italian.)

The truth was, what little English we learned during those years came from the streets or the playground. It definitely did not come from the classroom! It was this language barrier, the inability of both my teacher and myself to overcome it and my late start of the year that led me to repeat the 1st grade.

This was a calm time for my family. From 1923 to 1931 we continued to live in one of the four tenements on Main Street, and it was during this time that my three sisters were born. Each of them delivered by Dr. Frank Ross rather than the crazy Italian midwife that we older boys managed to endure!

My oldest sister, "Mary" Catalfo, was born in June of 1923. She was named Maria dell Elemosina Catalfo after St. Mary of Charity. As an Italian, she was called Elemosina, but in the English-speaking world, she was simply called Mary. The second born was my sister, Francesca Catalfo, who was born in April of 1927. She was named after Saint Francis of Assisi as well as our paternal grandmother, Francesca Catalfo, and was affectionately known as "Chicina." My third sister was Agatha Catalfo, who was known as Ida Catalfo in life, and was born in December of 1931. She was named after Saint Agatha, but ended up with the name of Ida in English-speaking America. Ida was the baby of the family and over the years she claimed a special place in my heart as my true favorite.

During these early years of 1923-1926, it became noticeable that the Italian population began to thin out as families moved away from Rollinsford to Portsmouth, Rochester and Dover, New Hampshire and Lawrence and Waltham, Massachusetts, and even Washington D.C. and California. Our people were beginning to spread out, and the tight knit community that we depended on began to disappear.

Then, on October 29, 1929, the United States suffered a catastrophic economic event. The stock market plummeted and that day marked the start of the Great Depression. Unemployment skyrocketed to unacceptable figures; people who were willing to work could not find jobs and banks went bankrupt. It was a time where there was plenty of food, but people had no money to pay for it. My father, Alfio, lost both his job in Dover, New Hampshire as well as his savings of

$900.00 in a Lawrence, Massachusetts bank. So here we are, living in a company property, no money to pay rent, no money in the bank, no job and a wife and five children to care for.

No matter how you look at it, this was not an easy time.

The history books talk about the Great Depression, but they do not give you a clear picture of what it was like to have lived it. We struggled simply to eat. Meat was a rare treat that found its way to our table maybe once a month.

And we were among the more fortunate. Our family had a large garden that kept us supplies with potatoes, tomatoes, pumpkins, lettuce and other fresh product items. My mother learned the art of canning and came up with creative ways to save what little food we had so that it might see us through the winter months.

She also learned how to bake bread without all of the necessary ingredients that she might once have used. Every Sunday she would work with whatever she had on hand to make our bread for the week. It usually started out fine, but was hard as a rock within a day or two. By the end of the week we were forced to soak it in sugar water just to be able to choke it down!

And let me tell you how I feel about squash. I HATE squash! To this day I will not eat it and really prefer to not even have it in the house. Why? Because when the squash was in season we were forced to eat it at just about every single meal. We would eat squash and eggs for breakfast, squash with vegetables for lunch and squash and pasta for dinner. It got to the point where I couldn't even stand the sight of it!

When I was little we were lucky if we had a little bit of chicken just one time a month. Meat was too expensive and there was no way we could afford it every day or even every week. It sounds sad, but that was just the way that life was. Our diet was pretty much pasta and veggies with some eggs thrown in for protein.

In short, we survived. This was before the days of government assistance and long before the days of unemployment benefits.

My father was finally able to find a job in Ipswich, Massachusetts. This provided us with much needed income, but it meant that we could only see him on weekends. During this time my siblings and I learned what it meant to be tough. We had to be if we wanted to survive.

Survival meant walking along the railroad tracks and picking up pieces of coal dropped by oncoming trains. It meant dragging a cart or sled out into the woods to find wood to burn. It meant doing whatever it took to keep warmth in our home and food in our stomach.

In those days our parents were forced to work long, hard hours at the cotton mill. This meant that the Catafalo kids were left to handle any chores around the house while also taking care of ourselves. We did what we could to chip in, but we were just kids.

The one thing I do remember is that every year when the blueberries were in season we would walk for miles and pick as much as we possibly could. Now, you might think that we would pick these as a treat for our own stomachs, and I'll admit that more than a few would make their way into our hungry mouths, but the point was to make money. We would pick the berries and then go door to door trying to sell them to our neighbors. It wasn't much money, pennies really, but in those days every single cent counted.

Winters were the worst. In the summer food was growing in the garden and heat was more than plentiful. In the winter we were faced with a whole different set of problems. First, the only heat in the house came from a coal stove in the kitchen. This meant that the bedroom was ice cold, cold enough that you could see your breath misting right in front of your face. The only solution was for all of the kids to sleep together in the same bed. Then instead of running out in the icy night to the outhouse, the boys would just make use of the second story window.

As bad as this sounds you have to realize that to us it was just a way of life. This was all we had ever known and, therefore, we accepted it as our life, not as some kind of tragedy.

And there were good memories to go along with the bad.

I can remember many cold winter nights when our father would tuck us into bed and tell us stories of Sicilian heroes. The trick was that he would never tell us the whole story in a single night. No chance! Instead he would get right into the heart of the action and then leave us hanging! Of course the point was to keep us anxiously waiting for the next installment, and I can promise you that it worked! We all loved those stories and I can still remember the sense of elation that would settle over me each time my father would finish a tale of heroic glory and honor.

I also remember that this was the point in my life when I developed a strong dislike for Santa Claus. When I was very young I convinced myself that if I was good enough then Santa would bring wonderful presents on Christmas morning.

He never came.

It didn't matter how good I was there was never a single treat waiting for me on Christmas morning. I was always disappointed and I was always sad. So I never forgave the fat man in the red suit. To the point that when my own children were small I always made sure that Santa left the worst presents of the bunch. The best gifts? They all came from Dad!

For us Christmas was a religious holiday. We would receive a small amount of candy along with an orange, but no real presents to speak of. Actually, there were no presents at all. Instead we spent time on fellowship. All of our neighbors would come together and we would just spend time enjoying each other and finding joy in the season its self.

Looking back now it strikes me how all of these couples would come together to eat, drink, laugh and celebrate, yet none of them spoke a common language. There were Italians, Greeks, Polish and French all in one house and all having a great time. I learned then that enough wine and enough sign language can cross any communication barrier!

One of the crazier things that my mother tried to make ends meet was selling illegal alcohol out of the garden. The way it worked was that she had a pint of whiskey buried under each potato plant. When a customer came to the house to buy a pint of whiskey, she would go to the garden with a paper bag in hand and come back with the pint of whiskey and potatoes in the bag. It worked for a short time, but the reality was that my mother was not a good criminal and was eventually arrested. And being arrested meant that she was taken to court to face charges.

It was in 1931 and I was 14 years of age. I watched her defense, by Attorney Everett Galloway, in the Dover District Court, and even then I knew that it was pathetic. I had not even finished grammar school yet and already I was critical of the way the case was handled. The case should have been negotiated or compromised. This was a woman who was then pregnant, the mother of five starving children, no job, and the depression in full swing. Hell, they should have nol-prossed the case. They should have given her a medal. This was not an act of violence. The trial last for a good part of the day unnecessarily and she was fined $20.00.

A real shining moment for the American justice system.

Now, this may seem like my entire childhood was one extreme tragic moment after another and this is simply not the case. Its just that these tragic moments are the ones that left a mark on my young mind and, therefore, are the ones that I can remember most clearly.

But there are some lighter moments mixed in as well.

Like the summer of 1929, the year that I was 12, Guiseppe 11 and Salvatore 9. That summer there was a small sand lot in front of our door where we would play. We loved our little sand lot, but we hated the noontime monster that stalked us every afternoon.

Let me explain.

Every noon hour in early summer, this male monster would come by our home and chase us into the house by running at us with threatening gestures and calling us "guinea wop." Well I can promise you that it didn't take very long before I had had enough of that crap.

So, we prepared to punish him.

We took some dozen building bricks from my father's collection located in the cellar and began to practice. First, we would pretend to act innocently in the sand in front of the steps and door. Then, at a given signal, we would run into the house and close the door. Finally the door would swing open and we would fire these brick projectiles out with great force at the oncoming intruder.

After I felt we were ready to take on this stupid, giant jackass, we set ourselves as bait.

We pretended not to notice him coming and spoke softly in Italian, "here he comes," and come he did, chasing us with threatening gestures and calling out "guinea wop, guinea wop."

We waited until the very last second, then raced up the steps and slammed the door. After allowing him to get just a few steps closer, the door flew open and this stupid giant was greeted with a barrage of brick projectiles. He couldn't duck fast enough and was struck about the face and head as he went down off the steps and onto the ground.

Now, let me admit to you that I did not know if we killed him and quite frankly I did not care at that moment. We simply collected the bricks and my two brothers took them to the sink, washed them and put them back in the cellar where they belonged. In the meantime, I grabbed a partly used gallon of homemade wine, belonging to my father, and poured it on the collapsed bum. I coated his face, hair and clothes with wine, then went back in the house and locked the front door.

It didn't take long for a knock to sound. When I opened the door a single police officer stood there. He asked a few questions about what had happened, and I responded to him, but only in Italian. I told him I did not know in Italian ("non-sachio") and added that he must be drunk ("qusto e ubriaco").

The officer seemed to accept my story. He helped our giant nemesis pull himself off of the street, and put him into the back of his police vehicle. After that, the we rarely saw him. And when we did he would walk across the street careful never to look in our direction.

Another fond memory from my childhood centers around a place called "Lucky Bucks."

It was the summer of 1931 and along with my brothers and our friends, we built a child-sized town on a nearby vacant lot. A town that we called Lucky Bucks. In no time, some 50 to 70 youngsters of all ages were involved in this adventure located some hundred yards behind the St. Mary's Catholic Church. We built two streets about eight feet wide and some hundred yards long. One street was called Main Street and the second was called Columbus Street. The person in charge of this construction was my friend, Louis Economos.

At first, I was simply recognized as the Mayor but a short while later we decided that we should hold an election. After the election I was officially the Mayor.

To us, this town was real. We were involved daily, seven days a week, from morning to near sundown. Most of the summer we all practically lived there. We constructed 21 buildings, which included a town hall, a restaurant and a church. These small structures were built of wood, cardboard and anything else we could get our hands on. My brother, Guiseppe, was the priest and my brother, Salvatore, was in charge of the army. He led 20 members in the military, all with proper identical hats and all with elastic guns.

The name for our town came from our chosen currency. We used "lucky bucks." These were printed by the Boston Globe every Sunday and the denominations were one, five, ten, twenty, fifty and one hundred dollar bills. It worked great for a while until one Sunday they printed a million dollar lucky buck. This caused immediate chaos and major inflation. To put it simply, chaos ensued.

As Mayor, I immediately called a meeting of my two brothers, Guiseppe and Salvatore, Peter Valhos, Lewis and George Economos, Robert Hudon, Roul Dupuis, Leo Lavigne, and August Dube among others and outlawed the one million dollar lucky buck denomination.

To use, our town was real. We had the church, we had the restaurant, we had our military, and we even had a navy consisting of eight older male youngsters. Our warship consisted of some 12 railroad wooden ties, bound together with cable wire, and floated in the Salmon Falls River just down the hill from Lucky Bucks Town. It floated as a raft and was powered by poles. The warship, as we called it, had a slingshot, a large V-shaped part of a young tree, and it had large rubber straps and a pocket large enough to hold apples or rocks to propel some appreciable distance. We never concerned ourselves with the danger that someone could get seriously hurt with this kind of firepower. Fortunately, we never were involved in any naval battle. However, our navy warship flew an American flag and the eight-man navy added prestige to our Lucky Bucks Town.

Alas, all good things must come to an end. In our case, the New Hampshire State Police in late August came to the scene and ordered us to remove the structures and clean up the place. We did not want any trouble, so we obliged and over the next several days, we demolished the structures and finally abandoned our project.

During the spring of 1931, when I was in the seventh grade, I suffered a bad experience with the headmaster, Guy Crockette. He was teaching 38 students at the time, 16 of which were in the seventh grade, while 22 were in the eighth grade. Both classes were held in the same room and mass confusion reigned supreme. To add to his problem, someone from the back of the classroom threw a spitball toward the front of the class. I did not do it. I never cared for this kind of foolishness. In fact, I was surprised when he ordered me to step out in the hallway. Suddenly, someone in the eighth grade from the back of the classroom stood up, called to Mr. Crockett, and told him that it was him, and not Fred Catalfo that threw the spitball. This did not change Mr. Crockette's decision. He forced me alone into the hall where he ordered me to stick out my hands, one at a time. Then, using an 18-inch wooden ruler he pulverized each hand with severe blows. After each blow I thought for sure he was going to break my hand.

To me, this was a criminal act. I felt discriminated against, abused and unjustly punished. I felt he used this as an excuse to strike me down because I was Italian. I was both embarrassed and in pain.

As a result, I transferred schools and in September of 1931, I matriculated to the St. Joseph Catholic School for my eighth grade. It was an academic year where I learned a little French and some of my French friends learned a little Italian. During the year, I did my Confirmation and was a member of the first graduating class of the Ecole St. Joseph in June of 1932.

During the Spring of 1932 several friends and I organized a Junior Birdmen of America Club. We learned about airplanes, what they were built of and what allowed them to fly.

Our plan? To build our own airplane!

And we did! We built an airplane with a fuselage of about ten feet, dual wings, fabric covers, dupe material applied to the fabric, baby carriage wheels, a single seat, no controls, a tail and a motorcycle motor to operate on old World War I propeller. It looked pretty good, but I was doubtful that it would actually lift.

But you know that we had to test it!

So early one Sunday morning we moved our contraption to the parking lot of the Boston and Maine Railroad Station. I personally had no plans to either fly our "plane" or even to get in it, but I was curious as to what would happen so I was more than willing to tag along for the ride.

One problem. No one else was eager to fly it either! After a long and heated discussion I agreed to try it. I climbed into the single seat while two of my friends held onto the bottom of each wing and two others started the engine. The propeller started to turn faster and faster until our plane began to move forward on its own. Soon the plane that I didn't believe could fly was lifting gently off the ground and moving quickly under its own power!

Now the new problem was that we had never planned on a way to stop the plane!

I managed to hang on until the plane struck one of the steel beams of a nearby water tower. Our contraption crumpled. Luckily I was just bruised, but I could have been hurt and hurt badly! My friends and I all thought we had stumbled upon a grand adventure until my father heard about our antics later that night. He was not amused and I was not amused with the beating I got because of it. That day officially ended my interest in the Junior Birdmen of America but it did not stop me from wanting to fly. I even held on to the propeller from our little makeshift plane until 2005 when I handed it down to my own son.

We were in the depths of the depression when I graduated from the eighth grade from the Ecole St. Joseph French Catholic School, in Rollinsford, New Hampshire on May 30, 1932. According to the grades, I just barely made it.

On March 4, 1933, Franklin Delano Roosevelt was installed as the 32nd President of the United States. He immediately started to restore confidence in our economic system of government and he proceeded to create a series of New Deal agencies in an effort to put our people to work. We had hope once again.

Chapter 3:

The Ugly Years

As I sit here today, I am often amazed by the world that we live in. Many of the young people that I come into contact with have no sense of accountability or even responsibility. They traipse through life with a sense of entitlement that they definitely have not earned and they are appalled at the idea that they be asked to carry their own weight, much less contribute to society as a whole.

I promise that this was not the case when I was a young man!

As soon as I turned 16 I was expected to start contributing to the family. I applied for and was given a job with the Pacific Mills in Dover, NH. It was second shift. It was five days a week, and it was a fully horrid experience that I hated from day one.

My title was "Floor Boy," and I promise that it was every bit as glamorous as it sounds! My duties in the cotton factory included moving bobbings and bales of cotton, cleaning the machinery, sweeping the floors and even cleaning the bathrooms. When I look back at this time, all I can see is that I succeeded at wasting three and a half years of my life. These were the dead years.

And how much do you think that I was paid for my toil? An astounding $14.40 a week! Of this I was given 40¢ while my father would take the rest of the money, no questions asked. It was my duty, my obligation by my father's Sicilian standards. I was too young to protest, and beyond that, I loved my family. But I felt like a prisoner.

After working for a full year, my father raised my share of the earnings from 40¢ to $1.50. He felt that he was both being generous and that I had earned it.

In the fall of 1933 my father purchased a 1929 four-door Chevrolet. The best part about this car was that I was able to drive it! Not often for entertainment, but I drove my mother and myself to work and back each day, and occasionally I would take my parents to Lawrence, MA so that they would have the opportunity to visit with their Italian friends.

One of my most vivid memories from this time is of my 17th birthday. Now, you might think that this day stands out due to a celebration of the joy that it held, but unfortunately this is not the case. It stands out because I spent the day feeling alone, unimportant and unnoticed. My parents allowed the day to pass without even wishing me a Happy Birthday. There was no cake, no card, no gift and no mention that this day was anything unique. And I can tell you now that while it may not have mattered to them, it mattered to me, and it still does to this day.

As immigrants living on American soil, we were struggling. Oftentimes we were undernourished and sometimes it felt as though we scraped by on hope alone. Looking back on it now it amazes me how man, regardless of their nationality, has such a capacity to find a way to survive. This was the case for the Catalfo family. We survived.

It was during this time that my father felt a calling to return to Italy and visit his aging parents. He had been planning for sometime to journey to his ancestral home and had scheduled a 6-month trip. Unfortunately, Benito Mussolini and his fascists destroyed those plans.

My father was apprehended by Mussolini's men while on a train from Naples to Catania. He was searched and flatly accused of being an American Spy. When the police accusations seemed to fail and be without merit, he was then held for dodging military service with the Italian Army. They claimed that since he was still an Italian citizen and he had not served his country, that he was guilty of fleeing to America to avoid military service. He was arrested on these charges and his American passport was confiscated.

It was only due to the help of the American Counsel and the American Red Cross that he was released from prison!

Before this incident, my father had great respect for Mussolini. However, being arrested on false charges and treated with long-term imprisonment or inscription into the army instantly and permanently destroyed that respect.

Can you imagine the idiocy of the Fascist Italian Government to accuse my father of being a spy? My father only knew a few words of English. He certainly could not read English and, in fact, with his one year of schooling, he could not even read in Italian. It was because of this incident that he was forced to cut his visit short and returned home in two months instead of six.

Our family was of course grateful to have him back home. We were also happy that he came home sooner rather than later. When he returned, the first thing that he did was tear an Italian calendar from the wall with Mussolini's picture on it and throw it to the floor.

On Saturday, October 27, 1934, I suffered a traumatic experience due to an unfortunate confrontation with my father, Alfio. For several weeks I had told him about two specific problems that I was facing. The first was that I had only one pair of trousers, which were worn out and displayed several patches on them. The second problem was that our 1929 Chevrolet needed antifreeze to prevent the radiator and the engine from freezing. My father continued to ignore my pleas.

I decided to take matters into my own hands.

Now, up until this day I would always turn over my entire earnings to my father. Every Saturday morning I handed over the entire $14.40 and he would give me back $1.50 as my share.

This day was different.

On this day, I kept the entire pay envelope. I drove to Dover and purchased $2.00 worth of antifreeze for our vehicle and paid $2.50 for a pair of trousers. I then kept $1.50 for myself and gave my father the balance of $8.40.

When my father realized what I had done, all hell broke loose. He was irate that I would have the nerve to defy him as the head of la familia. He began to scream and rant as he grew angrier and angrier, demanding that I give him the money that I had removed from the pay envelope.

I no longer had the money. I kept trying to explain to my father what I had done, and why I felt justified in my actions, but my words fell on deaf ears. It struck me in the middle of this chaos that my father was standing in front of me dressed in a nice suit as he prepared to go out with several of his friends. He had the money for a suit, but I was not allowed $2.00 for a 2nd pair of pants to replace the ones that were more patches than they were fabric.

At nearly 18 years old, this was almost more than I could take. I loved my father, but his standards were balanced for no one but himself.

It got worse.

At the height of the fight my father snatched up a full glass bottle of milk off the table to throw at me. As he raised it above his head, the paper stopper slipped out and milk poured out all over my father and his nice suit. As you might imagine, this did not help his mood. I did the only thing that I could. I ran straight out the door!

Later that afternoon the police stopped by the house and left a message for me to go by the police station as soon as I got home. It turned out that my father had called them and they asked me what had happened. As clearly as I could I relayed the events of the day and explained my actions. I had done nothing wrong and the police agreed with me. They let me go and asked that I call them if my father gave me any trouble.

Looking back on this now I can find small traces of humor in the situation, but I can promise that this was not the case as it was happening. I could not believe that my father would treat me this way or that he would call the police over me spending money that I had earned on necessities. My sacrifice to my family was not appreciated....it was expected. It was just one day, but it was a day that forever changed the way that I looked at my father. I lost respect for him, and it was a long time before I was once again able to look at him with love.

But this day also served as a stimulus for me and started the wheels of change, for it was on this day that I suddenly realized that I might do better by leaving home. My interest in getting an education began to grow and thrive inside me until it was a need that I could no longer ignore.

What can I say?

A few days later, once everyone and everything had cooled down, I had a conference with both of my parents and it was agreed that my weekly earnings would be divided. I would give them $10.00 a week, I would retain $4.40 from my earnings, and I would take care of my own clothes, the expenses of operating our 1929 Chevrolet and my personal expenses.

Now, $4.40 a week was more than I had ever had, but I still had a desire to earn more money. To do so I decided to enter the ring once again.

Once again you ask? Well I guess that this is a good time to let you in on one of my little secrets. You see, by this time I had already won all eight of the professional fights I had been engaged in. I had a manager, Pete Burley of Dover, great guy, I had a training regimen and I was good at what I did!

The night of my fight my opponent was a person by the name of Kid Clayton. He made me earn it, but I won.

I remember the fight, but I also remember that in the dressing room was an older guy in his late 30's. He was shadow boxing over in the corner and cursing to himself. Watching him I honestly thought that he had some sort of brain damage!

It horrified me that he was about to get into the ring and looking at him I saw my future. This was definitely not the road that I wanted to go down! So, I split the $30.00 prize with my manager and told him that I was done. I knew right then and there that their had to be a better way to earn a living rather than paying for it with a pound of flesh!

In May of 1935 my family achieved a milestone that we had dreamed of from the moment my parents first stepped foot on American soil. It was at that time that my parents purchased a 36-acre farm in Rollinsford, NH. Known as the Frank Wentworth farm, the property consisted of a small house and carriage house along with a large barn.

As excited as we all were, I have to give you a clear understanding of what this house looked like. There was no bathroom, in fact there was no running water of any kind, no electricity and no electric wiring. Our water came from a hand pump out in the lawn and we lit the house with candles and lanterns when we first moved in. My parents did have the house wired for electricity and had a water pipe connected from the well directly into the house. However, it was several years before either a bath or shower was installed.

By the time August rolled around I had made the decision to leave my job in the cotton factory and start high school. The yearning I felt to get an education was growing stronger with each passing day and I knew that I did not want to spend my life slaving at the mill. To me my timing was perfect, to my family it could not have been worse.

My father was unemployed because he accidently cut his foot with an axe, my mother was unemployed, and my brother, Joseph, had lost his job in the mill. So my hope of a formal education ended for now for the sake of la familia.

Over the next year I worked hard. My income did not increase, but it had to stretch further as I was the only breadwinner in the family for most of this time. I was grasping at straws trying to find ways to earn money.

So I came up with a plan...and I was proud of my plan! I

decided that I would be a chicken farmer. I mean, we had the land, so why not become a chicken farmer? Slowly I saved up money until I had enough to buy 400 baby chicks.

Now, two things that you should know here. First, I knew less about raising chicks than my father knew about raising cows. Second, 400 baby chicks is A LOT of babies. And, third, it takes an increasingly large amount of corn to feed this many animals.

In short, I had no idea what I had gotten myself into!

As the weeks passed, my chicks seemed to eat significantly more as they grew. They made a huge mess and, to my complete surprise many of them began to randomly drop dead no matter what I did.

Extremely frustrating to say the very least!

It didn't take long for me to throw in the towel. I quickly lost patience and sold the survivors to my father for one lump sum of $20.00. A loss, but one that I was more than happy to accept.

By the time spring rolled around in 1936 my life had come to a crossroads. I was 19, and as tends to happen, I wasn't getting any younger. Therefore it was now or never if I wanted to start high school and get any kind of an education. I began to take inventory of my life on a daily basis. It didn't take long for me to decide that if I wanted to improve my circumstances, then I had to obtain a formal education. No shortcuts, no side roads. Let me tell you, all that hot air you hear about being a self-educated person is junk. You can teach yourself anything you want, but unless you have the credentials to back it up.....it means nothing.

Nonetheless, everyone I knew thought that I was completely crazy. When I would tell them what I had planned the response was always the same, "Do you realize how old you will be in four years!?!"

I didn't argue with them. What was the point? But the thing was, I knew that I would be four years older in four years with or without a high school education. I had already seen what my life would become without one, now was the time to try something different.

There is only one road to travel my friends. Anyone that believes that one can reach an intellectual plateau by life's experience alone is both full of it and kidding themselves.
What caused this epiphany? Well, it wasn't a sudden burst of light. It was more like a seed. One that had been planted years before and had grown to take root and thrive as the time passed.

But my outer confidence shielded serious inner fears. How was I to overcome such horrendous limitations? I was 19 ½ years of age and four years out of a grammar school where I did not get much of an education. During these four years, I attempted to teach myself but eventually realized that to teach myself I should be a teacher. How in hell can I teach myself? I lack the qualifications to teach myself. I need teachers to teach me.

God gave me one life on earth. Without an education, what could I achieve in life? It dawned on me while I worked in a cotton factory among common laborers with little or no education that I did not want to be one of them. They are nice people - so what? Educated people are also nice people. I hate factory work. For me, it was a form of imprisonment or slavery.

Don't get me wrong...I'm not discriminating against people who work hard and earn their living through blood, sweat and tears. They are good, fantastic people who are family oriented, law abiding and God fearing for the most part. Nothing against them, it's just that I wanted more out of my life. I wanted more than this form of existence.

One thing that I knew for certain, there were no shortcuts on the path that I had laid out for myself; high school, college, law school, in that order. I did not know how I could possibly attain such a lofty goal, but I knew that I had to try. I knew that I could not submit, surrender or give up along the way. The challenge was mine, and it was one that I was ready to face.

The first step was to obtain that all important high school education. And the first step towards obtaining that goal was to develop an honorable method to leave my lowly job at the cotton mill and deceive my parents. My plan was to tell them about the Civilian Military Training Corps and that I had chosen to join this group. It was such a patriotic step that would both please my family and me.

At the time, I was so academically limited that I had to enlist the help of a nurse at Pacific Mills to help me fill out my application. She was the only person I knew at the time who had a high school education. The next day I took my application down to City Hall, had it notarized and mailed it off. If all goes as planned I will be a soldier in the civilian army...if they will accept me!

On Friday, July 3, 1936, I spent my last evening, from 3:00 to 11:00 p.m., at the Pacific Mills as a lowly employee after over three wasteful years of my life there. I had convinced my father that now that I had signed up to join the military, I had no choice but to go or be sent to jail as a deserter. Between you and I, this wasn't true, but it was my out. And I took it. I also ensured him that I would get a new and better job when I returned home, but truly I had no such intentions.

So on July, 9th 1936, at the age of 19 ½ and with only an 8th grade education I, gleefully, left for Maine by way of a special train from Dover, NH. I sat there with hundreds of young men just like myself, all of us trying to move forward with our lives and find something better. Together we would become part of the 700 member Civilian Military Training Corps, free....free at last!

Training was amazing. I loved it, if for no other reason than the food was fantastic. Our days were spent passing physicals, practicing with our weapons and learning how to be men. They gave us rifles, they gave us bayonets, they gave us cartridges and they showed us how to use them. This was the first time that I felt as if I was a part of something that mattered. I was filled with patriotism and the sound of taps echoing through the fort sent a shiver of pride down my spine. It was like hearing a musical prayer and I was so grateful to be a part of this adventure.

One of my proudest memories of being a student soldier was playing soccer with Company L. Our team won in double overtime, and in spite of a leg injury, I was all over the field. The game was down to its last seconds and my teammates and I drove down the field when I slammed in the last goal on a sharp pass. I was lifted onto the shoulders on my teammates and officers as the cheered and congratulated me. We had won...and I had done it!

This may not sound like much to the average person, but to me this was a defining moment that I can remember with amazing clarity. It was the first time that I felt that kind of joy, and even though the emotion was new, I could tell that it was one that I wanted to hold on to with everything that I had.

Chapter 4:

Berwick Academy

Most of us have defining moments, or even defining chapters in our lives. The moments where our life hits a crossroads and we are forced, for better or for worse, to make a choice, a choice that has the power to change the course of our lives.

For me, Berwick Academy was just such a moment. When I made the decision to go against the wishes of "La Familia" and create my own path, I brought myself to a crossroads. One where I could either go back and consign myself to living a life that I hated, or move forward towards the dreams of my heart.

As you can probably guess, I chose the second.

So, there I was, a 19½-year-old first generation Italian immigrant who had finished grammar school 4 years earlier walking in to start my first day of high school. I can't even imagine the picture I must have made to my peers, much less my teachers! Today, I can admit to you that I was afraid. I was terrified that some type of disaster would strike, preventing me from going through with what I was determined to do.

But I was no longer willing to allow fear to rule my life. I was finished listening to the counsel of fools as they whispered to me that an education was not an option. Because no matter what my father or anyone else thought or said, I knew that the key facet to achieving my hopes and dreams was education.

From the very first time I walked through the door, I knew in my heart that I had made the right decision. Berwick Academy was a magical place that simply boiled over with ideas, thoughts and theories that I had never even heard of before. I was inundated with intellectual curiosity and I wanted to know more. More about people, governments, science, geography, psychology, philosophy, geology, history, languages and any other subject that my mind might jump to. But above all this, I wanted to fight my way through the path that would lead me to law school.

It seemed that everywhere I turned, someone made a point to try and discourage me in my quest. I was repeatedly reminded that I was already almost 20 and that it would take me four years just to finish high school. And that was just one of many objections. At the time all I could think about was overcoming the obstacles others laid in my path, but now I see a different truth.

You see, the one common denominator present on all sides of this situation was fear; my fear of failure and of being forced to live a life that I hated, and my parents' fear of the unknown. My parents were strong, good-hearted people who truly wanted the best for their children, but they did not understand what level of difference an education would make in my life. Plus, my father had dreams of his own. He had dreams of grandeur that he would become a landlord, a land baron and a successful farmer. There is nothing wrong with this, but his path to achieving his dreams was through the expense of his children, me included.

Therefore, my father and I were locked into what felt like a never-ending conflict. He wanted me to work in a factory, help support him, his family and his dreams and, of course, help him operate the farm he was planning to develop on Oak Street. My going to Berwick Academy did not fit into my father's plans. To the contrary, he wanted me to give up this "stupid" adventure and devote myself to working toward his dreams rather than my own.

My decision was easy. On September 14, 1936 I reported to Berwick Academy. And, while this brought me one step closer to achieving my goals, it also significantly increased tensions with my father. In short, things were no longer friendly at home. My father was quite open in his hostility, and I was no longer welcome at the dinner table with my family. Instead, I would have to go out into the garden and eat what I could find.

I still did my share of the chores. I cleaned the barn, fed and watered the livestock and did my best to stay clear of my father at all costs.

School was another matter entirely. As bad as things were at home, going to school proved to be an oasis of sorts in my life. I actually enjoyed my time there so much that the 4-mile walk I faced each day didn't bother me. I was so far behind the other students that I didn't even know a verb from a noun, but it didn't matter. I acknowledged my shortcomings, and was determined to learn and overcome.

More than just an education, going to the Academy also provided me with a new love...football! I started out as the second-string quarterback, but it wasn't long before my Coach moved me to the line. He was impressed with my courage, my determination and with my unrelenting love for the game of football. So, he decided to start me at guard and tackle. This I liked. No, it was more than that. This I loved! I loved the down and dirty reality of football in the trenches and I was good at it!

But that disaster I was waiting on? It arrived just a few weeks into the school year. As I walked though the door one afternoon my mother informed me that two members of the Town of Rollinsford School Board came to our farm on Oak Street and informed my father and mother that they would be held responsible for my tuition at Berwick Academy. As a result of this information, brokenhearted, I went back to the Academy to return my books. With all of the hostility around the idea of me attending the Academy, there was no possibility of my father being willing to pay my tuition.

Not sure what to do, but needing to talk to someone, I stopped by and poured my heart out to my English teacher, Ms. Frances Babb. She helped me to calm down and assured me that I could make tuition arrangements with the Academy that would fit within the budget that I had. Or, even better, I might qualify for a scholarship.

Next I went to see my coach. His answer? For me to suit up and make sure that I got back to class.

Their response floored me. Never before had I had the experience of someone not only supporting my dreams, but believing that they could be achieved and being willing to help me find success. It was both humbling and exciting all at the same time.

In fact, it was because of the actions of these two individuals that a few days later, when we suited up to play the first game of the season, that I was part of the starting lineup. We lost, but it didn't matter. I enjoyed playing football and I played my heart out on every single play. Even better was the fact that my brothers and some of our friends were in the stands to watch the game. It made me feel like a star.

We got better with every game. My own personal goal was to hit harder with every play. I might have weighed only 130 pounds, but I felt like a giant and tried to hit like a 200 pounder!

To me, each time I stepped on the field, it was much more than just another game. It was a chance for me to prove myself. To prove that I was part of the team, to prove that I was good enough and most of all to prove that I belonged at Berwick Academy.

Once I learned that I would be able to stay at Berwick, I had a new horror to face, Freshman Initiation. And, this was an especially embarrassing right of passage to me as I was so much older than the average Freshman!

The way it worked was that all week we had to wear these ugly green paper ties everywhere we went. We also had to carry 4 books to and from school, have a plaque with our names on our backs and always open the door for upperclassmen and address them as "Yes Sir," or "Yes Miss." Definitely not the high point of my academic career!

Then came the best part, a full school assembly. On Friday afternoon the entire student body and faculty assembled in the main study hall. Some of the freshmen had been called upon to perform in front of the whole school, and my time was about to come. The task didn't seem all that hard, I simply had to broadcast the Berwick Academy – Somersworth High School football game, but you have to keep in mind that this was just the 4th week of school and my English skills left much to be desired.

As I walked onto the stage, my legs felt like Jello. I decided that the only way to succeed was to just go all out. Go big or go home, right? Well I definitely went big. I jumped around and carried on until it probably sounded like an Italian soccer game being broadcast for a full stadium crowd. And, I guess it was a hit because by the time I finished, the entire building was shaking with laughter.

But class clown was not my goal. I was determined that by the time I graduated from Berwick Academy I would have earned the respect of my peers. Football helped. Gaining respect on the field proved to be the front-runner of earning respect in the classroom.

The only problem was that many of these battles were hard fought.

I remember one instance in particular where a particularly dense opposing lineman spent the entire game dedicating himself to calling me a "wop." At first I was able to let the slur slide off, but as the game wore on my patience grew thin. So I bided my time. I waited until there were less than 2 minutes left in the game and we had a strong lead. The entire Berwick Academy line was down low waiting for the snap. I held my position until the last second when I raised up like a giant and grabbed the little fat bastard that had taunted me one too many times.

I held him by the helmet and drove my right knee right into his face as hard as I could. He instantly dropped like a rock as blood poured out over his face and onto the ground. Whistles sounded off all over the place, but it was like I could barely hear them in the distance. It is a given that I was pulled from the game, but I can promise you that it was a long time before that moron ever let the word "wop" slip back into his vocabulary!

Today I can tell you that I'm not sorry for what I did. I inflicted a well-deserved injury and was proud that I had stood up for myself. I helped to win the game and at the same time helped win one for the Italians.

If there is one person who believed in me more than anyone else at Berwick Academy, and in my entire life for that matter, it was my English teacher, Frances Babb. When I first walked into Berwick, I spoke extremely poor English. It was more than a simple language barrier; at this point in my life it had become a handicap. I could read and speak fluently in Italian, but knew very little of the English language. Mrs. Babb went out of her way to work with me, and to encourage me to speak proper English.

In an effort to overcome my extremely limited English vocabulary, I purchased a secondhand Webster's English Dictionary for just 25¢ as well as a pack of hand cards. Then the real fun began! I challenged myself to learn every word in the English dictionary. This was not an easy or a quick task to complete. It was long and laborious no matter how I chose to divide it up. In order to keep track of my progress, I challenged myself to learn at least 20 new words every day. I would speak them out loud, write them down and then try to build a sentence around each word to give it meaning. There was so much to learn that at first I became discouraged and intimidated by the task as a whole, but I didn't give up. Over time it got easier, I quit misusing so many of the words and I learned how to both write and speak the English language.

During this time my two brothers, Sam and Joseph, were working at the Eliot Rose Farm in Dover Point. Even though they continued to live the life that my father chose for them, my brothers were my biggest supporters and they honored me by taking every Saturday afternoon off to watch me play football.

In late November, 1936, our highly respected Berwick Academy headmaster, Ercel M. Gordon, called me into his office. He informed me that the trustees were giving me a scholarship to pay for one-half of my tuition. In addition, I was given a job at the school to work Saturday mornings and several days a week after school in the chemistry laboratory as well as in the Academy library 15 hours a month. This arrangement was more than I could have ever hoped for. I did not mind the work in the least as it was much easier than what I was accustomed to and allowed me to continue with my education.

One of the highest points for me during my freshman year was receiving my varsity B certificate in football. I had started every game and was the only member of the freshman class to receive this award.

One of the lowest moments happened, of course, at home. Being around my father, it often felt as though I was taking part in a horror show, but this cold December evening was far worse than the rest.

It all started innocently enough. I was standing in the kitchen making an egg sandwich to take to work with me the following morning when my father walked in. He did not say anything, but he took the dish from my hands and dumped the cooked egg onto the floor.

I have, and had, no idea why he would do this, and in all honesty he probably didn't either, but I knew that there was no good end to this situation. My temper got the best of me and I spouted off loudly in Italian. I shouldn't have done this, but in all honesty, the words were out before the thoughts had fully registered in my head.

Trying to end the confrontation, I turned and tried again to make my sandwich for the second time. This time my father came after me with a four-foot sawed off broom handle. My first reaction was shock. My own father stood above me like a madman swinging the broom handle and trying to hurt or even kill me. I felt defenseless and confused then suddenly everything went black.

I woke up on the kitchen floor covered in blood. There was a deep cut in the side of my head and blood was everywhere. I tried, but could not stop the bleeding.

To make matters worse, my father had called the police. He told them that I had fallen against the stove and my mother backed up his story. After the officers left the house, my mother helped me to stop the bleeding and bandaged the side of my head.

I couldn't help her. I couldn't pull myself far enough out of my own thoughts to make sense of the situation, much less what to do about it. Thoughts just raced through my mind at a rapid pace as I couldn't decide whether I should leave home for good or just do away with myself.

In the end I realized that this was my father's problem to bear, not mine. And, while he had the power to make me feel small and insignificant, he did not have the power to control me. This was the root of the problem. I had made my own choices and my father was unable to deal with that reality. What little power my father had over me, he lost that day. Our relationship changed in a moment, and it would never be the same.

After all the chaos at home, it felt good to be back at Berwick Academy following the holiday break. School was my refuge, home was my battlefield.

Not long after the spring semester started, my father suffered a heart attack. This was hard for me, but not for the reason that you might think. I felt bad for my father, but could not muster up the level of emotion that the situation warranted. In the back of my head I had doubts. Was my father truly sick, or was he simply looking for sympathy from the rest of the family in the wake of our current conflict? Without a real answer in site, my only answer was to stay away as much as possible. I did everything in my power to avoid my father and to avoid the situation as a whole.

Then, one day, I walked into the house just as my father entered the front room. We both stopped as if we had walked into a wall and simply stared at one another for a moment. Out of reflex more than anything I asked my father, in Italian, how he was feeling. He replied that he was alright and told me to go into the kitchen and get something to eat.

I'm not sure where the real change came from, but the tension eased that night. It was a small step, but it was one taken in the right direction.

Now, if there is one thing that every American boy knows, it is that springtime means Baseball! I had loved playing football in the fall, loved the feeling of being part of the team, so I decided to try out for baseball in the spring. I made the team as a catcher, and even though we didn't win many games, I loved it! The games were fun, the friendships gratifying and I loved the feel of the untied school spirit that came with being part of the team.

By the time the semester rolled to a close, I had made the honor roll at the Academy. To have started the year as an overage student who could barely speak English to ending it on the honor roll is still one of my proudest achievements. It proved to me that I could make something of myself and that I was on the right path. It proved that all of the struggle had been worth it, and it proved that I was worth the effort that everyone had put into me.

The headmaster rewarded my efforts with not only a full scholarship, but also an after school job where I could earn extra income. My freshman year may have been hard, but the success that I showed provided me with a scholarship for the rest of my time at the Academy.

My success at the Academy changed the course of my entire family. Suddenly I was not the only member of the family who saw education as a gift rather than a curse. My brother Joseph enrolled for his freshman year at Dover High School, and with both of us in school my father's attitude began to change. He even admitted to me that he would have loved to have sent me to high school and even to college but could not afford it so had pushed those thoughts out of his mind. Then, when I was able to do it on my own, his pride was somewhat bruised.

I listened and began to understand where he was coming from. The thought of sending 6 children through school just as we were coming out of the Great Depression must have been a daunting one to say the least.

But I stood my ground.

I told my father that all of my brothers and sisters had the ability and the capacity to learn. Getting an education gave all of them the chance to take control of their own lives and create a life of their choosing rather than one that was forced upon them. They may have to find the path on their own, but they should be given the opportunity to do so.

My second year at the Academy was full of joy for me. Much of the struggle was behind me as I was beginning to master the English language and earn the respect of my peers. I did not realize how far I had come until one day when I was called to preside over an election for a student teacher in my English class. My job was to be the moderator, but the outcome was far different than what I could ever have predicated.

What happened?

I was elected to teach the English class for the entire hour in the following week. It felt like a milestone to me. To have come so far in such a short amount of time and to have had my hard work recognized by my peers was more than I could have ever asked for.

The day that taught went beautifully. My classmates were interested, the headmaster stopped by and was impressed and I felt like I finally belonged in this school with these people.

Of course, by this time I did have a slight advantage over most of my very intelligent classmates in that I had a larger vocabulary than they did. Studying the dictionary had served me well, and I became known for coining phrases such as "ostentating an ameliorated lexiconic structure."

In fact, my command of the English language grew so much that by the time my class decided to publish a class paper, they named me as the editor in chief!

By this point in my high school career, my conviction in importance of education grew with each passing day. I felt strongly that a high school education, at the very least, should be mandatory in our country. For without it, a young life is doomed to obscurity in the army of unskilled laborers. Without an education there is no security and there is no true option of growth.

People who choose to immigrate to this country have no real concept of what it means to be educated. To this day I truly believe that my parents lacked the basic comprehension of what it meant for their children to become educated. They had no idea why their children would be better off and therefore could not understand the desire to peruse higher education.

And they are not the only ones. This is a pattern that I have seen repeat its self time and time again over my lifetime, and it is not always isolated with the older generation. In fact, during my sophomore year of high school a good friend of mine, James Dunbar, told me that I should just give up on the idea of going to law school

He had plenty of good reasons behind his argument. My age for one, the daunting reality of having to pass the bar exam and the fact that he claimed to personally know several "starving" lawyers in the Dover area along.

I appreciated his input, the reality remained the same, I knew what I wanted and was not willing to allow anyone to sway me from my course. This type of opposition is something that we will all face at one point or another, what separates us is how we chose to handle it. Some will choose to give up on their dreams and follow the path of least resistance, while others will push forward and fight their way to victory. I sincerely hope that you will always find yourself in my company, in the second group. The world needs more of us.

I can promise you this, it will not always be an easy road to follow. Even in my own life learning to have the strength to fight for my dreams was not a simple thing. And, every time I thought that the battle had been won, some outside influence would come along and stir things up once again.

During my Junior year of high school this seemingly ever present devil's advocate took the form of my father's Italian friend, Frank Cincotta. Mr. Cincotta was not a quiet man and he told my father that I was nothing more than a "bluff" that would never have what it took to become a lawyer. Now, it is bad enough that he would say something like this in the first place, but even worse, he said in my presence so that I was forced to look my father in the eye as these words were spoken. He went on to say that it was high time that I let go of this foolishness and go back to work for the family.

I tell you, two steps forward and three steps back. Every time my father and I made any progress something would happen to breathe new life into the same old arguments.

This type of rollercoaster relationship continued until that fall when my father's health took a quick and very serious turn for the worse. As I sat in our tiny kitchen and watched tears fall from my father's face I was over come by sadness and grief. He held out his arms and begged me to forgive him, but in truth there was nothing to forgive. I loved him and had forgiven his actions and his stubbornness long ago.

Because there was no damn telephone in the house, I had to run all the way to Broadway to call the doctor. In all honesty I did not know if my father would have the strength to survive the night, but under doctor's care he was able to pull through and his health improved over the next handful of days.

Despite the fragile state of my father's health, living though my Junior year was a form of triumph for me. I was the only 3rd year varsity letterman on the football team, I was elected for the 2nd year as editor of THE TATTLER, a publication that had grown immensely popular and was known to sell out in mere minutes, I was elected as vice president of the student council and my English had improved to the point that I was even able to write poetry!

And I don't mind telling you that I am proud of my poetry! In fact, I would like to take a moment to share a bit of it with you now

The following poem was written in March of 1939:

What Is Life?

* * * *

What is life?
>The man who drifts from day to day
>Finding happiness where he may,
>Living on a poor hebdomadal
>compensation,
>Usually meeting unexpected
>consternation.

>>Is that life?

What is life?
>The man with tremendous influence and
>prestige,
>Who financially could move all but age;
>The social gentility with enormous
>wealth,
>Still trying to make more, neglecting his health.
>>Is that life?

What is life?
>The man who stresses contemplation
>Who seeks fame and tremendous
>compensation,
>And even with indisposition moves intrepidly
>forth
>To accomplish what he may not.

Is that life?

What is life?
>The man who thrives but for a thrill
>Defying and laughing at death and they
>will.
>Their yarns are taken with exaggeration
>And compensated with a tingling
>sensation.
Is that life?

What is life?
>The man of nature - the vagabond,
>Whose moral code is but a song.
>The man who watches the world roll by
>And at night - in his bed beneath the stars he
>lies.
Is that life?

But this is life!
>An amorous man, living for what he has by his
>side,
>And for its cause willing to die;
>His wife, his children, his home and his land,
>You'll find him most a middle class man.
That is life!

* * * *

This second poem was written in 1940:

MY DREAM SHIP

* * * *

My thoughts and my dreams are like ships tossed at sea
-
And the captain aboard is but a poor humble
me.
With sails of pure white and ambition
prevailing,
I must bring safely to port the ship that I'm
sailing.

How am I - in this so raging a storm -
My body so cold and my heart so warm.
How am I going to conquer the sea - ?
After all who am I - but a poor humble me?

The sails not so rigid - the mast not so strong,
My sailors all tell me - I must be wrong.
Without a strong captain - to the bottom we'd depart,
But the captain of that ship is my own warm
heart.

My thoughts like a ship - may be washed
ashore,
Still they may sink and be seen no more.
But if I captain that little ship right,
I may - with God's grace - win my fight.

But even if I do lose my ship at sea -
And my plans sink with it - whatever they be,
I'll still build more - and send them away -
And perhaps one of them will sail home one
day.

My undaunted heart will never be moved,
Even if my hopes - the world has disproved.
Too busy he rolls - minding his cold affair,
To rigidly oppose him I wouldn't dare.

We shouldn't build ships and drift them to fate,
And then all we do is sit there and wait.
And here am I - whose ship may conquer the
sea,
And that the blessings of God - may spell
victory.

But even if all my ships failure they bring -
My last ship will said toward a heavenly ring;
And the angels will blanket and calm the blue
sea,
My soul on that ship - God waiting for me.

This my friends is the power of education. For it is only through education that a poor boy like me can find the power to fully transform himself in just two years time. As a Freshman I could hardly speak or understand English and as a Junior I could write poetry flush with words that many of my classmates were forced to look up.

Again I say that this is that power of education and again I say this is what it feels like to succeed!

The summer before my senior year was a busy one. For one thing, my headmaster once again showed his unwavering belief in me by allowing me to complete an independent study Senior Physics course over the summer. I would meet with him each week to turn in the work that I had done while receiving new assignments. This is not something that he had to do, and I owe much to him that he would be willing to provide me with such a service and an astounding opportunity for growth.

By this time I am 22 and my parents decided that it was high time for me to marry. In this vein they engaged in a form of

Sicilian conspiracy involving me, the idea being for me to marry Frances DiSalvestro. Frances was a beautiful Italian girl, wonderful and kind, but I was not interested. After fighting so hard for my education, I was not interested in marrying until I had the chance to finish. Luckily I had the chance to explain my feelings to Frances in private away from the prying eyes of our families. I told her that by passing on her hand in marriage that I was taking the chance of never meeting another person as sweet and wonderful as she was, but it was a chance that I had to take.

As I started my senior year at Berwick Academy, my life was focused on finishing this crucial step that would bring me closer to my goal of becoming a lawyer, but the world was focused on other things. For it was in September of that year that the War started in Europe.

What war? Why World War II, perhaps you have heard of it?

The war started when the Nazi army and air force attacked Poland on September 1, 1939 without a declaration of war and by September 3rd, Great Britain and France declared war on Germany. A German submarine torpedoed the British liner, Athenia, with 1,400 passengers as it was sailing for Canada and by September 16th, Russian divisions marched into Poland.

It was so different in those days, there was no Internet, not even any Television really. Our only link to the war was what we could read in the papers and that information was delayed by days, sometimes even weeks. I can remember reaching for the paper each day, almost dreading to read the words that would be printed there.

The British sent the Royal Air Force into Germany to bomb industry and German warships and in an early raid six of 24 bombers were shot down. The English then decided to drop leaflets instead of bombs. The British Parliament had the fantastic idea that the industrial might in the Ruhr should not be bombed because industry was considered private property. Have you ever heard of such stupidity? I suggested they start blasting before they get consumed.

It was not long before Poland was overcome. My father made a prediction, and he was right. For it was at this moment that he stated that only America would be able to save Europe.

But it is amazing how even in the face of chaos, life goes on. At this point all six of my parents' children were in school, a feat that consistently brought positive attention to our family. My parents were praised by their friends for managing and, amazingly enough, they began to actively support our desire to get an education rather than try to road block it. It took me many long years to achieve this, but that simply made the victory all the more sweet!

My Senior year was like living in a state of continually celebration. My brother Salvatore and I were able to play football together, I was elected to the position of secretary of the student council and once again I was elected to the position of editor in chief of the school paper, this year named the ACADEMY QUILL.

The only downside to the year was the knowledge that it would be my last at Berwick. I had grown so much at this school, achieved so much and received so much support from both students and staff that it was a bit daunting to face the prospect of starting all over again in the college arena. But perhaps the hardest moment of the year came in the form of the final game of the 1939 football season. Facing the reality that this would be my last game was exceptionally difficult as being a part of the team had always brought me so much joy.

My father's sudden change in attitude was also a source of great joy. I can remember one cold January evening sitting in the living room having a long talk with my father. He had asked me about school and what we were studying and I become so excited that he was interested that I tried to tell him everything all in one fantastically long breath. I entertained him with my knowledge of the solar system, the plague, and other subjects that he had an interest in and eventually the conversation evolved into my desire to go to college. He informed me that if he was in a position financially, he would help me.

He would help me.

Even if there was no real money to speak of and knowing that going to college would be something that I faced on my own, just the fact that his attitude had changed that drastically was more than I could have ever asked for. It was a huge change from just three and a half years before and I was grateful for it.

But college was definitely and important topic in my life at this point. Step one to becoming a lawyer was to finish my high school education. With that hurdle practically behind me, now was the time to set my sights on higher education.

The fantastic part was that I was receiving offers. The mother of one of my classmates inquired if I was interested in a full four-year scholarship at the University of New Hampshire. This was an amazing, and generous, opportunity, but my goal was to attend college away from home and I wanted a chance to look around a bit before I made my final decision. Also, my former English teacher, Miss Frances Babb had encouraged me to become a Catholic priest. If I were to choose this route then I would have my tuition paid at Trinity College in

Vermont. Even though I decided not to enter the priesthood, Miss Babb was able to get me a scholarship to the University of Vermont.

But the offers did not stop there. I was also given the opportunity to accept a scholarship to Bates College through the efforts of my headmaster, Ercel Gordon, and I had another scholarship to Washington and Lee University through Attorney George Varney of Portsmouth, New Hampshire.

For the first time in my life I was truly blessed with options! To be surrounded by so many people that believed in me and believed in my potential was an amazing experience. I had proven myself during my four years at Berwick, and this was the payoff for all of the long hours, hard work and tense moments that I had been forced to face to reach this moment.

After considering all of the options open to me, I had settled on one of two schools, the University or Alabama or the University of New Hampshire. The upside to the University of New Hampshire was the fact that I had been promised a full scholarship. The downside was that I would have to live at home and commute in each day.

The upside to Alabama was that it was very well ranked and I would be able to experience campus life to the fullest. The downside was that I would face tuition.

In the end, I chose Alabama, and, as luck would have it, they chose me too. On June 1, 1940 I was admitted to the University of Alabama!

The rest of my high school career was marked by strong, memorable moments both of happiness and grief. I watched as several of my good friends chose to leave school and join the US Army. The war was moving forward and it was bitter sweet as I shook each of their hands, gave them a hug and wished them good luck.

For many, it was the last time I would see them.

Then there was the moment when I was allowed to defend my father when he was discharged from his job at the Pacific Mills in Dover. They used the excuse that he lived in Rollinsford instead of Dover. After representing him at a hearing before the Independent Textile Union and arguing for some 20 minutes, he was allowed weekly workers compensation and later given his job back.

That day my father looked at me with pride in his eyes, and that is a day that I will never forget.

And finally, there was the day that I graduated from Berwick Academy. It was Friday, June 14th 1940, a warm, sunny day that was as beautiful in reality as it is in my mind. As I sat there among my peers, I was filled with happiness and repeatedly thanked God for the opportunities that he had given me and all of the help that he had offered along the way.

In all honesty, it was difficult to understand that the four years at Berwick Academy were over. Time truly does fly! I was 23 ½ years of age and I would have been this age anyway, with or without a high school education.

My parents were at my graduation, along with my brothers, sisters and friends, and I can remember feeling such pride as I looked at them in the audience. My parents shared that pride. They even gave me a beautiful Westfield wristwatch along with a white sweater that my mother had knitted by hand as a graduation present.

I Alfio Cataflo was finally a high school graduate. I had done it, and I had done it on my own terms. Finally my life belonged to me, and I could not wait to get started!

CHAPTER 5:

College...A Dream Come True

Have you ever held a ticket in your hand and wondered where it might take you? I mean, it's just a simple piece of paper, but the words that are written on it truly have the power to change your life forever.

For example, on September 3, 1940 I held a ticket in my hand. It was small, rather wrinkled and one-way. It was quite possibly the most important piece of paper that I had owned up to that point in my life, for it was that crumpled bit of cardstock that was destined to take me to the University of Alabama.

That day as I stood on the platform at the Greyhound Bus Station, I knew my life was changing forever. My two brothers were there with me, and we were all so incredible excited about what was to come. After all, if I could do it, then why couldn't they?

I knew that I would miss my family, but I also knew that this was my chance to strike out on my own and discover myself. It would be a new environment, a new challenge and, with all hope, a new start to my life as a whole.

As the bus moved away from the little city of Dover and stopped here and there on the way to Boston, my mind began to wander from one subject to another. I thought about the trials I had faced to bring myself to this point. I thought about my family and the life that I was leaving behind. But, most of all I thought about the opportunities ahead and how I might use them to get me one step closer to my dream of attending law school.

This train of thought continued until I arrived in Boston at 8:30 p.m. Now, keep in mind that traveling by bus, especially in those days was very different than traveling by plane or even private car. This trip was not to be a quick one, and Boston was simply my first stop on what turned out to be a tour of East Coast high points.

It started in Boston where I was given the chance to walk around in Park Square, Boylston Street and sightsee along the way. The idea was to spend the daylight hours taking in all that I could, so that I could sleep on the bus at night.

The next bus left out at midnight that night and took me all the way to New York City. This was an amazing treat, and a part of the trip that I was looking forward to because I got to spend the day in New York. It was so impressive! My goal was to see as much of the city as I possibly could, and I spent the day traveling by bus, subway and foot in an effort to cover as much ground as possible. I saw Times Square, Central Park, Grand Central Station, 42nd Street and the Empire State Building. To this very moment I can remember that day and the way that it felt to walk around that city on my own. I felt young. I felt free, and I felt invincible!

That evening I hopped on my next bus. This leg of the trip took me from New York to DC. As amazing as it was to be in New York, it's hard to say whether or not I liked it better than I did D.C. New York was thriving and alive, but D.C. was so steeped in history and culture that it held a beauty all its own. That day I had the opportunity to visit places that I had only read about and it was a true treat to get to see the wonderful sites of our nation's capital.

One of the biggest reasons that I am telling you about this trip is due to one event that opened my eyes to a whole new world. A would that while I had heard about it, I had never seen it and had certainly never experienced what it might be like to live in it.

As I boarded my next bus, I looked around at the other passengers and was thrilled with my luck. This was another night bus, and it was nearly empty, meaning that I could take up the entire back row to sleep in and no one would care.

This plan worked great for a few hours, then suddenly the driver stopped the bus and slowly made his way down the aisle to speak with me. He tapped me on the shoulder and informed me that I would have to move up and take a seat closer towards the front of the bus. In his own words, not mine, the back of the bus was for "blacks" and that was who the seats would be reserved for. He informed me that this was the law and that I would be forced to observe it.

I was floored. I sat there speechless for a moment or two, and then it dawned on me.

I remembered the pre-Civil War history of our country and the Missouri Compromise of 1820. For those of you who may have forgotten, the Missouri Compromise established a boundary between slave states of the south and the free states of the north.

In the span of one short bus ride I had arrived in a whole new world, and it was up to me to adjust. I was grateful not to be black and not to have to face these kinds of limitations and rules. My friends, the culture change was dramatic and it was one that left a bad taste in my mouth.

My next impression of the southern culture was that they were somehow able to completely murder just about any word in the English language. But as strange as they sounded to me, I soon learned that I sounded just as out of place to them. For the first time in my life, I felt like a foreigner.

This all happened so quickly that I didn't have much time to adjust. Just a snotty bus driver who seemed to take way too much pleasure out of what could easily be identified as a difficult situation.

When the bus stopped at for the first time south of the Mason-Dixon line, I saw that the division between the races went far beyond a simple seat on a bus. The restrooms were marked with the now infamous black and white signs and the restaurant as the bus station was reserved for white people. The discrimination was massive, and it far surpassed anything that I had ever seen.

Walking around that rest stop, it truly felt as if the South had won the civil war and I was grateful for the first time for the color of my skin. I felt sorry for the people these rules were forced upon and I was appalled by the behavior that I witnessed. As the bus moved from North Carolina to South Carolina through Georgia and on to Alabama, it seemed as if the black people out numbered the white people.

But it didn't matter.

Because those black people lived under very poor conditions. Coming from someone who has lived through the Great Depression and has on occasion wondered where my next meal would come from, I can tell you that I had never witnessed poverty of this level in my life. These were very very poor people. It was another of those moments, and to revelations that works to shape you and sticks in the back of your head for the rest of your life.

When I arrived at the beautiful University of Alabama, there were then nine schools on campus. The Graduate School, Law School, School of Medicine, College of Arts and Science, School of Commerce, School of Education, School of Engineering, School of Home Economics, and School of Chemistry.

At that point that College of Arts and Sciences was the largest school on campus and is boasted an enrollment of approximately 1,830 students. The school was held in such prestige that its graduates were granted unconditional admission to any graduate school in the country. Can you imagine what that would look like today? Having the opportunity to attend a school where simply graduating would assure your acceptance into the graduate program of your choice? Amazing...truly amazing!

Since one of the biggest reasons that I chose Alabama was to have the opportunity to experience campus life, I was excited to receive my housing assignment at Ridgecrest Dormitories. I was given a room in Dormitory Q and was assigned to eat at the Ridgecrest Dining Hall.

Honestly, I was so excited about just being there that it is hard to separate one event from the next as they are all rolled together in my mind! I do remember what the dorm was like though. Very different from today's students, I thought that my room was very spacious with plenty of room. I was excited to have my own desk, to meet my roommate and to only be sharing a room with one other person! When I hear about kids today heading off to college, I usually hear about how tiny they think that their rooms are. Not to me. To me, it was paradise!

Going to college also gave me the chance to enroll as a cadet in the Reserve Officers Training Corp. or R.O.T.C. as you might know it. At that point it should not have surprised me, but when they handed out uniforms, they were confederate gray! I know that I had studied American history, and even doubled checked several times during my time at the university, and the North most definitely won the Civil War. However, this did not appear to be the case on the campus of the University of Alabama in the fall of 1940!

Wanting the chance to experience campus life to the fullest, I decided that I needed to report for freshman football. After taking the physical, I was given the chance to try out, but they did not have a uniform small enough to fit me! All of the ones that they had on hand were simply too large, and it wasn't until they got a uniform from Tuscaloosa High School that I had one to use.

This didn't bother me in the least! I tried out for quarterback and made the team – fourth squad! The main purpose of the fourth squad was to scrimmage against the varsity team. I bet you can guess how those scrimmages often went!

So, with that in mind, let me tell you about one particular scrimmage that will be forever burned into my mind. (Trust me, the varsity team made absolutely sure that this was a lesson I would NEVER forget!) During one of the scrimmages, the coach called a pass for my squad. The only problem was that there was no one open for me to pass to. I tried, ducked and weaved the best that I could, but in the end, I just ended up running for my life towards the end zone.

I scored. One would think that this was a good thing. It was not.

It would seem that scoring off of a run was enough to seriously injure the pride of our starting line-up. In fact, it was probably the worst thing that I could have done to that. After that play they every time we tried to run the ball I ended up with half of the line doing handstands off of my chest. We couldn't move that pigskin 10 inches without them pouncing, much less 10 yards!

By the time the afternoon was over, I could hardly walk. We may have scrimmaged after that, but I can promise you that I have tried to make another run like that! It was not worth the recovery time.

My next task to tackle was running for president, president of the freshman class that is!   I realized that I was the long shot, but lets be truthful here, I had been a long shot most of my life. Plus, I had two key advantages that the other candidates did not have.

The first was that I had a strong network of friends to support me, such as Hugo Black, Jr. a friend whose father was the current chief justice of the US Supreme Court, George Wallace, a future governor of Alabama and presidential candidate and Curtis Reading the president of our own student council. My other advantage, one that no one could consider or even know the extent of, was my own tenacity.

I knew that if I wanted to win this election, then I had to convince my peers that I was one of them. I had to convince them that I was a Southerner just like they were.

So here is what I did.

I told them that I was absolutely a Southerner, and that my credentials would prove it. After all, my parents came from

Southern Italy, I grew up in Southern New Hampshire and I went to school at Berwick Academy in South Berwick, Maine.

How much more southern could they possible want!

I won the election.

BUT, I did not win the majority vote. This meant that there would be a special run off election where I would compete against the second place candidate, Billy Hunt. Billy was everything that I was not. He was a fraternity man and southern gentleman with deep pockets and even deeper campus connections. I knew that this would not be a simple race to win, and that if I wanted to claim victory then I was going to have to continue to work just as hard as I had in the primary.

So I reinforced my campaign with the help of Ed Devlin, the third place candidate and continued to press forward. The day of the election I spent hours holed up in my Dormitory waiting nervously for the results. I had all but given up hope when Buddy Cleveland, Student Council President, came running in shouting that I had won the election by a landslide.

In an instant all hell broke lose! Cheers erupted from every direction and I was overcome with congratulations from all sides. On October 22, 1940 after not even two months on campus, I had been elected as President of the Freshman Class in the School of Arts and Sciences at the University of Alabama. It was a moment of affirmation that I will never forget or let go of.

The following day I withdrew myself as a football player. At 138 pounds there was no way that I was ever going to make the starting line-up, and as the recent election had shown, my strongest talents were found off of the field. In short, I realized that I was much, much more than just another tackling dummy.

Besides, I had plenty on my plate to keep me busy. For not only did I win the election, but I was also extremely honored to become one of the very few freshmen to be asked to be part of the University of Alabama weekly newspaper, *The Crimson White*. To me, this was like bringing a small bit of home away with me to school. After spending so much time working on the school paper for Berwick Academy, *The Crimson White* was an exciting new opportunity that still felt just a little bit like home.

On October 23rd, 1940, I received a letter from Gene Wortsman, Co-Chairman of the Association of the College of Arts and Sciences of the University of Alabama, which read in part as follows:

"Dear Alfred;

Congratulations on your election to the presidency of the freshman class in the Arts and Sciences School. By virtue of your position you automatically become one of the two freshmen representatives to the executive committee of the Association of the College of Arts and Sciences."

To say that I was honored by this recognition is an understatement of a lifetime. I took this position very seriously and was very active in the organization throughout my time at the University of Alabama.

One thing that holds true no matter where you go to school, your freshmen year is sure to be one filled with moments of learning, both in and out of the classroom. For example, in October of my freshmen year I learned very quickly that one thing that you never tell your college roommate is, "I have a date." Unless that is you want said roommate to immediately run and scream this announcement throughout the entirety of the dormitory.

Which is exactly what my roommate did!

As soon as I told George, my roommate, that I had a date he took it upon himself to scream it across the dormitory. "Freddie's got a date!" In a span of seconds it seemed like our room filled to the brim as my friends crowded around me to offer their advice. After all, this would be my first date with a southern belle, and they had to tell me the rules.

With my friends' help I put together what they thought was the perfect outfit of light gray trousers, a white shirt, black shoes and a "Red" Garafalo's green sweater. I looked sharp!

Her name was Mary Helen Chappell and we have a lovely evening. We spent some time visiting with her family then walked together along the edge of a cotton field beneath a full beautiful moon. She was a lovely person, but nothing more. While I enjoyed her company our relationship was strictly platonic and did not progress.

As much as I enjoyed my time at the university, it was like we existed in a bit of a bubble while on campus. For when we were on campus, that was our world. We were aware of the tension and drama taking place outside of our hallowed halls, but it was not our primary focus much of the time.

And then something would happen that would bring our attention sharply back to the war in Europe. The instatement of the draft was just such a moment. Sometime in the middle of September 1940, the US Government passes a law ordering all males between the ages of 21 and 35 to sign up for the military draft. Let me promise you something, receiving that card, and knowing that there is a strong potential of your number being called, is a very sobering moment to say the least.

I loved being at school. I loved the energy and rhythm of campus life, but it was also nice to go back home. I was actually relieved to get the chance to visit my family and friends over Christmas break my freshman year.

It was such a huge change from those tense early days at Berwick Academy!

My parents were thrilled to see me and couldn't wait for me to tell them about my time in Alabama. My brothers soaked up every word as they looked forward to their own turn to walk the hallowed halls. I felt, finally, like the returning hero who was loved by all. Going home for the holidays was a wonderful experience and one that I will always treasure.

And, as it tends to do when you are having fun, the time simple flew by. It seemed as if I barely had time to step off the bus before it was New Year's Day and time for me to head south once again. This time the trip was like driving through the pages of the calendar rather than down the lines of a map. With each mile the snow melted away and gave way to green grass and sunny skies!

I can promise you that this is one huge advantage of living in the South! There is no, well very very little, snow in the south! I loved that the sky was clear and the day warm even though it was still early January.

After going home for the holidays, I knew that I had a decision to make. I loved attending the University of Alabama, but I also had to face the financial reality that I had a full scholarship waiting for me at the University of New Hampshire.

This was not an easy topic for me to face, and it was not an easy decision for me to make. But, at the end of the day, I knew what I needed to do. It took me most of the semester to fully commit and make up my mind, but I decided that after the spring semester I would be transferring to the University of New Hampshire. This would take me closer to home and would also remove a great deal of the financial strain that I had experienced during my freshman year.

Coming to the University of Alabama had been an intellectual experience, one that marked my life and brought me significantly closer to my dream of becoming a lawyer.

That year my name and photo appeared in the 1941 COROLLA yearbook as one of the many undergraduates of the University of Alabama. It was printed as follows:

"CATALFO, ALFRED, JR.; Dover, N. H.; Freshman in Arts and Sciences; Crimson-White; Newman Club; Excelsior; President, Freshman A.B. Class; A.B. Association; Executive Committee; Associate Editor of Newman Club Publication"

The hardest part of my decision was informing my classmates. In all honesty, I was not expecting the reaction that I got. The big reveal happened when my college English teacher asked me if I was expecting to return to the University the following year. When I admitted that while I loved Alabama, I would not be coming back, my classmates were appalled!

I tried to explain to them that the reasons were mostly financial and had nothing to do with the school or with any of them, but it didn't matter. They were adamant that I belonged with them at Alabama and that they did not want me to leave. Truly their responses were flattering.

Ralph Budge, L. C. Adams, Rosco Williams, Elizabeth Chappell, and Dot Averall openly said, "I thought we had changed you into a good southerner", "Yeh", said Elizabeth, "You have been a pretty good southerner", "Oh, Freddie, don't change schools". I was moved emotionally by such spontaneous affection.

I left Alabama on the day that I finished my last final exam. The exam was no problem, I can't even remember much about it. But I can remember how hard it was to mount the steps that put me on the bus for the final time.

I didn't want to go.

As amazing and wonderful as it had been to arrive at Alabama the previous fall, it was that much harder to leave. I knew that I was doing the right thing, and that I had made my decision for the right reasons, but that did not make it any easier.

The fact that my family was so incredibly happy to see me made things easier. It was nice to be back among the familiar and even nicer that none of the old tensions had surfaced among us. But I would miss my new southern home, the friends that I had made and the freedom that I had found.

I took some time to grieve in my own way, and then closed the door and put it behind me. Because I knew, even then, that if I spent my time living in the past, I would never be able to fully embrace what the future had to offer.

And, if I am going to be completely honest I enjoyed my time at the University of New Hampshire just as I had enjoyed my time in the south. I was admitted as a second year student without any problem and all of my credit hours transferred.

To help make the daily commute I purchased a second-hand 1931 Chevrolet motor vehicle to carry me to and from campus. My goal had been to stay in the dorms as I had done at Alabama, but there were no rooms available at that time.

On Tuesday, September 17, 1941, I responded to my draft board in Dover, New Hampshire. My number was 1680. I was told to go ahead and enroll at U.N.H. for the first semester of my second college year, but for me not to expect to be deferred for the second semester. I did not expect to, but I wanted to join the Navy and especially the U.S. Naval Air Corp. I wanted to be a fighter pilot.

Until that time I continued to live my life as a college sophomore to the fullest. I tried out for the Junior Varsity football team and was giving the nickname, "Bama" by my teammates. I also joined the R.O.T.C., and, to my pleasant surprise, our uniforms were not confederate gray. They were standard U.S. Army and I loved them.

My big break on the football field came during our first game of the year. Keep in mind, I was the smallest member of the team, and I was not initially on the starting line up. As the game started, one of our players could not find his helmet and I was sent in as a temporary replacement until a new one could be found.

That was all the time I needed!

With every snap I exploded over the backfield until I had every eye in the stadium glued on me, wondering what I would do next. I did so well that after the game that my coaches handed me the playbook, told me to study it and I never looked back.

A few weeks later I was elected to be team captain and started every game from then on. In a span of 4 quarters I had gone from a Junior Varsity walk-on to a Varsity starting lineman. At the end of the season, it was even written that I was one of the most aggressive players of the year.

And, as if things couldn't get any better, I was even able to find a room on campus. My own brother, Guiseppe a freshman at the time, gave up his room so that I could be closer to campus and to everything that I needed to do. I have always loved my brothers, but this was a sacrifice above and beyond anything I would ever have asked him to do.

We made the exchange at Thompson Hall and I was given my brand new room number, 108. Life was definitely good!

Chapter 6:

The War Comes Home

Sunday, December 7, 1941 is a day that changed not only my life, but also the lives of every American both present and future. It started out innocently enough. That morning my brother, Joseph, several of our friends and I were all working at the American Woolen Company. Our job was to clean the machinery in the spinning rooms and we spent the time mouthing off as young men are prone to do. The work was easy and the company pleasant.

It took just a single moment for all of that to fall away.
At 12:55 p.m. Eastern Standard Time, Japanese planes from carriers attacked the U.S. Naval Station at Pearl Harbor, Hawaii, where most of the U.S. Pacific Fleet was anchored. Nineteen U.S. warships, including eight battleships, were destroyed or disabled, 189 planes were destroyed, 2,403 soldiers, sailors and civilians were killed, and over 1,200 more were wounded.

We were unaware of what had happened until roughly 2:00p.m. when someone ran screaming into the factory. "The Japs attacked Pearl Harbor! The Japs attacked Pearl Harbor!" In an instant all of us froze. It is one of those moments where you will never forget where you were or how you felt when the world changed.

I will never forget the smell of the machinery in that room, and I will never forget the anger that filled me as the shock faded away.

And I was not the only one.

Each of us was shocked that an attack had happened on US soil, but the shock wore off and in its place was a real and lasting anger that did not fade in the days and weeks to come.

As I wrote in my diary at the time, "While we have every intention of winning at this stage of proceedings we are told we have a chance to lose, but the United States cannot afford to lose and I was willing to give up my life for my country before I would allow that to happen."

I can remember that night, sitting there in the dark writing down the words that were pouring from my heart. Words powered by emotions such as fear, patriotism and sorrow. As I sat there I knew that I had a choice to make. I had to decide what to do, where to go forward from this moment. I knew that I didn't want to sit around and do nothing. There were plenty of people willing to that and I wanted to offer more.

After thinking it over I decided that I wanted to try and join the U.S. Naval Air Corps as a fighter pilot. To my young mind that plan was simple: join the Navy, kills Japs and help win the war!

One thing was for certain, the surprise assault on Pearl Harbor immediately ended the debate on whether or not America would enter the war in Europe. As soon as the first bomb struck American soil the time for talking had past. We were going to war and we were going voluntarily.

My brothers and I took some time and decided that the three of us would join the U.S. Navy. This decision and it implications brought out mixed emotions in my parents. My father was filled with pride, my mother with fear. Both reactions are understandable and both were echoed in our own hearts. We didn't know where this journey would take us, we just knew that it was one that we had to undertake.

The day after the bombing at Pearl Harbor, Franklin D. Roosevelt appeared before a special session of Congress to speak to the hearts of all Americans. He declared December 7th, 1941 to be a day that would live forever in infamy and called for an immediate declaration of war on Japan.

The United States Senate voted for war 82 to 0 while the House of Representatives voted for war 388 to 1. We had known it in our hearts and it was now official, we were going to war.

Following the Japanese attack on Pearl Harbor, Hitler made a grave mistake. He believed that America's early neutrality in the war denoted it as both weak and defenseless. Based on this belief he declared war on the United States on December 11th, 1941 with Italy following soon after.

In a matter of days it seemed as if the country had transformed. Cities and towns all across the nation were practicing air raid blackouts and suddenly my R.O.T.C. classes were taken more seriously than any other.

Just nine days after the attack I wrote a letter applying to join the U.S. Naval Air Corps as a fighter pilot. It was not long before I received the following message in reply:

"NAVAL AVIATION CADET SELECTION BOARD
150 Causeway Street, Boston, Mass.
December 19, 1941

Mr. Alfred Catalfo, Jr.

80 Oak St.
Dover, N.H.

Dear Sir:

Your inquiry regarding Naval Reserve Aviation Training has been received. Enclosed you will find a circular of information and a questionnaire.

After noting the necessary qualifications, if you feel that you meet the requirements, please fill out the questionnaire enclosed and return it to this office in order that an appointment for interview and flight physical examination may be made for you.

Thanking you for your interest in Naval Reserve Aviation Training, we remain,

Very truly yours,"

I felt that I possessed the necessary qualifications, I filled out the questionnaire and I was accepted into the training program.

Now, as I mentioned before, my brothers and I all made the decision to join the US Navy. However, we all received very different assignments. My brother, Salvatore, did his boot training at the U.S. Naval Station in Newport, Rhode Island. During the war, he served on a destroyer protecting convoys crossing the Atlantic to Africa and Europe. He made numerous trips across the Atlantic and was in combat with enemy submarines from time to time. Fortunately he was never injured during these battles.

My brother, Guiseppe (Joseph), was assigned to the Medical Corps of the U.S. Navy and served in the Pacific Theatre of War. His duty stations varied and serving time on several different aircraft carriers until the war ended. He was a pharmacist first-class.

Today, as a parent, I cannot imagine how my parents must have felt with the three of us scattered across the globe. I know that they were proud and that my mother had a three-star flag prominently displayed in the window. But it must have been extremely difficult to maintain a brave face in front of our sisters.

On December 31st, 1941, my friend, Joseph Charles Kafel, and I drove to Boston and I reported to the Naval Aviation Cadet Selection Board. I was to become a Naval cadet under the V-5 Program and to train to become a fighter pilot. I was told I needed a two-year college education and I had not yet finished the second half of my sophomore year. However, I received a letter from the Navy to deliver to my draft board. It was sealed. I was told that a law was passed on March 12, 1941 which permitted me to be deferred from the draft, provided I was admitted to participate in the Civilian Pilot Training Program (CPT) at the University of New Hampshire if it was available and I qualified.

I was thrilled to be part of the program and quickly began to look forward to my new classes. So three nights a week, from 7 to 10 you would find me deep in training to do my part for the war effort.

The ground courses were taught by Dr. Edward Stolworthy. Dr. Stolworthy was the head of the Department of Technology at U.N.H. This was combined with flight training five afternoons a week, weather permitting, at the Skyhaven

Airport in Portsmouth, New Hampshire (in later years known as Pease Air Force Base).

On January 7, 1942, I was deferred by the draft board until May 15, 1942. So, now I started my second semester at the University of New Hampshire taking R.O.T.C. (Reserved Officers Training Corps) and C.P.T. (Civilian Pilot Training Program), all at the same time.

I won't lie, it was a grueling schedule to keep, but it felt right. It felt like we were doing the right thing, and besides, by that time it was all military all the time on the U.N.H. Campus. The war, and the war effort were the number one issue on everyone's mind. And, even though we all managed to continue with the day-to-day necessities of living, this harsh reality was never far from the surface.

On February 21st, 1942, I accepted an invitation by the US Navy to report to the Naval Aviation Cadet Selection Board. I was given a physical, had my teeth checked and told that I had perfect vision. In short, I passed with flying colors.

I was pronounced to be a perfect physical specimen and was given the thumbs up to fly under the Civilian Pilot Training Program as a student pilot.

And though the situation that necessitated my flight was not ideal, my first time going up in an airplane was amazing. It was so beautiful up there! No matter which way I looked, the ground seemed to roll out endlessly below me. It just took one time, less than one hour behind the controls and I was hooked. Each time I landed, I began to count the hours until I could take off once again.

By April 7th I was able to solo. Soloing in an airplane is one of the most thrilling things that you can do. Even I was a little amazed that I could take off and land gently, safely and beautifully. When I taxied in after that first flight, I was immediately swarmed by my fellow students. To me it seemed that they did everything but break a bottle over my head! I truly was a pilot and now I wanted to become a fighter pilot.

On May 19, 1942, I took a full day of physical and comprehensive examinations at the Naval Aviation Cadet Selection Board and was
given the high sign late afternoon. This meant that I had successfully passed all my examinations and was ready to move forward with my training.

Because of gas rationing, I took the bus home that day. The war was effecting every area of our lives. I'm telling you, just when you managed to put it out of your mind, you would turn around and there it was again.

On Saturday, May 23, 1942, I was back at the Naval Aviation Cadet Selection Board in Boston. At 4:10 p.m. in front of everyone and in an office full of Navy personnel, myself and three others took the oath to serve my country, my president and my officers over me to the best of my ability, so help me, God.

Then it was sign the dotted line and that was all it took. Within a matter of minutes I was signed up for a four-year tour and told to expect to be called up for active duty within the month. I was now officially property of the US Navy and it did not take them long to claim their property.

On July 6th, 1942 I reported to Colby College, in Waterville, ME. This was a special nationwide program designed to accelerate the training of military aviators. My class was made up of 30 Naval personnel and 40 Army personnel, each of us hungry to make our own mark on the war.

I was given the rank of platoon leader of Platoon No. 2, simply because I had more experience than many of the other cadets due to my experience with the ROTC both at Alabama and U.N.H.

At Colby we were introduced to the new 300 horsepower bi-wing Waco planes and in what felt like no time at all, we were flying them. It took only three days for them to put us in the air. And 10 days after that, we were soloing.

On July 20, 1942, I practiced take-offs and landings with a cross wind and felt free as a bird and wonderful. My landings were strong and very soon after I was checked out by my instructors. They were pleased with my level of aptitude and my fearless attitude.

But learning to be a fighter pilot requires more than just flying and landing the plane. To be a fighter pilot you have to learn how to push your equipment to its limits and beyond. You have to be in tune with your aircraft and know how to squeeze every last ounce of ability out of both man and machine.

We had to learn spins, stalls, series of 8's, S-turns, spirals, slow rolls (hanging by my seatbelt, while I was upside down at 3,000 feet up), steep turns, lazy 8's, chandelles, pylon eights, half rolls and inverted reverses. I was able to literally throw the plane all over the sky and make it bend to my will. Three U.S. Naval officers led by Lt. Commander Bowers came to check on our progress on July 26, 1942. We were all complimented collectively.

By August 7, 1942, American Marines landed on Guadalcanal and two other small islands of the Solomons. The landings on Guadalcanal had little opposition and the next day the

Americans had overrun the Japanese airstrip on the island and renamed it Henderson Field.

Before leaving for home on September 3, 1942, I had accumulated 50 additional solo flying hours with a 300 horsepower plane (Waco). I also had been awarded my pilot's license to fly 300 horsepower planes and taken another highly important step toward Pensacola and to becoming a fighter pilot for the U.S. Navy. Achieving this goal would allow me to join my two brothers and to begin to make a difference in the outcome of this war.

Coming home from Maine was a harsh reality for me. As I walked down the street I felt as though I was walking through a ghost town. Everyone was gone. Everyone had been drafted. The running joke was that the Army had taken every single male, right down to the neighbors dog, but it was a bitter sweet joke.

Bitter sweet because it was practically true.

By then end of that month, it was my turn to go. The goodbye was difficult. I was the last of the boys to leave and my parents and sisters were left facing the unknown. They did not know when they would hear from us again. They did not know where we would be going. And, they did not know if any or all of us would be coming home to them once again. It was an emotional moment. One that I both never wanted to end and wished it would fly past all in the same breath.

Luckily I was not headed over seas right away. My first stop was the United States Pre-Flight School on the University of North Carolina at Chapel Hill. And, even though we were at Chapel Hill, we were treated as though we were cadets at the US Naval Academy. It was first class all the way right down to the uniforms!

We were issued cadet uniforms, naval dress blue and naval dress white with shoulder boards. Also, fatigue military clothing, shoes, socks, belts, guns and bayonets. We were fully equipped. We were housed four in a room.

The following days were a never-ending parade of both physical and comprehensive exams. It was like living through a marathon race that lasted for days.. Every moment was scheduled and if you were not in a constant state of rush, then it was guaranteed that you were going to miss something.

Also, we were always required to stay in formation and I loved it!

Now, any of you who have been in the armed forces know that being singled out is not usually a good thing. In fact, one of the last things that any cadet wants if for their instructor to call their name in front of the group of a whole.

It is almost never a good thing!

So, with this in mind, you can imagine my gut check reaction when one day, while in full parade uniform my name was called out, clearly and loudly. "Cataflo! Front and Center!"

Not good!

I racked my brain as I moved briskly to the front of the formation, but could not think of what I might have done wrong. I stopped, saluted and held my breath to await whatever was coming.

To my surprise it wasn't bad. The orders were shouted out in loud military fashion. "Cataflo, take this battalion around the field and return it back to the same station!"

What!?! No problem!

Just that quickly I took over the 10th battalion. I yelled out in true military fashion, "Battalion!" and waited for the company and squad leaders to yell back before commanding "Attention....Right Face!"

At my command the entire 10th Battalion Corp. of cadets turned right and, as I screamed out "Forward March!" the US Naval band blasted off with Anchors Away and we were off.

I had been well trained for this moment, both at Alabama and at U.N.H., but that did not diminish it power. It felt great to be recognized by my instructors and to be given charge of the battalion as a whole I was excited about the sudden promotion and excited about what it may bring.

First Cadet Battalion Commander and later Cadet Sub-Regimental Commander to my great surprise. I wore three stars on my clothing to denote my cadet rank, and I often wondered what I had done to deserve such an honor. But deserved or not, I appreciated the honor.

My time as a cadet gave me much to be thankful for. It instilled in me a new love of flying and it also gave me the chance to indulge in an old past time, football.

Even though I was the smallest member of the team, even of the entire league, I was often praised for my tenacity and grit. We won 10 games that season and only lost one. Beyond that I was voted captain of the team and was often singled out by the coach and his staff. They said that I hit like a 200 pounder and I loved the sting of battle.

The purpose of these types of schools was to develop men whose physical and mental strength as well as their inner fortitude would enable them to master the fastest, most vicious machines in the world - fighting aircraft. Out of its rigorous, comprehensive, competitive program came cadets who were strong, rugged, disciplined, intelligent and well on their way to becoming the smartest, most aggressive fighting fliers in the world - all officers in the U.S. Navy Reserves, or Marine Corps Reserves.

But don't think for a minute that they neglected our scholastic training. We hit the books just as hard as we hit the training field.

The hardest part of being a Naval Cadet was knowing that the war was moving forward and that we had not yet taken our places beside our brothers in arms. My own brothers had already gone through their basic training and had received their duty stations while I was still going through this extensive training process. The solace we found was knowing that this training was going to make us far more effective once we made our way to the front lines. What we learned now would have the power to make us more than just soldiers; it had the power to make us deadly.

On November 8, 1942, the Allied invasion of French North Africa began under the supreme command of General Eisenhower. Some 107,000 American and British troops landed at Casablanca, Oran, and Algiers. At the same time I was completing my pre-flight training at Chapel Hill. From there, on December 8th, 1942 I was moved to the US Naval Air Station in Memphis, TN.

This school was different from Chapel Hill in that it was to be more focused on combat training and the actual mechanics of flying. We would wake up each morning ready to face a full schedule and ready to eat, breath and, at some point, fly these big bad machines. To this end, our days were fully packed. We started each morning with a full half day of ground school then spent every afternoon training in the sky.

For many of the cadets this was their first experience with actually flying a plane. I felt like I was far ahead of the curve given that I had already earned not just one, but two pilot's licenses during my time in New Hampshire and in Maine. By that time I had roughly 90 flying hours to my credit and was licensed to fly both 90 horsepower and 300 horsepower planes.

In all honesty at that point I had more time in the air than many of my instructors!

But it didn't matter. I had to look at it like this. Even though I had already earned my licenses, every minute spent in the air training was one that would make me a stronger pilot. And I would need each and every lesson that I could get if I wanted to be effective and safe in the war.

So I spent several hours flying with my instructors then worked my way up once again until I soloed and was allowed to begin practicing maneuvers on my own.

By January of 1943 I had completed my training in Memphis and had over 130 solo flight hours to my credit. At this point I had just one additional week of ground school to complete before I would leave Tennessee behind and travel to the U.S. Naval Air Station in Pensacola, FL. I held the rank of Cadet Wing Commander and I was ready, more than ready at this point, to finally get to Pensacola and move forward with my training.

As I worked my way through the cadet program, my focus had always been to work harder than everyone around me and to make a good impression on those around me. Since I kept doing well, I felt that I was achieving those goals, but it was not until I received the following letter from my former football coach that I knew it for a fact.

Here is what he wrote:

"I know your training at Memphis will be as satisfactory and successful to you and your officers as your training was here. I need not encourage you in any way. We are all certain you will make a good flyer, and an even better fighter. I have coached football for the past 10 years and I have yet to coach anyone with more honest-to-goodness scrap, determination, and love for battle than you have. I enjoyed my work with you, as much as you could have possibly enjoyed yours with me."

At this point, I was flying high. I was successful as a pilot and was ready to move forward with my training and then take my skills to the front lines. But, this was not what fate had in store for me.

My life changed once again on January 25th, 1943. On that day my flight instructor in Memphis, Ensign Charles Mark, was given permission to take out a plane and asked me to join him. I was excited to do so as any excuse to fly was always a good one!

Together, we flew the plane out 25 nautical miles from the base to an outlying auxiliary field that was marked off like the deck of an aircraft carrier. This was where we had learned how to both take off and land within the distance allowed by the deck of a carrier, for as Naval pilots that would be our standard base of operation.

In fact, that was exactly what we were doing on that faithful day, taking turns practicing take-offs and landings one right after the other, touch and go's as the practice is often called. It was not difficult for either of us, and truly this was as routine as a training flight could possibly get.

Thinking back I can remember that it was cold that morning. Cold enough that we wore our heavy flight gear and that there was a frost still hugging the ground. But a cold sky is often a clear sky and it was beautiful.

We had gone through the routine some dozen times when disaster happened.

Ensign Mark was at the controls and he guided the plane into a steep climb on take off, just as we were trained to do. Everything was fine until we reached an altitude of between 200 and 300 feet.

The propeller stopped.

In a single moment we went from a standard climb to full and complete engine failure.

Instantly our Naval training kicked in and Ensign Mark put the plane into a steep nosedive in an effort to regain sufficient air speed and get control of the plane. The idea was to glide us to a safe landing. The only problem was that we did not have sufficient altitude for this plan to work.

The plane's left wing struck the ground like a hammer on an anvil. I remember the sound it made as we hit, and then the world went black.

I woke up some time later, dazed, in shock and pulling my self off the ground. My left humerus was broken, leaving my arm dangling down by my side. I tried to stagger back towards the plane, but I had no feeling in my legs or feet and could not see past the blood running down my face. I only made it a few feet before I collapsed.

The next time I came to, Ensign Mark was shouting at me. It sounded as though he was yelling through water and it was all I could do to focus on his words. He was trying to get me to free him from the cockpit. The danger in a situation like this is that the plane can catch on fire. If it did, while he was still trapped, then there would be no way that he would survive.

Hanging upside down, still held in place by his restraints, he was in worse shape than I was. His left arm was broken, as mine was, but he also suffered a broken left leg and a broken right ankle.

Slowly, fighting my way inch by inch, I crawled to the cockpit and managed to free him. Together we made our way away from the plane, literally dragging ourselves away from the remains of the demolished aircraft.

This time, then the lights went out, I did not wake up again for three days.

Later, I was told the story of how we had been found.

Apparently several black men had driven by in a pick-up truck. They saw the wreckage and figured out pretty quick what had happened. They picked us up and took us back to the air station in Memphis.

As the story goes, one of the men looked at me and wanted no part of helping me into the truck.

"I don't want to pick up that man – that man is dead!"

Luckily for me they not only did they pick me up, they got me to safety and to people that could help me.

I woke up in the medical dispensary at the Air Station. My left arm was strapped and stretched, my right eye was bandaged, both my legs down to the toes of my feet felt numb and my back ached continuously. My only relief from the pain was to try to sleep and that was only possible when I was given pain meds.

This entire time is hazy. It's like flashbulb moments of snippets that my mind captured while I was awake. But, the one thing that I do remember clearly was that I was given paperwork to sign that permitted the removal of my left arm.

I refused.

To me, I would rather die than go home without an arm. I was told that my arm was mangled beyond repair, but I was not willing to give up. To me, nothing was impossible, just look at my life!

Finally, the Navy flew in Lt. Commander John Rankin, an orthopedic surgeon stationed on in Pittsburgh. Lt. Rankin performed an in-depth surgery on my arm, implanting a series of screws to secure the bones into place. These screws would be permanent and would stay with me for the rest of my life.

I didn't care.

The surgery lasted for four hours. After it was over I was placed into a plaster arm and body cast with my left arm held at shoulder level. I was given the pleasure of staying in this exact position for the next 18 solid weeks.

I didn't care.

It itched, I suffered from occasional swelling and, as many of you probably know, the cast made me feel half crazy most of the time.

But I didn't care. I had gotten to keep my arm, and my hopes were high that I would be cleared to fly once again.

My classmates did their best to keep my spirits up. They visited often and provided me with nothing but words of encouragement throughout the healing process. My roommates from Chapel Hill even brought me my very own set of gold Navy wings after they graduates from Pensacola.

Then, my brother Joseph came to visit. He stayed with me during my operation and part of the recovery process. I can't remember much of his time there, but I remember that I was a complete mess. He later told my mother that when I came out of the operating room and began to recover that I spoke for four hours without stopping telling how close I came to meeting death, close enough that I poked her right in the eye and that Hitler was at the bottom of all my troubles. My poor mother laughed.

And still the war went on. On February 9th, 1943 the American forces recaptured Guadalcanal. During the battle the Japanese lost 10,000 troops, the Americans just 1,600; it was an important victory, strategically and psychologically.

But it was hard won, and the wounds were deep on both sides.

It was also hard for me to hear or think about the war. Before the crash, I would hear this type of news and I would think about being able to help. Once I had completed my training,

I knew that my skills would make a difference to our troops and to the war effort. Being chained to a hospital bed was a hard reality to accept.

My instructor, Ensign Charles Mark, and I occupied the same room until he was transferred to the Great Lakes Naval Hospital in May, 1943. The last time I heard from him was by a letter he wrote me dated July 27, 1943. He was then still at the Great Lakes Naval Hospital, but he was encouraged that he was no longer forced to use either crutches or a cane. Because he was lucky enough to suffer no back or eye injury as I did, he was planning to go back as a fighter pilot - great! At this time, my own future looked bleak, but I was keeping my hopes up high.

On June 17th, 1943, the U.S. Navy transferred me to the U.S. Naval Hospital at Portsmouth, New Hampshire in hopes that being closer to home would help speed up my recovery process. So, with my arm in a sling, a patch over my right eye, a bad back and injured right hip, I took a train to New Hampshire.

After the cast had been removed, it was discovered that my shoulder had healed in an abnormally high position. To rectify this, and return my shoulder into the correct position, the joint had to be broken and reset. Add this new injury to the fact that the joints in my wrist, elbow and shoulder had calcified during recovery and I was still facing a long road to recovery. It took many months for the pain to diminish and it made the trip to New Hampshire very difficult.

My back and hip have bothered me the rest of my life and no longer can I lace up my own shoes. I had to find someone to help each and every time I wanted to dress.

The rest of the summer was a never-ending stream of monotony. Each morning I would wake, dress in my white cadet uniform and report in for medical inspection. Then I would return home to sit for the rest of the day. I could come and go as I pleased, but with the extent of my injuries, there was not much that I could do at that point.

During this time I was also told that due to a scar on my right cornea, I would probably never fly again.

This was the devastating news that I had been dreading.

My mother was simply happy that I was alive. But I wanted more from life than to simple be alive. I wanted to live!

Long ago I heard a fantastic quote:

"One crowded hour of glorious life is worth an age without a name."

I agree, wholeheartedly with this. In fact, this is what I wrote in my diary at the time.

"The plane crash has probably given me a permanent cornea scar of my right eye. I received a laceration of the cornea in the plane crash from my goggles. This eye injury will prevent me from flying as a pilot ever again, in the military or in private life. All of my classmates are fighter pilots. Some are in the war zone. Some are dead. I am alive, if that means anything. It does not mean much to me."

And while I fought my own personal demons, my brothers and classmates fought the war. In early July, 1943 Sicily was invaded by U.S., British, Canadian and French troops in an offense that included 2,500 ships, 3,700 aircraft, and eventually 480,000 men. Opposition was light and several

108

cities in southern Sicily were captured on the first day. By July 22, 1943, General George Patton captured Palermo, the capital of the island.

My own future hung in the balance.

At this point I had two choices. I would either receive a full medical discharge or I would be reclassified within the Navy. To do either I had to travel to the Classification Center in Bainbridge, Maryland. In that moment, I did not know what I wanted to do. My dream in the military was to fly. To be a real part of the offensive and someone who would fight valiantly on the front lines.

It was not to sit at a desk somewhere and file papers.

I felt like I was back, working the mill, trying to find a way to make my dreams of going to school become a reality. The only difference was at that time, my actions and my future were under my own control. Today, it was up to the Navy.

And it was not destined to be a quick process. After days of red tape and being pushed from one person to another, I was finally discharged from the Navy on October 19th, 1943.

I received a Certificate of Discharge - service number 705-51-79 - Aviation Cadet - V-5 - U.S. N.R. - character of discharge Special Order (C.G.) under satisfactory conditions - Conduct 4.0.

On my way home it was difficult not to feel sorry for myself. I had a bad back, a bump knee, my left arm was like a Frankenstein puzzle gone horribly wrong, extensive uncorrectable cornea damage and to top it all off, I couldn't tie my own shoes so I was stuck wearing loafers.

I felt like a failure.

My brothers and my comrades were off fighting the war and I was stuck at home. I was stuck helping my mother peel potatoes and my sisters with their home work. It was fine, but it was not enough.

I wanted more, and now it was time to find a way to get it. I might not be able to fight, but my mind was still sharp and my will strong. I was down my friends, but I was definitely not out.

Chapter 7:

The End of A Goal....Now What?

By the middle of October I was no longer a member of the US Armed Forces. I was a civilian. I was back home with my mother and father. And, I was most definitely not happy about this turn of events.

Knowing that I could not stand to sit at home, day after day, doing nothing and rolling the events that had led to this point over and over in my head, I went to the local unemployment office trying to find something that I could do. They send me to an aircraft factory in Northwood, MS.

It was by no means a great job, but it was a job and it paid $68.00 a week more than I was making now. Which was a big fat nothing! I reported for work, but left feeling even more frustrated than even when I learned that I could not pass their physical requirements.

Somehow in the span of a single day my life had descended into the reality of a living hell.

Now, as I saw it, I had two options. I could sit around feeling sorry for myself and eventually go quietly insane, or I could go back to school and find a way to finish my education.

I chose option two.

So, by the end of that same month, I had returned to the University of New Hampshire to enroll as a first semester junior.

It seemed that no matter where I looked sites, sounds and news of the war, surrounded me but I had to put it out of my mind. I knew now that it was time to put that dream and desire behind me as I refocused my life and continued with my studies.

I was fortunate that the University was willing to work with me at all, because they were almost 8 weeks into the fall semester as I was just walking in the front door. I knew that I had to dedicate myself to my studies if there was to be any hope of successfully completing the year.

So that is what I did.

Each day I commuted to the school by bus or train, my left arm in a sling and my injuries still apparent. I got to school, I worked hard and I let nothing distract me. Not the fact that I had no income and could not have a job. Not the fact that I could not borrow money and was only able to attend school on deferred payments. And, not the fact that I was sitting at home while my friends and brothers fought on foreign soil.

This was my reality until I made one of the best decisions of my young life. I joined the American Legion, Post #8, Dover, New Hampshire, on October 26, 1943. The men at this post became family to me of another sort. They understood how I felt, they understood what I had gone through and they understood what it would take for me to move forward from this point.

To this day I feel as if I may actually owe my life to these men. If not for them I don't know that I would have ever truly put the plane crash behind me so as to focus on what life still had to offer. It was through their friendship that I let go of the bitterness and truly began to live once again.

It was also through their friendship that I was able to continue with my education. Because not one full week into my membership, three magnificent, generous members of Post #8, Gordon Booth, Cycil Bennett and Herbert Clark, all World War I veterans, volunteered to co-sign a note for $500.00 with me at the Strafford National Bank so I would be able to attend college until I got my tuition and monthly pension as a disabled veteran.

Now, keep in mind that money held a different value in this time, and $500.00 in 1943 is the rough equivalent of over $6000.00 today.

Their actions and generosity humbled me and made me determined to work that much harder to succeed.

As I sit here today, looking back on my life, it is interesting how "life" as a whole doesn't really seem to care what you are dealing with. It continues to move forward regardless of your state of mind and you are left to either step up to the plate or fall by the wayside.

At this point, living my life was somewhat like living on a roller coaster that never stopped. I would have these gut wrenching lows followed by amazing highs that I hoped would never end.

They did, and it felt like the moment my financial fears were lifted my life plummeted once again on November, 5th 1943. You see, on that day my father took ill. His health had been poor on and off for years, but this time felt different right from the start. I took him to the hospital hoping to find answers, but they had none to offer. My family gathered by his bedside hoping, and praying for a miracle to take place.

And, as days turned into weeks, that is where we stayed.

It was like our new routine. Each of us would do the things that we had to do, then the moment we were free, return to the hospital so my father would not be alone.

This was our reality for a full 45 days. Then, the hospital decided to attempt a gallbladder operation. To our surprise the operation was a success and on Christmas Eve, 1943 I took my father home. Having him home for Christmas was a small miracle that each of us held dear. With the war going strong, it was like our lives were laced with tragedy, and every new day would bring news of another life lost or missing. Pvt. Fred Simon, age 19, who lived on our street, was killed in Italy. Ralph Clark died of wounds. Ralph Ciardi and Wyatt Webb were killed in action. James Blaisdell is missing in action. Dick Couture was wounded. These were men that I knew, that I grew up with and I felt their loss in the depths of my heart.

World War II was so different from the War in Iraq or the War on Terror. Each day the newspaper was filled with lists of names. Long, seemingly never ending lists of those young men who wouldn't be coming home. You couldn't get away from it.

Even at the grocery store. The civilian population was forced to ration goods whether we wanted to or not. Meat, butter, eggs, coal, oil, fuel oil and tires were in short supply. Gasoline was rationed at a mere three gallons a week.

Why you ask? Because everything went to the war effort. This was one time when every man, woman and child was united in the support of our troops and the defense of our country.

114

The attack on Pearl Harbor was still fresh and biting in our minds and we were not willing to learn to speak German!

Still, even in light of my father's homecoming, it was a dark Christmas that year. The War still raged. My brothers were still away. All my father could do was sit or lay in bed. This was how the days passed, and this was how we welcomed 1944, with cautious hope and often bitter hearts.

There were moments of joy and even fun. Like the day I moved into my first apartment. A good friend, Danny Colokathis, and I had rented an apartment on campus with the understanding that we would act as janitors. They asked us to remove the garbage, mow the lawn, remove snow, change the screen windows, etc. This was fine, but we didn't want to do it. So, we paid the kid next door $10 a month and he did it for us. Win/win situation all the way around if you ask me!

Then, in March of that year I was finally awarded a 60% service connected disability in relation to my injuries. The money was retroactive from the previous fall and receiving it allowed me to pay back my $500 loan along with all related interest.

And then, there was Eddie. I met Edward J. O'Rourke, Jr (I know, it's a mouth full) in May of 1944. He was a pre-med student at Harvard University and we hit if off right away. In fact, Eddie become the closest friend of my life and I treasure our relationship.

So as you can see, happiness did happen. On rare occasions these types of bright shining moments would burst through the clouds allowing you to bask in their warmth.

They just didn't last long enough.

No matter where you turned or looked, the War surrounded you. By May 1944 the allied forced had launched an offensive designed to drive the Germans to the north and out of Italy. The campaign was successful and by June 4th, the first American units entered Rome.

The offensive was successful, but it was costly. A cost paid in the form of lives lost. Here at home, we did our best to honor the fallen through both thought and action. One of the things that we did at U.N.H. was hold a memorial service in front of Thomas Hall. As taps was played and the firing squad sounded off we remembered not only the 3,040 U.N.H. students currently serving in the war, but also that 41 who would never come home.

Little did we know at the time, but those days marked the true turning point in the war. As I completed my third year at U.N.H., the allied troops stormed the beaches of Normandy as D-Day began.

It was June 6th, 1944. Just after midnight two U.S. airborne divisions sank silently to the beaches to be followed in the early morning by 4,000 invasion ships, 600 warships, 10,000 planes (only one of which was shot down), and 176,000 allied troops.

The landings took place along a series of beaches in Normandy between Cherbourg and Le Havre - the Americans' code-named Utah and Omaha, the Canadians' Juno, and the British Gold and Sword. The Germans had six infantry divisions near the beaches and others within range, but due to Hitler's interference and their failure to pinpoint invasion plans, they failed to stop the first troops. Despite heavy casualties in some sectors, U.S. losses on Omaha Beach were 1,000, by the day's end there were 150,000 allied troops dug in, with thousands of vehicles and tons of material. It was the largest invasion in history. A day marked by both epic movements and individual heroism.

Back home, I marked a victory of a different sort. On June 9th I accompanied my father to the Strafford County Superior court where he applied for his American citizenship. Then, we made the journey to U.N.H. campus where I gave him the full tour and showed off the extensive library. We walked around campus, had lunch and I even showed him my apartment. It was the first time that my father showed real pride in what I had accomplished on the academic front and it is a moment that I will never forget.

On June 22nd, 1944, President Franklin D. Roosevelt signed the Servicemen's Readjustment Act providing financial aid to veterans for education, housing, and other needs. This act would become widely known and admired as the GI Bill. Because of this law, I had the balance of my tuition paid, as well as my entire law school education.

I have to admit, with the introduction of the GI Bill, my finances were healthier than ever. My education was paid for, my apartment was covered, and I even had a job.

I had been appointed to the position of supervisor of Bellamy State Park in Dover. The park had a bathhouse, restrooms, included a lunchroom for refreshments and a public beach on the Bellamy River. The great thing about Bellamy was that is was easily accessible. With the gasoline rations still in effect, people needed somewhere to go that offered a break from their daily stress without using more gas than they had available to them. Bellamy was the answer to this riddle.

My salary was $122.00 a month, plus 50% of the profits on sale of refreshments and I was thrilled. Plus, the position did not interrupt my attending summer school at the University.

Of course, the job did not end up being exactly what I had in mind. I thought that it might be sort of glamorous and fun, but really by days were spent chasing dogs off the beach, selling candy, providing fatherly advice to youngsters and flirting with the pretty girls.

Not too bad really.

But, as I have said before, this was a time of taking the good with the bad. As I was enjoying my summer at the park, I learned that one of my best friends, Fernand Roberge, was killed during the Normandy Invasion. On the second day of the invasion, he was killed in an air battle in the skies over France when his plane was shot down by Nazi fighter planes. He was 21 years of age at the time and it was an assignment he had volunteered for.

On July 11th, President Roosevelt announced that he would run for president once again, "if the people command me to continue in office....I have as little right as a soldier to leave his position in the line." President Roosevelt was in fact nominated for an unprecedented 4th term in office, but what the public did not know was that his health was declining rapidly. Several presidential insiders were aware of the issue and urged that the vice presidential candidate be a man acceptable to the broad majority of Americans. Senator Harry S. Truman from Missouri was the chosen to be just such a candidate.

Now, this does not really fit with the flow of the story that I am telling here, but it is a moment that I feel compelled to include. That summer at Bellamy was filled with all sorts of interesting people and situations, but there is one that stands out starkly from the rest.

One afternoon when I was working at the park, there were a couple middle-aged women hanging around telling people's fortunes. They had that kind of strange gypsyesque look, and to me it was simply a bunch of bunk. I didn't believe in it, and I didn't want anything to do with it.

However, several of my employees ganged up on me and laid down a dare for me to let one of the women read my palm. I gave in, more to make them happy than anything else, and sat down to submit myself to the wishes of this fortuneteller.

She grabbed on to my hand and spent a few minutes oohhhing and aaahhhing over things that I definitely could not see. Honestly I was just glad that my hands were clean. After awhile she looked up and announced to the room that I was going to live to a ripe old age, have a very successful life, and I would enjoy two marriages, both happy unions. I thanked her and didn't think much of it for years to come.

Now, fast-forward about 70 years as here I sit at age 93 telling you my story. I have in fact lived a very successful life, I am enjoying a ripe old age as we speak and I love my second wife as I did my first.

Friends, this did not dawn on me until I started to write my book. I had not thought of this woman in probably 50 or more years, but today I find that she was right. So now, I pose the question to you. Was it an accident of chance and luck? Or are there people out there who really have the power to read a person's future simply by looking into the palm of their hand?

I know what I think, but you are going to have to decide on your own.

As summer came to a close so did World War II. True, there was still work to be done, but the nail biting tension that had dominated the previous months and years was starting to fade as the allies continued to make progress and thwart the German offensive.

We thought that we had seen the worst of the war. We did not know how wrong we were.

On August 29th, the Russians and Polish discovered Majdanek, a disgusting example of German depravity that shocked the world and cost the lives of 1,500,000 people. Unfortunately this was the first of many such harrowing discoveries. These were the acts of this self-acclaimed super-race society under Adolf Hitler. The bastards.

With each new discovery my relief grew that the world as a whole had had the strength to stand up to Hitler's deranged sense of entitlement. It was not an easy fight, but it was one worth stepping into.

Also during that summer, I made my name available to the University Bureau of Appointments for a possible teaching and coaching job. One of the letters of recommendation read as follows.

The Bureau of Appointments
University of New Hampshire
Durham, New Hampshire   July 24, 1944

Gentlemen:

It is with pleasure I offer you this letter of recommendation in favor of Mr. Alfred Catalfo, Jr. He has written me of the possible opportunity to coach and teach this coming Fall.

I had Mr. Catalfo in my platoon at the U.S. Navy Pre-Flight School, Chapel Hill, N.C. The association of a platoon officer with the members of his platoon is extremely intimate. The officer, through observation and study, learns to know and understand each of his men thoroughly, as it is his duty to determine what qualities each man possesses as to character, leadership, courage, honesty, cooperation, etc. An officer accomplishes this through day-long association with his men.

I do not hesitate to recommend Mr. Catalfo to you gentlemen. He is a born leader, possessing the finest of ideals and most certain to accomplish whatever it is he sets himself to. There can be no question of his sincerity, determination, willingness to cooperate and of his innate ambition to succeed.

I have taken my part in the training of approximately 1,500 Naval Aviation Cadets in the past two and a half years, and I assure you gentlemen Mr. Catalfo rates at the top.

As to leadership, while at Chapel Hill, Mr. Catalfo rose from Cadet Company Commander to Sub Battalion Commander, and upon graduation to the rank of Cadet Sub Regimental Commander, the second highest rank any cadet is eligible to hold at the Pre-Flight School.

As to athletics, he performed well in basketball, soccer, swimming, wrestling and boxing, and played an outstanding game at left end and on my squadron football team. Lacking size, Catalfo more than compensated for this handicap with his fiery and inspired play, and took the first string job away from men who possessed better physical attributes and the benefit of more extensive college coaching. You undoubtedly are familiar with Mr. Catalfo's athletic record at Berwick Academy, where he was a three sports man, and of his work at the Universities of Alabama and New Hampshire.

If there is any further information I can furnish you, I shall be glad to do so.

> Sincerely,
> Robert J. Meyer
> Lieut., USNR

Receiving this letter meant quite a bit to me. Lt. Meyer was a man that I both respected and looked up to. His praise meant more than what ten other men could have offered, and it did me a world of good. At a time when I felt like my options were beginning to dwindle, Lr. Meyer breathed new life into my dreams and reinvigorated my self esteem.

Plus, it is largely due to this letter that I was asked in September of 1944 to serve as the head football coach at Berwick Academy. I was thrilled! I was excited! I was scared to death.

I had never coached a day of football in my life and I had no desire to fall flat on my face in front of my Alma Mater. So, I did the only thing that I knew to do.....I read.

In the spam of a single weekend I devoured three different books on coaching football. They were, "Winning Football" by Bernie Bierman, "Practical Football" by Herbert Crisler, and "The Control of Football Injuries" by Stevens and Philips. My plan was to mix my experience as a player with their training for a coach and come up somewhere in the middle with a winning strategy.

Sounded like a good plan to me.

So, now armed with my brand new knowledge, I traveled to my old stomping grounds to meet with the potential squad.

They all called me "Freddie."

I explained to them that off the field I didn't care what they called me, but otherwise they would address me as "Coach." And my trials as "Coach" started from the very first moment.

I had a youngster, Laurent Michaud, who wanted to play, but his parents feared he would get hurt. I went to their home and convinced them that football was no more dangerous than crossing the street, climbing a flight of stairs or riding in a motor vehicle. It had all of the dangers that accompany life itself. Once you are born, each of us are subject to being exposed to danger, and the biggest danger is to live in fear of danger.

It was a tough sell, but I finally convinced them. They allowed him to play, he was a good player and he never got hurt. In fact, none of our players got hurt during the season.

On September 21st, 1944, I told my entire football team at practice that Berwick Academy would be playing St. John's of Concord, New Hampshire on November 11, 1944 and that we would be going to Concord with an undefeated record. That was my goal! And that was our goal.

But it was not going to be easy.

Our Academy team had only six players that returned from the prior years. The equipment was inferior. It was falling apart in my hands and there way no way that I could send my players out onto the field looking like this. It was definitely a problem, but it was one that I could fix.

I began to call in every favor and friend that I had in an effort to help out my team. The progress was slow, but steady. I got Olie Adams, coach of Dover High, to give me much of his discarded equipment, such as eight pairs of cleated shoes, eight pairs of shoulder pads, eight pairs of football pants, etc. Carl Lundholm, Athletic Director of the University of New Hampshire, also gave me discarded equipment, which was helpful. Plus, Ercel Gordon, our headmaster, was able to purchase extra equipment and jerseys so our team looked great and protected, including winter gear.

Our season was a success. And, while I would love to give you the play by play, I think that the follow excerpt from the 1945 Berwick Academy Yearbook does a better job than I ever could. Why don't you read it for yourself.

THE FOLLOWING APPEARED IN THE
1945 BERWICK ACADEMY YEARBOOK

"Unbeaten, untied, and but once scored upon 1944 's eleven enjoyed a season of seven victories in Berwick Academy's most successful gridiron campaign in thirty-five years.

'Freddie' Catalfo, Academy alumnus and all-around athlete, who recently was graduated from the University of New Hampshire, coached the team.

From a squad of thirty-five Coach Catalfo came up with a well-balanced and consistent eleven that ran up 132 points to its opponents' six.

The Berwick boys, averaging 146 pounds, trounced Eliot High, Exeter High, Brewster Academy, Hampton Academy, Somersworth High and St. John's High of Concord in that order. St. John's was the only team able to score on the Academy gridsters.

Stellar performers included Co-captain Bill Morgridge, 180 pound fullback acclaimed by many as one of B.A.'s all-time grid greats; Harland Cheney, triple threat quarterback, who really lived up to the athletic name of Cheney; and tremendous Ernie Littman tipping the scales at close to 200, a tower of strength in the guard slot."

At football practice on October 25, 1944, the headmaster at Berwick, Ercel M. Gordon, complimented me. His words were simply, but they stood out and they meant a lot. He told me that a good coach makes a great difference. To date, we had not suffered a single injury and had won every game.

I'll take it.

On Wednesday, November 1, 1944, we scrimmaged Dover High for the second time. My Academy team, two teams deep, was able to push Dover all over the field. The Dover coach was amazed. He couldn't believe the difference in the team and that these were the same players from 5 weeks earlier. Shaking his head, he shook my hand and said, "This team is exceptional."

My life was starting to take off and I felt like I was flying. I was in my senior year at U.N.H, I was a successful football coach and I had a girl friend.

She was 20 years old and her name was Jane. Jane Cooper to be exact. Believe it or not, one of the things that we bonded over was cigarettes. Back then it was popular to smoke and no one thought about the health risks. It was just fun. Not something that I had ever done before, but Jane liked to smoke and she liked that I was able to provide cigarettes for her.

Being a civilian, this was a luxury that she could not easily get her hands on. Cigarettes were rationed and were kept in large part for the sole use of the Armed Services. Being a veteran, I could get them with no problem, and I did. For her.

In a span of weeks we became inseparable, spending every free moment together and enjoying each other's company.

I fell in love. A first for me, but I embraced this new emotion with both hands.

Everything was wonderful for about 8 months. Then my relationship started rolling through dramatic ups and downs that eventually threw it off track all together.

The heart of the problem was that Jane's mother did not care for me. And, if truth be told, my mother did not care for Jane. I was willing to stand up to my mother. Jane was not.

After nearly eight months of dating, Jane informed me that the two of us were different. Different? I was a Catholic and she was Protestant. I was a Democrat and she came from a Republican family. I was Italian and she was a Yankee. I never considered these alleged handicaps significant. I loved her. These differences were probably important to Jane or they were just another excuse.

Finally I asked her point blank, would things be different if her mother felt differently about me. Jane didn't hesitate. "Of course!" she said, "but she doesn't."

And that was that.

Jane wanted to continue to date, but she wanted to be free to date others as well. This arrangement didn't work for me.

Not even a little bit.

So, that was the end. I had fallen in love with her without reservations and, of course, I was emotionally devastated for a while, but it was time for both of us to move on. As Alfred Lord Tennyson once wrote, "It is better to have loved and lost than never to have loved at all".

On November 7th, 1944, President Franklin D. Roosevelt won an unprecedented fourth term, with 25,602,504 popular votes to Thomas Dewey's 22,006,285. The electoral vote was 432 to 99.

By this time my college career was coming to a close. I had a single semester left at U.N.H. before I moved on to Boston and to law school. Not truly knowing what the future would hold, I was honored to be chosen as one of 20 students at U.H.N. to be named in *Who's Who Among Students in American Universities and Colleges.*

You know by now that my goal all along has been law school. This was the prize from day one and now I was closer than ever to achieving my dream. There was just one more hurdle to   overcome.

I had to get the approval of a member of the U.S. Veteran's Administration in order for the government to move forward with my G.I. Bill. I though all along that this would be the easiest part of the process.

I was wrong.

Some young druggist showed up on campus and informed me that I did not qualify to be a law student. I sat there, said nothing and then promptly went down and had all of my records transferred to Massachusetts. The transfer went smoothly and within a few short days, I had my approval!

On November 29th, 1944 I was officially admitted to the Boston University School of Law.

This was a defining moment in my life. On that I had been working towards from the very first day I set foot in Berwick Academy. Against all odds and despite the hurdles life had thrown at my feet. I Aflio Cataflo had been admitted to law school and I would become a lawyer.

Stepping onto that campus for the first time felt like victory, and it was a great great moment.

Chapter 8:

The Beginning of a New Life

On Monday, January 29th, 1945 I became a student at the Boston University School of Law. I was accepted, I registered for classes and I was finally and officially going to become a lawyer.

Now I would like to ask you to do me a quick favor. Stop for a moment and imagine what this felt like. A first generation Italian immigrant that wasn't even supposed to be able to finish high school? This was a defining moment and one that I was and still am very proud of. My friends....I had made it.

The next day was a big day for me as well, for not only did I start my classes, I also met my future roommate. A good friend of mine from the University of New Hampshire, Louise Flynn, had asked that I meet up with her brother Tom and get to know him a bit. Apparently Tom was not known to be very outgoing. Louise thought that I would be a good roommate for him at Law School and that I would help him to break out of his shell. Tom was on board with this plan and agreed to find us a room on Beacon Hill near the law school. He could pick the place and we would share the expenses.

While going through the process of applying to law school, I was thrilled to learn that I would be getting my full tuition and books paid as a service-connected disabled American veteran and in addition a total of $134.00 a month from the U.S. Veterans Administration ($65.00 for sustenance and $69.00 for my pension). This was a huge relief! Now, I could take this time to focus on my studies without having to worry about working so that I could survive.

And, to tell you a bit about my brothers, and the type of men that they are, it was during this time that my brother Joseph wrote me a letter and offered to loan me his entire savings of $900.00. Since he had no idea about the GI bill or about the money that I was receiving from my pension, he thought that I was trying to find a way to pay for school. He was a truly wonderful brother and I greatly appreciated the offer, it's just that I didn't need it.

It didn't take Tom long to find us a room. I took a quick tour, liked what I saw and we were moved in by the end of the week.

On January 20th, 1945, U.S. President Franklin D. Roosevelt was inaugurated for his fourth term. It was because of this election that in 1951, the U.S. would adopt the 22nd Amendment limiting a president to two consecutive elected terms. In April of 1945, President Roosevelt died of a massive cerebral hemorrhage. Vice-President Harry S. Truman was sworn in a few hours later to assume the monumental task of replacing a world leader in closing out the most devastating war in history.

A War that was finally coming to a close.

On April 29th, 1945, Adolf Hitler married his companion of many years, Eva Braun, and prepared his political testament in which he appointed Admiral Doenitz as his successor. He blamed both Germans and Jews for failing to help him in his struggle to defeat Bolshevism. The next day, Hitler and Eva Braun committed suicide (Hitler by shooting himself in the mouth, Eva by poison). Their bodies were taken outside the bunker where he had led the final stand of the Third Reich, doused in gasoline, and burned. No traces of the bodies were ever found by the Allies.

On May 7th, 1945, German Admiral Friedeburg and General Jode signed unconditional surrender of Germany at the headquarters of General Ike Eisenhower in Reims, France. The war in Europe had come to an end.

Wait...let me just say that one more time so that it has time to sink in. The WAR in EUROPE was over! Unconditional surrender of Germany. This was amazing news! But, it was only half the battle for the Japanese had yet to surrender.

That summer my roommate Tom and I decided to try and improve our living arrangements. We liked our apartment fine, but were starting to feel cramped. Well, imagine our surprise when we were able to find a significantly bigger apartment, one that was closer to campus at one third of our current rent. My friends, this one was a no brainer!

We moved onto the fourth floor facing the street into a space with two desks, two bureaus, two couches that opened up into full size beds, a large dinner table and six chairs, a walk-in closet, a small kitchen and a large bathroom. The main room was so spacious that there still was plenty of space left over. We were now paying $30.00 a month ($15.00 each) where we were paying $90.00 a month at 33 Revere Street for half the space.

But even with all of this happiness in my life, there were still moments of darkness. Such as the day that I learned that John Valhos, a friend I had known all my life, was killed in the War. That wasn't the bad part. The bad part was that John's family was notified of his death by the local undertaker, not by the US Army. There is no excuse for this level of disrespect.

August 6th, 1945 was the day that the world was forever changed. For it was on this day that the USAF plane the Enloa Gay dropped an atomic bomb on the Japanese city of Hiroshima. The bomb was a new uranium fission type that delivered a blow equivalent of dropping 20,000 tons of TNT straight to the heart of the city. Sixty percent of the city was destroyed in the blast and firestorm that followed; some 80,000 Japanese were killed; many thousands more were burnt or developed radiation poisoning.

But still the Japanese did not surrender.

So, on August 9th, 1945 the United States Air Force dropped the second, and final atomic bomb, this time on the city of Nagasaki. With the second bombing 40,000 Japanese were killed.

A few short days later on Tuesday, August the 14th, the world did more than change, it was turned upside down, sideways and every other direction you could think of. I remember that it was hot and that I spent a good portion of the afternoon studying by the river before eating dinner out on the town. In fact, I was walking home from dinner when I saw a group of people gathered around a parked car listening to President Truman address the nation. He had but a single point to his message, the war was finally over.

On that day Japan had surrendered unconditionally and the war that had hung over our heads for so many years was finally over.

My body was tingling, my head was reeling, it was hard to know what to think or even where I should go. I just stood there for a moment as a thrill of satisfaction rolled up and down my spine and my whole being was overcome with an extreme feeling of patriotism. In a daze, I stumbled my way back to my apartment, watching the news spread through the city like wildfire as I walked. Around me Boston was going mad as people reacted to the reality that the fighting was finally over.

On Charles Street, servicemen blocked the traffic, jumped on cars, cars tooted their horns, fire trucks loaded with servicemen blared their sirens through the streets and paper rained down the buildings like snow. The people were related, relieved and thankful all in one blinding moment. People were kissing, Park Square was jammed, Tremont Street was blocked off and noise poured in from every direction.

Headlines screamed, "THE WAR IS OVER!" Women in tears, people drunk, police disregarding regulations; all of Boston's conservative people going mad. Everyone was dancing with joy. The noise went on into the night. It increased with activity. Flags waving, sirens, horns blown by many people - the war was over! This war was over! Liquor stores were crowded. The crowds on Tremont Street grew with rapidity and the place was jammed. The night was hot. The outdoor breeze was good. Fights, more drunks, more paper, more kissing, embracing and loving. Good old U.S.A. was back to normal, back to the days of celebration.

As I walked the streets that night with my friends, I felt like I was walking on air. I felt as if a huge weight had been lifted from my shoulders and like I was floating more than I was walking. Truly it is hard for me to find the words to covey the emotion and the reality of that night. I can't find them, because they do not exist. There are just some things that you have to live.

The next day President Truman declared a national holiday, giving me time to go home and share my joy with my family. My brother, Salvatore, was home. He had been in the Atlantic

133

on destroyer escort duty. He held the rank of motor machinist third class and was now an instructor at the U.S. Naval Base in New London, Connecticut. My brother, Joseph, was with the U.S. Navy, but on his way home.

Here on the home front one of the first real physical sign of the end of the war was the end of gas rationing. For the first time in years I was able to pull into a gas station and call out "Fill it up!" That my friends felt really good.

It was during this same time that I learned that I was being considered for the position of head football coach at both Maynard High School and Mission Catholic High School. Coaching football was something that I loved to do, so this was fantastic news for me. But, while I wanted to coach, I also had a chance to head to New Orleans with my friends for a quick four day trip.

Unfortunately I couldn't do both. So, when I stopped by the school for the final word and found out that I had in fact been chosen for the position, I decided to stay in town and take the job.

Now, I didn't know it at the time, but that was a very important day in my life. That was the day that I first met my future wife, Caroline Joanne Mosca. Caroline, who preferred to be called Carolyn was employed in the history department of the library, and she and I had struck up a conversation that day as I happened to walk in when she wasn't busy. What started out as a quick chat turned into a two hour talk and I was instantly smitten.

She was Italian.

She was smart.

She was beautiful, and I was desperate to make a good impression. I'm guessing that I did, even if I wasn't sure at the time!

It turned out that the Mission High School football position suited me just fine. I could get there each afternoon after law classes by subway or trolley and then back again when I was done. Classes started at 8:00 a.m. and ended at 1:00 p.m. each day so I was free to coach football at Mission Hill Catholic High School in the afternoon.

Before I went to coach the Mission Catholic High School football team in Roxbury on Monday, September 10, 1945, I stopped at the Boston Public Library to talk to Carolyn. We went to the interior quadrangle of the library where I shared her sandwich. Early that evening I took her to see a movie at the Metropolitan Theatre. I accompanied her by trolley to Waverly Square and I met her mother, Giovanina (Batoli) Mosca.

One huge point in my favor was that I was able to speak with her mother in her native tongue. Being born in Sicily, Giovanina was a native Italian and I had grown up speaking Italian as my first language. I made a great impression and it felt fantastic! Unfortunately I did not get to meet Carolyn's father that evening as he was working.

I did however get to meet him the following Sunday when I was invited to have dinner at their home.

The night? It was a smashing success! I spoke Italian, I was a Catholic, a law student, good credentials and Carolyn was good-looking, educated, morally sound, an only child. Her parents loved me, and I was completed impressed by her entire family.

In the meantime, in spite of a busy coaching job at Mission Catholic and being inundated with law studies, I was still able to be with Carolyn Mosca several evenings a week and especially on weekends. Our relationship began to blossom throughout the year and I looked forward to the time that we got to spend together. It wasn't long before Carolyn told me that she was interested in going steady and that she loved me.

I knew that I loved her and I knew that I wanted our relationship to continue to move forward.

By October our relationship had become serious to both of us. We went to dinner one night to talk about what we both wanted and decided that it was time for us to go steady. I gave her an 8 x 10 photo of myself in military dress by a U.S. Naval plane and I wrote, "Carolyn, I thought flying was the most wonderful thing in the world until I met you" and signed it, "Love, Fred". I think she was by far the best girl I had ever been out with in my life.

In November we took the next important step in our courtship...I took her to meet my mother! The day started when I took her to the University of New Hampshire to see the school and to meet my friends. Next, we went over to Berwick Academy and watched a football game at my alma mater. Then, we went home to meet my family. That night Carolyn met my mother, Vincenza Catalfo, my father, Alfio Catalfo, my sister, Mary, age 22, Francesca, age 18 ½ and Ida, age 14. They all loved her!

And what was not to love?

She was a good-looking Italian girl who was well dressed, well mannered and well educated. But more than that she was fun, sweet and pleasant to be around. They truly did not come any better than her and as I often told her, Carolyn came with a touch of class.

I knew that I loved Carolyn. More so, I knew that she could offer me all of the emotional security and happiness that I could every want, and I admitted this to her, but I was in no financial position to marry yet. We would have to wait.

But there was one thing that I could do for her.

On Monday, December 24, 1945, I went to Boston with Eddie O'Rourke and his brother, Hughie, by train. I had a purpose that day, one that required me to seek out Carolyn and ask her a very important question.

I got down on one knee and presented her with a ring, asking her to marry me and to be my wife.

SHE SAID YES!

Let me tell you friends, that moment was almost as sweet as the one that ended the war. It was like fireworks exploded inside my body as I was filled with joy. |

I was engaged!

I had a fiancé!

And I loved her with all of my heart.

Later our families got together to celebrate our happy news. How did we celebrate? Like any good Italian family, with a party stocked with plenty of food! My family made it known that all of them loved Carolyn and highly approved of her joining the family. She was very kind, unselfish, loving, intelligent, morally sound, educated, good-looking, Italian and Catholic. Her parents went back home to Watertown that evening, but Carolyn stayed with us and shared my sister Mary's room.

Christmas day, 1945 was a fantastic day at the Catalfo home. I remember that day and how happy and proud that I felt. Pride in both my family and in Carolyn. Carolyn was as in love with my family as she was with me, which just made her that much more wonderful. She loved how close we were and was in awe of the strong bonds between us all. She loved how there were so many people in the house and how all of my siblings brought friends in and out throughout the day.

My Christmas gift that year is something that I still have and still treasure. Carolyn gave me an engraved identification gold wrist chain which read on the front "Alfred Catalfo, Jr., Boston University School of Law, 1947" and on the back "Loving you is my supreme happiness, Carolyn".

That Christmas was also special because both of my brothers were finally home from their time in the war.

My brother, Joseph Catalfo, was highly decorated. He was honorably discharged from the U.S. Navy as a pharmacist mate first class. He saw combat in the invasion of the Marshall Islands while on the aircraft carrier, U.S.S. Corregidor, and was attached to the Fourth Marine Division during the invasion on Iwo Jima.

My brother, Sam, was highly decorated, as well. He was honorably discharged, having served on a destroyer accompanying convoys to Africa, England and some of the war zones in Mainland Europe.

Sooner than I would have liked Christmas break was over and it was time to fall back into the real world. School was starting once again, and I had a full schedule of classes lined up.

It was a busy time, but Carolyn and I made time to see each other nearly every day. We would often spend our time together studying either as the B.U. Law Library, the Boston Public Library or at her home. I can remember that giddy feeling of first love and how much joy it brought me just to be in the same room with her. When we had time away from our studies, we would go out to lunch or dinner and see an occasional movie. We were young and in love and it really didn't matter what we did, just that we were together.

Love must have been in the air that year, because it wasn't long before my sister Mary announced her own engagement to Roland Oates. I was so happy for her and I was impressed by Roland. He was a Veteran who had served in both the African and European theatres of the war for three and one half years.

From there on out it felt like it was raining weddings and wedding related events around my house. There were bridal showers, fittings, receptions and every other kind of get together that you could think of.

I had hoped that my good friend Eddie would be able to serve as my best man, but he was called to duty in May before the wedding. While I hated that he couldn't be there, I was also pleased that Tom, my roommate from law school would be able to take his place.

On Saturday, June 1, 1946, my baby sister, Mary (Maria dell Elemosina) was married to Roland Oates at St. Mary's Catholic Church in Dover, New Hampshire. The reception took place at the Dover Municipal Auditorium and it was a lovely wedding.

On Sunday, June 9th, it was my turn. I married my beautiful bride in the St. Luke's Catholic Church at 4:30 p.m. in the afternoon. The church was packed! Every pew seemed to be full and someone told me later that there were over 850 people present.

A large part of the audience came from the University of New Hampshire, Boston University School of Law and Emanuel College. Carolyn and I had made many good friends over the years and they were there to support us.

Father Dennis Sullivan performed the services and the music was melodious and inspiring. In fact, the wedding as a whole was impressive, and exceptionally beautiful. The organ was played by Mrs. Doherty while Catherine Hickey sung. They played *Panis Sanglicus, Ave Maria, Here Comes the Bride* and so many other beautiful songs.

When I look back on this day, I remember thinking about how blessed I was. The church was full. Every row from the front altar to the rear of the church was filled to capacity. Carolyn and I both knew and cherished them as friends. We were showered by wedding gifts and money.

I also remember that I wasn't nervous at all. We marched in front of the altar. I took Carolyn from her father, Thomas Mosca, and a few moments later, I put a three diamond wedding ring on Carolyn's finger, which was not yet paid for. She put a wedding ring on my finger, which was also not completely paid for. I think that quite a few marriages start out that way!

The wedding turned out exceptionally. Carolyn looked radiant, beautiful, facially picturesque, lovely. Her gown was exquisite. The ushers all looked good and so did the bridesmaids and the best man and maid of honor. When we came out of the church, confetti rained down on us like a snowstorm.

Next, the wedding party went to Emanuel College where we made a traditional trip down the altar and back to the delight of the nuns. More confetti and more music!

The next stop was Sargent Studios where we were seated under the torrid heat of those photographer lights and then it was on to the Hotel Myles Standish where we were marched in by wedding march of the orchestra. We then lined up to receive the many, many guests, loads of handshakes and kisses. There were over 600 people at the reception. Also, there was plenty to eat and drink. The wedding cake was 60 pounds. We got a little over $3,500.00 and other wedding gifts.

Then there was the dancing.

I swept Carolyn off her feet with the dancing. But the big surprise was the honeymoon. I wouldn't let anyone know what my plans were or where we would be going. My friends tried to get a rise out of me by spreading the rumor that my plane reservations had been canceled.

Let them talk...I knew the truth!

So, at about nine o'clock, with no warning what so ever I dashed Carolyn out of the reception wedding dress and all! My best man, Tom Flynn was waiting in his car and he took us over to our apartment where we were able to change cloths and then it was off to the airport.

The reason that I kept my plans secret was that I had heard a plan circulating among our friends that some of them wanted to separate us so that we would miss our flight. They thought this would be a wonderful joke while we didn't find it funny.

So, we flew out of our own party, and honestly, everyone was having so much fun that I don't even know that we were missed!

We boarded our four engine Sky Giant of the Northeastern Airlines and we were aloft. It was Carolyn's first experience flying and I was excited to share my passion with her. With my encouragement she looked out to see New England sprawling below us on this beautiful clear night. I held her close and we shared some beautiful moments. Our first as husband and wife.

Where did we go for our honeymoon? New York City!

We were there for a full week. The city was full of life and we were young and in love. The week flew by faster than either of us wanted it to and we wished that it would never end. One of those moments where you want to freeze time and hold on to it forever.

There is so much to do in New York that we almost didn't know where to start. One of the things that had been recommended to us was to take a double-decker bus to do some sightseeing. It was a fantastic idea and one that helped us to get a feel for the city to decide what we wanted to do with the rest of our trip. After that, we visited Times Square daily, shopped on 5th Avenue, saw movies, went out to eat, went to Yankee Stadium to watch the Detroit Tigers defeat the Yankees 8 to 2, and saw the play "Hamlet" at the New York City Center. We visited Grand Central Station, the Empire

State Building, Staten Island, the Statue of Liberty and Coney Island. We rented a convertible for a day and drove to Jersey City to visit my former football coach in the Navy, Lt. Commander Robert Meyers. He lauded my courage and superior qualities to my wife, Carolyn, and told her I was the most outstanding of all the cadets he ever led. We drove to West Point Military Academy. We saw the Rockettes and a movie at the Radio City Music Hall and had nice dinners.

And believe it or not, we were able to pack all of this into a single week! Plus, I even found the time to brief a few law cases.

Carolyn and I were both happy and truly in love. She was just perfect. It was a perfect honeymoon. It was the happiest week of my life and I was so lucky to have her as my wife. I was beginning a new chapter of my life, and I could not wait to get started.

Chapter 9:

A Dream Come True

As much as we dreaded it, our honeymoon came to an end, and life moved forward. Forward, in this case, to a new house, a new job and the start of a brand new future.

Carolyn and I started our life together living in a single remodeled bedroom in her parents' home. It may seem strange, but this was the perfect start for us. I was still trying to finish up my time at law school, while my wife spent the summer studying at the Hitchcock Secretarial School. We did not have the money to move out on our own, and living with my wife's family allowed us to finish our education without putting unnecessary strain on our finances.

I appreciated this, appreciated having the option to live with my wife and her parents, but you should know that these accommodations were not in any way free. During this time we were required to pay $25.00 a week for our room and board. This may not seem like a big number, but it was big enough and all that we could afford during this time.

Also, my father-in-law informed me that if I wanted to leave the house with his daughter, then I was required to ask his permission.

What? This absolutely floored me! I was required to ask permission to leave the house with my own wife!

And it didn't stop there! Not in the least.

I was also given a list of chores that I was expected to completely on a weekly, if not daily basis. My chores included keeping up with the garden as well as mowing the front and back lawns. It's not a huge job, but it was one that I could not do because of my back injury. I tried, I did the best that I could, but each day made me more and more determined that my wife and I find out own place as soon as we possibly could.

This is the exact reason why most of my time was spent studying. I studied at the library, at home and with several of my friends and classmates at my old apartment.

My dream of becoming a lawyer was so close that I could taste it, I just had a few more hurdles to clear.

The biggest of these was easily the bar exam.

Passing the bar, as many of you probably already know, is the last step in becoming a lawyer. If I was unable to pass this test, then all of my time and hard work would have been in vain.

Let me just make one thing clear....not passing was not an option. There was no way that I had dedicated this much of my time and effort only to fail at the last moment. I didn't care if I had to study 24 hours a day right up until the moment that I sat down for the exam, I can promise you that I was not going to fail.

And I was willing to take whatever help I could get. That is why, when a local attorney, Richard Cooper, gave me a copy of his New Hampshire Bar review material, which was composed of about 600 lead cases. I briefed every single one of them before I took the New Hampshire Bar Examination.

Over time, my professors began to take note of my dedication. I can remember one day when I was called on to speak on the case of Gibbons vs. Ogden in front of my class of over 100 students. From the moment I began speaking, I had the attention of the entire class and it felt good to be in command of the subject matter and to talk intelligently on the topic. My professor praised my abilities and I was more thankful than ever of the time that I put into preparing for each and every one of my classes.

My last semester of law school was one of the busiest times of my life, but there was one commitment that I could not bring myself to give up. Throughout this time I continued to serve as the head coach of the Mission Catholic High School football team.

Thirty-two students reported for the first day of practice at Mission Hill, and I will admit that this lead to a large amount of hope and wishful thinking on my part.

The reality was that the cards were stacked against us from the very beginning.

First off, Mission had no home field. This meant that all of our games were played on the road. We did have a practice field, but it boasted more sand and pebbles than it did grass or dirt. Plus, there were no lights. This meant that our practice time was limited to the time between 3:30pm and sunset. Not a huge amount of time during the winter months in the North East.

What did this mean? I meant that while I enjoyed coaching the team and building relationships with each of the players, our season was not a success.

In fact, we lost almost every game. Our record looked something like this:

Mission - 0   - St. James High - Haverill - 21
Mission - 6   - Immanuel Conception - Revere - 6
Mission - 0   - St. Clement's - Somerville - 12
Mission - 13 - St. Patrick's - Stoneham - 7
Mission - 7   - Malden Catholic - Malden - 20
Mission - 13 - St. Mary's - Waltham - 19
Mission - 0   - St. John's Prep - Danvers - 34
Mission - 0   - Keith Academy - Lowell - 34
Mission - 0   - St. Mary's - Brookline - 14

Back at law school I was working my way ever closer to graduation and to taking my turn to sit for the bar exam. One of the last projects that I faced as a part of my law school career was to oppose Tom Flynn, my good friend and former roommate in MOOT COURT.

This meant that each of us would take a position on a case and then argue in it in front of a "judge" and our peers. In this case, Tom took the part of the plaintiff and I of the defendant before Judge Kabatznick of the law firm of Kabatznick, Stern and Gesmer of Boston. We both had two witnesses for the trial.

The battle was fierce, but fun. We were determined to keep our conflict professionally friendly, as we felt good lawyers should. In the final argument before the court, I was equally prepared. I was loud, loquacious, emphatic, resounding and confident. I drove each of my points home with ostentatious gestures, angry passions, occasionally slapping the table and keeping my eyes focused on the judge. A week later, I found out that I had won the decision, but both of us got an A+ for the subject.

Honestly I could not have asked for a better outcome. I wanted to win, but Tom was like a brother to me and I wanted to see him succeed as well. I knew that Tom would make a great lawyer and I never wanted to stand across from him in a real court of law!

Monday, January 13, 1947, was the beginning of my last week at Boston University School of Law. Starting Monday, January 20, 1947, we took three-hour final examinations in each of the courses assigned to us. My last examination in law school took place on Saturday, February 1, 1947. As I walked out of that test I realized that I had done it. I would graduate from law school and I would become a lawyer!

True, I still had that bar exam in front of me, but there was no way that I would let myself fail in the final hour!

Want to know something that I am extremely proud of? When I walked out of law school on that cold February day, I had officially completed a three-year program in just two calendar years.

Once my exams were over, it was time to focus on studying for the bar exam. I went to Concord, New Hampshire in February and got a position with the law firm of Coferan and George for $20.00 per week. As part of my new job, I was given a key to the office so I could go there evenings to use the New Hampshire Reports and brief all of the lead cases, some 600 of them, in preparation for the Bar Examinations.

To celebrate finishing law school and being able to finally move forward with my career, I purchased a beautiful fur coat for my wife on Valentine's Day. The coat was on sale for $500.00 and Carolyn could not have been more surprised. I will never forget the way her eyes lit up when she saw the coat and ran her fingers through the rich fur for the first time. She said that the coat was beautiful, but as she slipped it on and twirled around the room, she took my breath away. It was she who was truly beautiful.

It was also during this time that my wife and I moved out of her parents home and into our first apartment. It was a fully furnished space located close to my new job in Concord, NH. I loved it, but as the days passed, it became clear that my wife was not happy.

She was homesick.

As an only child, she was the focus of her parents' lives, and it was hard for her to be away from them. I tried to be kind, but I had to tell her that as much as I enjoyed her parents, I did not plan on living with them throughout our marriage. In fact, I had no intention of going back. We could visit as much as she liked, but our days of living under their roof were over.

Between my new job and studying for the bar exam, it felt like I never had a single moment to spare. Tom Flynn had moved into a nearby apartment and the two of us began studying 9 hours per day, learning cases and preparing to sit for the exam. We would do three, 3-hour session per day, breaking between to eat and clear our minds before the next set.

I was glad that Carolyn was able to get a position with Blue Cross Blue Shield so that she could leave the apartment and not sit for days at a time watching the two of us struggling to learn the details of over 600 different cases. The days were a blur, and before I knew it May had arrived and with it my official graduation from Law School.

On Monday, May 26, 1947, I attended the Boston University graduating exercises at the Boston University arena where I received my law degree. In attendance were my wife, Carolyn, my mother-in-law, Giovanina Mosca, my mother, Vincenza Catalfo, my father, Alfio Catalfo, my sisters, Ida and Frances, Mrs. Frances O'Rourke, Joseph Kafel and Attorney Anthony Mosca.

By June 3, 1947, Tom Flynn and I had finished briefing the 600 lead cases in New Hampshire and we then began to memorize them. We kept up our grueling schedule and continued to work three hours in the morning, three hours in the afternoon and three hours in the evening to prepare for the Bar Association Examination.

Sitting for the Bar Exam took three full days. Each day we were subjected to three two-hour periods of exams or six hours each day.
For those of you who haven't had the pleasure, let me give you a brief look at what it means to sit for the Bar Exam.

Now, I have already told you that the exam takes three days and lasts for 6 hours each day. This is a total of 18 hours worth of exam time for 90 questions, or 12 minutes per question.

Each question must be answered in essay form and the answer can be found among the 600 lead cases. This means that the more you know about the lead cases, the better chance you have of passing the exam. This sounds straight forward, but the reality of learning the details of 600 different law cases is daunting and it is a huge amount of information.

All of this and there is still a very good chance that you will not pass and will have to attempt the test a second time.

As I worked my way through the questions, I tried not to feel overconfident, but I recognized every one of these questions. The marathon study sessions that Tom and I had worked through were paying off and I felt at ease during the test and confident in my knowledge.

I was almost positive that I would pass, but I would have to wait. The results would not be published until July 1st, when they would be printed in the Manchester Union Leader.

Does it surprise you to know that I couldn't sleep on June 30th? After all these years, my results were out there and I could not get my hands on them until the papers hit the stores! I cannot even put the frustration I felt into words!

It was so bad that I dragged my wife out of bed at 5:30am to see if we could go find a paper anywhere in the city!

None were available.

So, we went down to the beach and waded in the Atlantic while we dreamed about the future and waited for the paperboys to finish their morning runs.

By 8:20 I could see the papers being unloaded and raced over to buy two copies. Carolyn and I raced through the pages, but she was the one to find my name. I hadn't even found the right page when I heard her screaming, "Fred you passed! You passed!"

She then promptly dropped the paper, threw her arms around me and burst into tears.

I was stunned.

I was speechless.

And, as the dust settled I was both at peace and bursting with happiness all at the same time.

152

In truth I felt good. I felt damn good and I knew that I deserved it. No human being has ever worked as hard as I had and I deserved every second of the happiness that I now felt.

It took a moment for both Carolyn and I to calm down enough to decide what to do next. First, we went back inside and purchased more papers. Then, we went to tell our families.

It didn't take two weeks for me to find a job. By July 14th I was working for the prestigious law firm of Burns and Calderwood directly over the Strafford National Bank.

My compensation?

As a new graduate I was paid $80.00 per week.

Now that I had finished Boston University Law School in two years rather than the customary three years, and *passed* the bar, I had some unfinished business to attend to. I went to the New Hampshire VA and had the man who had rejected me for law school under the G.I. Bill fired.

But it wasn't about revenge.

I did it for the sake of other Veterans who, like me, face this kind of prejudices each and every day. Who knows how many dreams were affected by the shortsightedness of this one man? In those days you were required to have pre-approval before you were eligible to use the G.I. Bill. I made sure that his pre-approval days were over!

Chapter 10:

Me – Attorney at Law

As a lawyer my goal was never to spend my life working for someone else's law firm. I wanted to be my own man, make my own way in the world and start my own firm. So, in September of 1947 I opened my own law office.

It wasn't huge, but I couldn't have been more proud of my new space. There was one large office, a long waiting room, a smaller extra office, a kitchen and a bath. Everything that I needed, and even a bit of room to grow when the time came!

Carolyn and I were so excited! She had started a job teaching 7th grade and we were able to have lunch together everyday as well as spend our evenings as a family.

In the early days, I spent most of my time putting my new offices in proper order. This meant installing wall-to-wall bookcases and carpeting, ordering new furniture, improving the kitchen and setting up the waiting room. The good part was that I did not have to do all of this on my own. My brother-in-law, Roland Oates, and my two brothers and friends helped me with the repairs.

There wasn't much happening around my office in those days. It truth it was often quite boring and the money was definitely not rolling in just yet. I can remember this set of burners that I kept in the back room just so I could cook up some spaghetti at lunchtime. I also remember the crazy old typewriter.

In those days typewriters had carriages. When you typed a line, the carriage would move until you reached the edge of the page. Then you had to reach up and push the carriage back so you could start a new line. Well my typewriter? It had style! On my typewriter the carriage would FLY off the end and crash into the wall if you didn't hold up a hand to keep it in line!

Trust me when I say that my secretaries LOVED this! They all tried to avoid it, but I would tell them to put some paper in and pretend to type if a client happened to come in. I wanted people to think that we were insanely busy because we were in such high demand.

And then my first case walked through the door! I was hired to represent a group of workers who were not paid their final checks when a local factory closed down. I did the job and then one day opened the mail to find a whole slew of checks made out to me as well as each one of my clients. I was so excited that at first I didn't know what to do!

My clients were all extremely happy and they began to spread the word that a new lawyer was in town!

Slowly I began to make a name for myself as a lawyer and to build my own clientele. One case that stands out was argued on October 24th of that same year. It was a domestic case where the husband wanted to walk away from the marriage and leave his wife with nothing.

What the husband thought would be a quick case ended up taking several hours and in the end, the judge granted the wife everything that she had asked for. That day I was called brother attorney by Judge Ovila Gregoire and complemented by the husband. He told me that I must be a good attorney or he would have gotten everything from his wife.

Well, in retrospect, I don't think that he meant it as a complement, but I sure took it as one!

On Wednesday, December 24, 1947, I made the jump into criminal law. Our law office was closed that day, but my wife and I were there cleaning things up a bit when suddenly the telephone rang.

A woman called in telling us that her brother had been arrested for defacing property. The County Attorney, Frank Peyser, of Rochester, was the prosecutor. The charge of defacing property was nol prossed and immediately after, he was arrested for armed robbery and taken to the Somersworth Municipal Court. The State's witness identified my client, but under my cross-examination, the witness was not certain and before I completed my cross-examination, the witness admitted that the defendant, was not the man.

The verdict?

The case was nol prossed and my client went home. I received $50.00 for my work.

Around this same time I learned some fantastic news. My good friend Eddie O'Rourke sent word that he had married a U.S. Navy nurse by the name of Frances Torkelson. The two had met while serving on the U.S.S. Cavalier and best part was that she outranked him! Torkey, as we affectionately called her was a wonderful woman and my wife and I loved her from the very first time that we met.

In March, 1948, I filed a Petition for a Writ of Habeas Corpus for a defendant I represented who was locked up (without a hearing) by a mittimus issued by the Dover Chief of Police. The defendant was originally given six months in jail, suspended, by the Dover Municipal Court on condition he pay $20.00 a week to the Probation Department for support of his children. Failing to pay his $20.00, the chief issued the mittimus, or arrest warrant, and he was taken to jail without a court hearing.

I felt the Court had no authority to delegate this quasi-judicial function to the police chief or anyone else under statutory or common law. I felt a mittimus must have the hand and seal of the Court for it to be valid and the defendant was entitled to a hearing before this type of order was issued.

The ability to comply with a court order is always an issue. I hated to name the Superintendent of the County Jail, and the Chief of Police, as defendants, but I was left with no choice. Chief Justice Stephen Wheeler of the Superior Court heard the Petition the following day and transferred the case directly to the New Hampshire Supreme Court.

Due to the unique nature of this case, it was heard before the full bench of our New Hampshire Supreme Court on May 5, 1948. My loving wife, Carolyn, attended the hearing, and I was more than ready for it. I was well prepared. My presentation was ostentatious. It was dramatic. And it was full of both color and life. I argued that if the Court could delegate its judicial powers to the chief of police, why not the janitor as well. I mean, why not? They are picking and choosing who is given their power, so would it really matter if they gave it to the man who sweeps the floor? At this point, even the five conservative, sophisticated judges broke into laughter.

When I informed the Court that the mittimus was issued without the seal of the Court, the drama reached a high point. One of the justices stated, "Certainly Brother Catalfo, you don't mean to tell this Court that the mittimus left the clerk's office without a seal?" Before I could answer, Attorney Frank Peyser stood up and told the Court that the mittimus had no seal. I added, worse than that, the mittimus was not issued by the Court.

I had them, I thought.

I won.

My wife had heard several other cases argued before mine, and she concluded proudly that I was the best. I loved her. As I got in my vehicle, I was approached by Attorney Frank Peyser. He shook my hand and said, "Good job, Fred, good job." I thanked him.

On May 21, 1948, the New Hampshire Supreme Court denied the dismissal, but that did not discourage me.

My parents Alfred and Vincenza Catalfo

Passport photo from left to right: Giuseppe (Joseph), my mother Vincenza Catalfo, on her lap Salvatore (Sam) Catalfo and me Alfio (Alfred) to her right

The Family: Front row - my father Alfio, Ida and my mother Vincenza. Back row left to right: Frances, me, Sam, Joe and Mary

U.S. Naval Air Corp Cadet

U.S. Naval Air Corps June, 1943 Arm and Body Cast

Colby College Waterville Airport U.S. Navy. Catalfo on the left

Naval Air Training 1943

In my dorm at the University of Alabama

University of Alabama me on the right

My campaign committee at the University of Alabama. I was elected Class President

Me at the University of Alabama 1940

Waiting for the bus home after finishing my year at the University of Alabama

Berwick Academy Football Class of 1940

Before I started high school with my sister Ida. Civil Military training Portland, Maine, Ft. McKinley 1936

My mother with me at my graduation from Berwick Academy 1940

Graduation Berwick Academy 1940

Coach Mission Catholic 1946 Boston, MA

Atty. Alfred Catalfo, Jr. Candidate for U.S. Senate from N.H. 1962

Alfred Catalfo, Jr.

Attorney at Law
Dover, New Hampshire

DEMOCRATIC CANDIDATE

for

COUNTY SOLICITOR

For Efficient, Distinguished,
Capable Service.

(over)

Running for County Attorney

Dept Commander NH D.A.V. 1956-1957

My future wife Carolyn Mosca
Emanuel College

My wife Carolyn, myself, my best friend
Dr. Ed O'Rourke and his wife Marion
(Torky) in Dublin, Ireland 1955

Wedding Day June 9, 1946 Carolyn Mosca Catalfo
and Alfred Catalfo, Jr.

D.A.V. Department meeting at my law office 1960

Greeting JFK in Manchester, NH 1960

Me at my office 1962

Practicing law 1971

Jimmy Carter candidate for President of the U.S. visiting me at my law office.

The marriage of Atty. Alfred Catalfo, Jr. and Atty. Gail Varney Catalfo May 14, 1988

Gail's favorite pictures on vacation in Norway and Florida

I decided that the only way to proceed was to bring about a motion ab initio in the Dover Municipal Court.

The issue at hand was whether or not the defendant had been adjudicated as being the father of these children, all born out of wedlock. Certainly not! At least not on December 1, 1947. He was not married to the mother and a common law marriage did not exist unless the parents lived together as husband and wife for three consecutive years. So, at the time the court order was made in December of 1947, there was no formal marriage and no common law marriage that existed.

Both experienced and able lawyers, City Attorney T. Casey Moher and County Solicitor (County Attorney) Frank Peyser failed to convince the Court otherwise. The Court discharged the defendant from prison and dismissed the Court Order and the mittimus.

And basically that is a lot of legal jargon for saying that I won the case and the defendant went home.

On Saturday, June 26, 1948, while I was attending the New Hampshire Bar Association State Meeting with several of my friends, one of our Supreme Court judges approached us and informed me that I had given an excellent argument before the Court on the Carpentier case. He said I had created a difficult problem for the New Hampshire Supreme Court and apologized that they had ruled against my client.

But there was a reason for it.

Had the court voted in my favor in the Carpentier case, then roughly 90% of those individuals currently in prison would have to be released. This was a risk that they could not afford to take, no matter how well I argued the point.

As I sat there, listening to the judge several different responses rolled through my head. I should have told him about the defendant being released and that I had ended up winning the case through a different avenue, but I didn't. I held my tongue, thanked him for his kind remarks and moved on.

Would have been fun, but probably not worth it in the long run.

On Wednesday, April 21, 1948, I tried my first jury trial. This took place in the Rockingham County Superior Court in Portsmouth, New Hampshire.

A friend of mine, Attorney Robert Shaw, sat with me and gave me a hand with this trail and I don't mind admitting that I was slightly nervous. Luckily, my wife was on spring vacation at the time, so she was able to witness the entire trial. Just having her in the room gave me an extra confidence.

My client was indicted for lewd and lascivious conduct with a 15-year-old girl. Judge Stephen Wheeler presided. The prosecutor was Attorney Wyman Boynton. The trial ended at 3:00 p.m. and the jury found him guilty at 7:00 p.m.

Doesn't sound like much of a success does it? But there is a bit more to the story.

One of the witnesses for the prosecution was the chief of police associated with the case. Under cross-examination I had him frustratingly angry. While the jury was out, he approached me, shook my hand, and told me that he hoped the next time we met in court that I would be on the same side. My client received a six-month suspended sentence and went home.

All in all, that was an outcome that I could be pleased with.

In April of 1948, I tried a criminal case in the North Berwick, Maine Municipal Court with Judge Paul Harrington presiding.

Now, I tell you about the judge because the trial it's self was heard in the Judge's living room. This may sound strange, but at that time there was nothing unusual about this. In fact it was quite common for trials to take place in the homes of various Judges.

In this particular trial the charge involved was sodomy on a goat. An interesting charge for sure, but one that did not have much fact based evidence to back it up.

Here is what had happened. My client and his friend were visiting a friend who was not home at the moment. The goat had broken loose and my client and his friend caught the goat and secured it.

The State had only one witness to the proposed crime, a retired groundskeeper at Harvard University, who did not speak English very well, but did speak Italian. There was no physical or forensic evidence of any kind and the witness was roughly 200 yards away from the scene.

After going through all of the evidence the defendant was found NOT GUILTY and was free to go!

The most interesting facet of the case was that my wife was present throughout the entire trail and was visible embarrassed by the language involved. She made it through, but not without a few very evident blushes.

About this time Carolyn and I celebrated our 2nd wedding anniversary. It was a time of many changes in our life, not the least of which was that we moved into a new, larger apartment in Dover, NH. I wanted to do something special for my wife so I brought home flowers and we went out for a fun night on the town.

Another big change was that both my wife and I enrolled in summer school at the University of New Hampshire. Carolyn took a course called "Education Psychology," while I took graduate courses for a possible Master's Degree.

And, to keep things interesting, I decided to run for the office of Strafford County Attorney, or County Solicitor as it is more commonly known, as a Democrat. I did not think that I could win, but I wanted to try. My competition came in the form of a friend of mine, Attorney Lewis Fisher who was favored to win the Democratic primary.

When I first started to campaign, it appeared hopeless. The Democratic machine decided who would and would not get nominated and Attorney Lew Fisher appeared to have the position all but in the bag.

The task seemed to be all but impossible.

I had only one year of experience as a lawyer. Attorney Fisher had been practicing for eight or nine years. He is a good lawyer and a close friend of Attorney John Bemis, who was Chairman of the Strafford County Democrats. And, even if I got the nomination, I then would have to face the incumbent and a very able lawyer, Republican Frank Peyser.

So, I went back to my roots so to speak.

I called on the veterans. I made a point to travel to each and every veterans' organizations in the county. Attorney Fisher was not a veteran and neither was Frank Peyser, the incumbent County Attorney (County Solicitor). At that time, after World War II, that was important facet to one's political credentials.

Credentials that I had.

For two straight weeks before the election I campaigned vigorously. I went in front of factories, visited the American Legion posts in Rollinsford, Farmington, Rochester, Somersworth and Dover a number of times. I was also an American Legionnaire.

My next step was getting the primary voting lists of the area. This gave me all the names and addresses of every registered Democrat so that I could target my campaigning and advertising efforts. I mailed 2,000 cards and 3,000 letters and I had advertised in all the papers in the county. I had a lot of help from my wife, Carolyn, my mother, Vincenza, my three sisters, Mary Oates, Francesca, Agatha, as well as many, many others.

It was work. It was hard, tedious work that seemed to be never ending and that we all knew might not pay off.

But it did!

I won the nomination! I won the county by 495 majority. I had 1,571 votes to Fisher's 1,076. I took Rollinsford 155 to 13. I took Farmington 22 to 0. I won in all three cities. In Rochester, I won 251 to 247, in Dover, 388 to 350 and in Somersworth 868 to 415.

That night was all about celebration! My friends and family all gathered in our new apartment to congratulate me and to show their continuing and unwavering support. There were over 35 people packed into our tiny little space, to the point where it was standing room only.

I still had a long way to go, but that did not diminish the joy and the feeling of accomplishment that I felt that night. The Democratic party leaders were not happy with the results and Sheriff Stephen Scruton informed me shortly after that he'd see to it that both Moe Pare and I would go down in defeat in November.

I didn't expect them to be happy about it, but I did expect them to prepare for a fight!

One thing that broke in my favor the last week before the primary was that Wilfred "Moe" Pare, a novice Democrat, was running for sheriff against incumbent Democrat Sheriff Stephen Scruton. A well-known man who had been in office for 16 years.

By joining forces, both Moe Pare and I hoped to make our campaigns stronger. So, to that end on Primary Election Day, September 14, 1948, we provided his political organization with five motor vehicles and five workers for all of the wards in Somersworth. We had workers in front of all of the wards in Dover, Rollinsford and Farmington and at Ward 4 in Rochester.

On Saturday, September 18, 1948, the entire family and I went to Wolfeboro to witness my brother, Sam, marry Patricia Wilkinson at the Episcopal Church. Following the wedding, my brother, Salvatore Catalfo, and his bride, Patricia, left for the University of Alabama where he would start his freshman year. I was proud of Sam for continuing with his education even after his time in the navy. He was following his dreams and that was all I could ever want for him.

By October 6th, we had ordered 10,000 political cards and 20,000 letters for this campaign. We knew that was a lot, but we never thought about the reality of what it would take to address each and every one of those envelopes. My wife, bless her, took on the task and was seeking help from any and every one that she could think to ask. It was a chore that seemed to be never ending but they worked through to the end and I was forever grateful for their dedication.

But no matter how hard we worked, it all came down to one thing....Election Day.

All of the hours, the blood, sweat and tears, that had been poured into this campaign all came down to one day and even one moment.

I'll admit that I was nervous, that I hadn't slept the night before and that I felt as if I spent the entire day sitting, standing or walking on pins and needles. But I also knew that I was well prepared.

For that day alone I had 26 cars and drivers in place to help ferry voters to and from the polls. I had 10 volunteers manning the phones and trying to encourage people to vote. And we even had a truck fitted with a loud speaker driving around soliciting votes throughout the area. Truly I had more help than I could have ever hoped for and I was grateful for every person that gave of their time and energy.

I had to chase down the truck with the loud speaker! One of my friends, who was a little drunk, had control of the microphone to the loud speaker. He was riding threw town shouting, "Vote for Catalfo! He is a persecutor not a prosecutor!" As you can guess, we took him off the microphone and passed those duties to someone a bit more sober.

My wife even went as far as to take the day off from school so that she could help out with the campaign. In all honestly she was the heart of the whole movement and settled into the law office for the day to oversee the entire organization.

One would think that all of these elements would work in synergy to alleviate my fears and help to boost my belief in success. After all, with this kind of help in my corner, how could I lose!

I promise you, I could and it was a fact that never left my mind even for a moment.

I spent the day campaigning, literally working until the very minute that the polls closed. I went around to the wards in Dover, Somersworth, Rochester and the Towns of Rollinsford and Farmington, with Nick Shaheen and James Koromilas. The goal was to put my face in front of as many people as possible and to encourage them to get out of their homes and out to the polls.

By 8:00 p.m. it was over. The polls had closed and at that point there was nothing else I could do but wait for the votes to be counted and the results announced. I went home and passed the time with some 50 friends who had crammed themselves into our tiny little apartment. We had good food, good drinks and good company. Truly there is no better way to keep your mind occupied than to surround yourself with people that you both love and enjoy.

But no matter how you look at it, the wait was excruciating!

At that time Strafford County had paper ballots. This meant that each vote had to be counted and tallied by hand. And the count had to be exact. So there was simply no way to hurry this process and nothing to do but wait.

172

So we did. We waited. And waited. And waited. And then, just about the time we were all ready to lose our minds, the results were announced at just after 5:00 a.m.

I HAD WON!

Cheering, rejoicing, chaos all around as we sat stunned with the enormity and victory of the news.

One year out of law school and I was officially the County Solicitor of Strafford County. This is the equivalent of County Attorney or District Attorney in other States. I won over the Republican incumbent, Attorney Frank Peyser,
10,818 to 9,040 - by 1778 votes.

By this time, only Carolyn, my mother, Vincenza, my mother-in-law, Giovanina, and I were still up to hear the news. And somehow, I think that we for the best. Even though so many people had given of their time and effort, it was nice to share the first moments of thise victory with those who I was closest to.

I can remember sitting there that night, just letting the feelings of victory and accomplishment sink in. I had been literally showered with help and support, and I was so grateful for each and every person on my team who gave their time free of charge. I had every intention of serving in this capacity with professional dignity. I was prepared to prosecute the guilty and to protect the innocent.

Early the following morning, well in truth just a few short hours later, congratulations began rolling in from all sides. People from all walks of life reached out to me, sharing their joy in my success. I was so humbled by the outpouring and awed by the sincerity of the correspondence. In those moments it was driven home to me that the importance of this post was not what it could do for me, it was what it would allow me to do for my community as a whole.

Going into my new post I took dedication, discipline and a strong sense of duty. The one thing that I did not take was experience. But I was not going to let that fact deter me. For if there was one thing that I had learned it was that experience would come with time and the strengths that I brought to the table could not be taught.

On January 1st, 1949 my wife and I made the trip to the Strafford County Superior Court where I was sworn in to the office of County Solicitor. In that moment I became the chief law enforcement officer in Strafford County.

Again, I was just one year out of law school my friends. One single year.

My father was so proud of me for what felt like the first time in my life! Everywhere he went he was now an important man, and because of me, people fought over the honor of buying him a drink at the club. He would come to my office to visit, reinforcing his position as my father and his connection to me.

The learning curve was steep, but I was infinitely fortunate to have some outstanding mentors in my corner. One of these men, Superior Court Justice Stephen Wheeler, arranged for me to watch Prosecutor Attorney Bill Craig of Hillsborough County present some of his cases before the Grand Jury. It was just a few hours, but I learned more that day than I ever imagined possible.

Judge Wheeler also invited me to his home in Exeter to acquaint me with the duties of County Solicitor because he was once a County Solicitor himself. He was very instructive and very helpful and I was profoundly grateful.

One of the first cases that I had to tackle as County Solicitor made me quite unpopular even though I only had the best interest of my constituents as heart. It was called the Pyramid Club.

Ever heard of it?

I'm sure that you have in some form.

These types of schemes, or "clubs," call for members to send goods or money to those members above them on a list. In short, it is a form of illegal gambling that is cloaked as a get rich quick dream.

I got involved when several local law enforcement officers began to complain to me about the situation, one that they felt was getting quickly out of hand. Now, while I understand that many people out there need these kinds of dreams to hold on to, the reality is that the scheme was weighed heavily against late joiners.

So, on March 22nd, I went to the papers, the radio stations and every other format that I could think of to label these schemes as illegal.

This did not make me popular.

Well, I did become the most talked about person in Strafford County, but not in a good way. In fact, almost all of the outcry was negative. We were receiving some 50 to 60 telephone calls a day, all argumentative and all questioning my authority. A few brave souls took things one-step further and came down to my office to personally blast me with their thoughts.

This was what was known as trial by fire!

Even my poor wife was forced to face their wrath as some of her students' parents took their irritation with me out on her.

In the end, the interest in this issue died off quickly, and with it the majority of the interest in the Pyramid Club. I was glad for the reprieve, but I was also at peace with my decision. I knew then, and I know now that I did the right thing for the population of my district. They might not have liked it, but it was the right thing to do!

This just goes to show how everything in life is a cycle. For every high there is a low, and we must embrace the highs in order to survive the lows.

My low? It wasn't the Pyramid Club.

It was the death of my father.

The beginning of the end started in my own living room. That evening my mother and father stopped by to have dinner with my wife and I, but my father didn't seem to have any appetite. Carolyn went back to the kitchen to make him a large bowl of chicken and rice soup, but it didn't help. He ate, but it was halfhearted at best.

They left, with my father promising that he was fine, that nothing was wrong, but I knew it wasn't true. I just had this feeling that something wasn't right that I couldn't get rid of. So, later that night, my wife and I went over to my parents' home, just to check on him one more time.

He was so sick, and we made the decision to take my father straight to Wentworth Hospital. Things did not go well throughout the night, but by the next morning the staff assured us that his condition was improving and that we should go home to get some rest.

We did.

Four hours later my father had passed away.

I had almost finished my haircut at the Kimball Hotel barbershop on Third Street about 9:30 a.m. when my wife called me. She said, "Fred, I have some bad news for you." I responded, "I know - he's dead." I felt so bad. My father dead. Finally I broke down and cried and cried.

Looking back on it now, I know that we did everything that we could and I was at peace, but that did not change the reality. My father was gone, and there was absolutely nothing that I could do about it. I could not change this fact and I could not imagine the world continuing on, when such a large part of my world was gone.

A horrible scene followed at 80 Oak Street. It was a clear, beautiful day, but ugly and sad. My mother, Vincenza, was sick all over. My sister, Mary fainted onto the kitchen floor. Joseph was crying upstairs.

I felt helpless.

Before I could reach my sister, my mother, my own mother, fell onto the kitchen floor motionless. I screamed for help, "God, where are you?" My sisters, Ida and Frances, helped with Mary and me and my brother, Joseph, helped my mother.

From there it was like everything happened quickly.

I was given the task of informing my brother Sammy and his wife about my father's passing and trying to help them find a way to come home. Sammy was attending the University of Alabama and, as a full time student.

Then it was time for my brother Joesph and I to plan the funeral.

All of these details blend together in the stark grey of the day, but the one moment that stands out was when the undertaker arrived at my parent's home with my father's casket.

Watching them bring the body into the house drove home reality in a way that nothing else could. A mere 24 hours before my father had lived in this home. Now we would have his wake.

My father laid in a mahogany open casket. Many, many people. Many, many flowers. From Massachusetts and elsewhere many Italians who were friends of my parents or who were related to my wife attended the wake. The Catholic priest came to the house each evening for prayer services.

On the morning of April 13th, 1949, my brother, Sam, and his wife, Patricia, arrived at my parents' home. They made it just in time, with literally just minutes to spare before the funeral was to take place.

The services took place at St. Mary's Catholic Church in Dover with Fr. Thomas Connors, D.D., celebrating high mass. His remains were put to rest at St. Mary's Catholic Cemetery. There were about 20 vehicles in the procession. I instructed the funeral director not to lower the casket until everyone had left the cemetery.

That is something that my family did not need to see.

But life, as is its way, moves on. And, in my case, it moved on to a new adventure whether I was ready for it or not.

On Friday, April 22, 1949, my teacher wife, Carolyn, and I volunteered to chaperone the Dover High School Class of 1949 on a visit to New York City and Washington, D.C. I was not completely on board with the plan, but I wanted to make my wife happy and I knew that the trip would be interesting at the very least.

We boarded the "State of Maine" train on Third Street at 11:00 p.m. with 78 students. Our hope was that they would sleep on the train, but that hope was in vain. Most of the students did not sleep at all and some of them came armed with water guns, which they used to annoy their fellow classmates.

A very long night my friends!

We finally arrived at Grand Central Station, New York City, at 7:30 a.m. the next morning. There were joined forces with about 500 students from other schools and were taken by bus to the Piccadilly Hotel right off Time Square.

When we arrived at the hotel, we had thought that we would check in and then be given time to settle in before heading out to see the sights.

This was not the case.

Standing in the lobby, someone from our Green Tour Company yelled at those sleepy and confused students that those that wanted to see the Statue of Liberty should follow him. And, almost half of them did, my wife and I among them.

This was chaos! No organization, no structure and no way to tell if we had the students in our group or not. Literally 500 students, over 500 suitcases and not a single room prepared until after 1:00 p.m. Beyond that, a single guide yelled to a lobby full of people to follow him and then just walked out, leaving the rest to their own devices.

What a mess!

As soon as we returned to the hotel, I called this Green Tour man to the side. I introduced myself as a chaperone, but also as a lawyer and I told him I was in possession of a check for over $4,000.00, but that they were not going to get it unless their company would fulfill their part of the contract.

Things improved immediately.

The rest of the New York leg of the trip went off without a hitch and we headed off to D.C. on a pleasant note. Even better, we delivered every student in our care safely back to their own families.

All in all, I would call that a success.

Would I do it again? Not on your life!

A few months later I received a nasty little medical surprise of my own. My wife and I were driving home from spending the weekend with her parents when I began to suddenly experience severe, constant pain in my side.

Rushing to the hospital we learned that my appendix had ruptured and that I would need immediate surgery. Luckily it was something that could be dealt with rather easily, but it was still almost a full month before I was able to return to work.

In my post of County Solicitor, one of the things that greatly concerned me was that the police departments of Strafford County and New Hampshire lacked coordination. In short, there were too many departments competing for jurisdiction of serious crimes.

Think that I'm kidding?

Well, then consider this. For any given crime, the State Police, the Sheriff's Department, the local police, the Motor Vehicle Department, the County Solicitor, the City Solicitor, the medical referee and the Attorney General's Office all rushed to be first on scene and then proceeded to ruthlessly compete for jurisdiction. There was no coordination and, as such, there was no organization.

From what little experience I had, I could see at some of these crime scenes there were seven or more divisions or departments arriving and they were all operating independently from one another.

There had to be a better way!

One would think that this type of suggestion would be a no brainer type thing. After all, our job as public servants is to find the best use for the taxpayer's funds and to be fiscally responsible with how we allocate our resources, but believe it or not, I too received flack for my stance.

In fact, here is an example of an editorial that appeared in the Rochester Courier on March 18, 1950. This column stated in part:

"It Takes Training

Youthful Strafford County Solicitor Alfred Catalfo, who is as full of ideas as a dog is of fleas, thinks the investigation of major crimes should be entirely in the hands of the county sheriff and bolsters his argument on the grounds that most major crimes bring out local, state and county officials, whom he feels merely get in one another's way."

Yes...he was exactly right...it is much better for seven different agencies to show up to work one crime scene and fight over evidence. Cooperation is boring and out dated.

Open your eyes people! This shouldn't be that hard to figure out!

Well, that was an issue that was not going to be resolved any time soon, so I simply put it on the back burned and began to focus on new cases that were walking through my door.

One such case involved a local children's home.

It all started that March when a lady by the name of A.F. came to me with a complaint. She felt strongly that a crime had been committed at the Dover Children's Home and was adamant that I take the time to look in to the matter.

When she first walked in, I admit that I was trying to hurry her through the meeting because I was pressed for time that day and had quite a bit on my plate. But, once she began her tale, I was glued to my seat at the unbelievable chain of events that she imparted.

Here were the basic facts.

Mrs. F. told me that a matron of the children's home, N.G., had struck a ten-year-old female child repeatedly with a stick.

Beating the child badly and then proceeding to lock her in the attic of the children's home for three full days.

My first reaction was that the story, while horrible was exaggerated. But, as the chief law enforcement officer of the area, it was my job to get to the bottom of the matter. So, I suggested that we pass the case off to the Dover Police Department.

Again, Mrs. F. insisted that I look into the matter personally as the police had already been involved and had done nothing.

My next step was to contact the Dover Police Department Chief of Police, Andrew McDaniel. Chief McDaniel was surprised at my call. It was obvious through the course of our conversation that he knew little to nothing about the incident, and even inferred that I was interfering with his department by contacting him on this matter.

Now I was intrigued.

I politely hung up the phone the continued to question Mrs. F. about the facts of the case. She remembered that one of the officers on scene was named William Bigger.

As far as leads go, this was a great place to start.

I called Mr. Bigger at home and he informed me that he and Officer John Wormell were working the third shift a few nights ago when they were called to the Dover Children's Home at approximately 3:00 a.m. Once on scene they found a young girl with large bruises on her left hip. Upon questioning the child, it was determined that a matron of the home, N.G., had assaulted her.

The weapon? A wooden club roughly two feet long and two inches thick.

They then determined that the minor child was in fact locked in the attic, the only door secured with a chair propped up against the knob.

Now, here is where the tale got interesting. This incident was reported in detail by both officers AND N.G. readily admitted to committing the assault.

No one was arrested for the crime.

The child was still in the home.

No medical care had been given or offered to the child.

I don't think that I have to tell you just how unacceptable I found this to be.

The next morning I went to the Dover Children's Home along with a secretay. We were shown the attic in question and I spoke to the minor child in the presence of my secretary and one of the women of the home.

The young victim told us that she received permission to go across the street from Mrs. A.F. to buy some candy, but the matron told her not to cross the street. When the matron learned that she had in fact crossed the street, she beat the child with a "paddle." The beating was so severe that the child could not sleep on her left side or climb up or down stairs for several days.

That beating left the child so injured that the only way she was able to go up or down the stairs was to crawl on her hands and knees.

184

I was absolutely disgusted. I was even more disgusted once I was shown to the attic where the girl had been kept.

As a result of my visit, the matron admitted to the assault and was discharged from her position. She was also arrested for aggravated assault and released on bail.

On Monday, March 27th, 1950, I appeared in the Dover Municipal Court with the minor child, her father, and Mrs. A.F. Since this was an alleged felony complaint, the only issue was to hold the defendant, for the Grand Jury. At the request of defense counsel, Attorney Fisher, the case was continued. The State had no objection to the continuance.

Then, the case hit the newspapers and the whole thing was blown completely out of proportion!

Over the next several days it seemed like every newspaper that was even somewhat close to our area covered the story.

It was so over the top that I went to visit the State Attorney General and seek his advice. On his recommendation I reduced the aggravated assault charge to simple assault. I also advised the father of the minor child, who had a court order of sole physical custody of the girl, to remove the child from the Dover Children's Home and place her at the home of the paternal grandmother, who lived in Exeter.

The case was tried in the Dover Municipal Court on Monday, April 3rd, 1950. My loving wife, Carolyn, and my two friends, Dr. Edward O'Rourke and James Koromilas, came to court with me that day to show their support in a difficult situation. I reduced the charge to simple assault then called Chief of Police Andrew McDaniel as the State's first witness.

Next, I put the youngster, age ten, on the stand. She told about the assault and identified her assailant, the defendant. For someone so young, she did a great job of describing the situation, outlining her injuries and explaining what it was like to be locked in the attic for three straight days. She looked straight at the courtroom and told them about being in so much pain that she was forced to climb the stairs on her hands and knees.

Under cross-examination, she could not identify the instrument and was not sure whether she was struck by a stick or a paddle. She was asked, "Were you beaten or spanked?" For a ten year old, she did very well and I could not have asked her for more.

For my next witness, I put Mrs. A.F. on the stand and her mental competency was a topic, but eventually the judge ruled that she was competent and she was permitted to testify.

The case was continued for a second day. I put Police Officer William Bigger on as the State's final witness. He testified that he and Officer John Wormell went to the Dover Children's Home at 3:00 a.m. to answer a complaint for an assault and then went through the full story that he had shared with me during our previous conversations.

Officer Bigger was concise. He was well spoken and he gave a relevant and detailed testimony. He was even able to give details about how the defendant, who was 220 pounds, had admitted to striking the child repeatedly with a 22-inch long stick that was submitted into evidence at that time.

After his testimony, the State rested and the defense moved that the case be dismissed for insufficient evidence.

The motion was granted.

I was absolutely *shocked*! How much more evidence could you ask for. An eyewitness, a confession and the weapon in question and that was ruled to be not enough evidence? Preposterous!

To make matters worse, at that time, the state had no right to appeal. It was in that moment that I came to realize what my law professor, Bernard Marvin, meant on our first day at Boston University School of Law when he philosophically stated, "I want all of you members of this class to understand that the law is anything, but just."

By September of 1950 I was up for re-election in my post at County Solicitor. My opponents fought hard, citing the Children's Home case and trying to make the claim that I was an atheist, but their struggle did not stop me from winning the primary. On Tuesday, September 12th, 1950, I was named to be the Democratic candidate.

The only problem was that with every win I accumulated new and more dangerous political enemies.

By October I was convinced that I had been targeted to be defeated in my campaign for re-election. This time the Republicans had reached out to local Democrats in their quest to defeat me.

Here is an example of one of the tricks that they pulled. On the Wednesday before the election a full-page negative advertisement appeared in the Foster's Democrat with a second full page ad following the next day in the weekly paper.

I tried to respond, but both papers refused to print my rebuttal because they allegedly did not publish political advertisements after the Wednesday prior to the election.

Their plot worked and I lost the election. The only up side was that the Attorney I lost to was a good lawyer and a nice person. I believed that he would work hard for the people, which helped to make the situation slightly easier to bear.

I wrote him a letter of congratulations and moved on.

Chapter 11:

Success

The year was 1952, and it began with my winning a jury trial in Strafford County Superior Court. But life was not lived exclusively in the courtroom.

I was blessed that my own life was especially full. I had a sweet and loving wife who enjoyed my company. I had a close family whom we visited with often. And, I had almost completed work on my own Master's Degree in History.

Life was definitely not boring!

Being a full time husband, full time lawyer and full time student was quite a bit to handle on any given day, but I loved it. I loved being busy and quenching the thirst for knowledge that only education can bring. I loved wearing different hats throughout the day and doing my best to not only succeed, but to thrive in each and every role I took on.

In short, I loved my life.

Carolyn was busy teaching the 7th grade at the Sherman School, a job that she enjoyed and looked forward to. For me though, the best thing about her job was that it was located only about 200 yards from the front door of my law office. This meant that we were able to have lunch together almost every single day.

I looked forward to that noon hour more than any other throughout my busy day.

And believe me when I sat that busy was in fact a serious understatement! I was inundated with law work, writing the original history of Rollinsford as part of my graduate work and taking on a full semester of classes. I did not see winter come and go, although I knew it had passed, just like the ghost of a dream slipping by me in the hallway. With so much pressure beating at me from all sides, I truly did not even notice the change in seasons. I doubt if I slept more than six hours a night.

The easiest way to describe what I was living through, and how I would often describe my life at the time, was to quote the classic work of Edna St. Vincent Millay. Who in 1922 wrote the following:

"My candle burns at both ends
  It will not last the night;
  But, ah, my foes, and oh, my friends -
  It gives a lovely light."

By February of that year I took it upon myself to add to my already full plate by becoming involved in the first national primary in New Hampshire. We built a targeted campaign, and executed it well, but in the end our candidate lost. Senator Estes Kefauver from Tennessee defeated our chosen candidate, President Harry S. Truman.

Sometimes success is not possible, even with the best intentions and the best laid plans well in place.

As my wife, Carolyn, was a school teacher, she had the benefit of being giving all of the vacation that her students were. I

190

was only fortunate that she was willing to use that time to help me.

Need an example?

Well, her spring vacation in 1952 was spent helping me complete the first draft of my thesis, *The History of Rollinsford*. Keep in mind that this was well before the days of computers. Meaning that my wife typed, by hand, each and every one of the 18 chapters and 341 pages of that book. She was my right hand, helping me every step of the way with my thesis and with my quest to earn my Master's Degree.

I owed her greatly and can readily admit that I would not have been able to do it all without her help.

We did spend the week at her parents' house, but we spent it working. Morning until night, all we did was organize research and type out that book. It took all week to finish, but both of us felt as if a huge weight had been lifted off of our shoulders when it was!

Luckily it was time well spent, because on May 5th I received word that my thesis had been approved. Futher, my professor viewed me as such a good student that I would not have to take any additional final exams. This meant that I had finished all required course work and would be receiving my Master's of Arts Degree in just about a week.

My wife literally jumped for joy at the news!

We dropped everything and headed out right then and there to celebrate the good news. How does one celebrate this type of accomplishment? Why with a lobster dinner and a movie of course!

From there you would think that Spring would have slowed down. After all, I had cleared a huge hurdle and should have more time free to spend with my wife, but that just didn't turn out to be the case. In fact, if anything it felt like someone had hit the fast forward button along with piling on extra work at every turn.

A lot of things happened that spring!

Here are a few examples:
- I tried a jury trial in Essex County and another in York County. I won them both.
- I handled 11 divorce cases in a single day.
- I served as the Grand Marshal of the 1952 Memorial Day Parade.
- My wife and I took her entire 7th grade class to Fenway Park to see the Red Sox play.
- I drafted a new set of by-laws for the Department of New Hampshire Disabled American Veterans.
- We attended the D.A.V. State Convention.
- I was re-elected to the post of Department Judge Advocate.

And this was just in a month or two!

Our days were busy. That was why it was so important and so precious to us when we had the time to slow down and enjoy the company of our family and friends. Those days were few and far between, so they were meant to be treasured!

The day that I received my Master's Degree turned out to be just such a day.

It was Sunday June the 8th, and people that I loved surrounded me. My wife was there, along with her parents and my own mother. My best friend Eddie was there along with his wife and his two young sons. My sister Ida was there as was Mr. and Mrs. Frank Scifano. Each of these people made the trip to come and watch as I received my degree. Their support was important to me and I have never forgotten the way that it felt to receive my honors while each of them stood by to watch.

At this point my wife and I felt that we had earned a vacation. We had been working non-stop practically since the moment we had married and it was time to play for a bit!

So, we met up with our dear friends Eddie and Torkey O'Rourke, piled in my Pontiac Sedan and took off. There were 4 adults and two infants in the car, and we were ready to go!

The trip started with a quick stop by Carolyn's parents home in Watertown. We spent the night with them, enjoyed our visit and then loaded everyone back in the car to head to Florida.

The idea was to visit Torkey's mother in Key West, drop off the children with her and then fly out to Cuba!

Oh...Cuba! A warm topical paradise the likes of which none of us had ever seen before. And this was Cuba at its peak, a scant year before Castro and the communist party took over the island and forever changed its reality. We could not wait to get on that plane and to sink our toes in the warm sand of a sugary beach.

The drive was easy. We made our way to Key West without incident, dropped off the O'Rourke's two small sons with their grandmother, then headed to the airport.

We flew from Key West to Havana, Cuba, in a two-engine prop plane that seated just 24 people. Once our plane touched down, we knew that we only had 4 days on the island, and we wanted to make the most of each and every one of them.

To do it right, we had to come up with a plan of action. So, as soon as we checked into our rooms at the Regis Hotel in Havana, we made arrangements with the concierge to hire a taxi for our own personal use during our stay.

It was a perfect arrangement!

For just $6.00 a day we had our own personal taxi at our disposal morning, noon and night. All we had to do was walk downstairs and our driver would take us anywhere we wanted to go.

And we wanted to go everywhere!

We traveled all over the island, taking in every experience we had ever heard or thought about. The amazing thing about Cuba is that everywhere you look it is like a postcard, a true picturesque tropical paradise from every angle. Yet, as beautiful as it was, the native people lived in very poor conditions. The divide between the tourist areas and the native population was huge and the contrast stark.

Being there it was obvious that something was going to have to change. I just wish that the politics had turned out differently.

But all of that took place after we had left, and it did not impact our trip or the fun we had.

We went all over Cuba, visited the University of Havana, the capitol building, the Colon Cemetery, and rum factories to drink free rum. I purchased five bottles of 25-year-old rum (supposedly) at $1.75 a bottle. We saw a cockfight and a burlesque show.

Finally, we went to the Sam Souci tropical outdoor nightclub. We drank, we ate, we dance and then we settled into our seats to watch the live entertainment for the evening. It was here that I unwittingly became part of the show in a grand moment that my friends will never allow me to forget.

Here is what happened. Throughout the night of frivolity, I became quite inebriated. What can I say? I was on vacation! Well, one of the live acts featured a man dancing with a "woman." What we didn't know at the time was that the "woman" was really a very life like rubber doll.

The whole point of this act was the man made it appear as if he were sexually assaulting his dance partner. This was supposed to be funny?

Well not to me!

I could not allow this! I jumped from my seat to race out on the floor and smash into the man in a valiant effort to rescue the woman. The act was so real that I bought into it lock, stock and barrel. My wife's jaw dropped to the floor as I was quickly restrained and brought back to our table.

In that moment there was plenty of laughter at my expense, and none laughed harder than my own dear friend Eddie. It may sound a bit harsh, but if I'm being honest then I have to admit that if the tables had been turned, I would have been rolling on the floor at his antics.

I think that at this point several of the other guests thought that my interruption was just part of the act, but to me it had been an act of rescue.

It was a fun and fitting end to our trip and it also made a great story to tell for years to come.

The next day we left the beautiful Cuban beaches behind as we traveled home. From there we picked up the kids and then it was a long drive north to fall back in to the daily grind.

A daily grind that included arriving home just in time for the Democratic primary.

It was already almost too late. Only some 18 days for the primary election and I had considerable opposition with Attorneys Philip Keefe and Leo Cater. By August 26, 1952, I was campaigning with my wife, Carolyn, in Rollinsford, Somersworth and Dover. In the next several days, I went to Middleton and New Durham and visited 19 separate families in Lee, went to Rochester and, of course, I visited all of the prominent Democratic leaders in Strafford County.

On Election Day, September 9th, 1952, I had our organization out in full force. We had 42 cars, drivers and 19 ward workers for the Democratic primary. My entire family helped, except my sister, Frances, who was away on her honeymoon.

It was a close one! That night I found out that I had won the primary by just 122 votes. A close race, but a win nonetheless. Unfortunately all that work did not translate to a win on Election Day. While I had high hopes for my campaign as a whole, I ended up losing the election by a margin of 621 votes.

Looking back on it now, I can see that 1953 was an interesting year for me, one that was filled with challenges and forced me to grow as a lawyer. I was working on a huge variety of cases, with each one seeming to be more in-depth and technical than the one before.

The first took place in February of 1053. That day I tried a jury trial, defending a second offense DWI. The officer on the case attempted to stop my client on Central Ave, but the defendant did not stop. The officer then stopped an oncoming vehicle and ordered the driver to follow the defendant for the next four miles.

For my first witness I called the owner of the vehicle who was asked to follow my client. He testified that in the four miles that he followed him, the defendant did not violate the laws of the road and there was no appearance of the defendant being under the influence. Additionally, I was able to find two additional witnesses that both observed the defendant before he got in his vehicle and they both testified he appeared sober to them. The jury got the case at 8:00 p.m. on Friday night and returned a NOT
GUILTY verdict at 11:00 p.m.

My next jury trial lasted for an entire week.

In this case, my client was charged with three separate Indictments. After a long and drawn out fight, the jury delivered a NOT GUILTY verdict on the charge of first degree manslaughter, a NOT GUILTY verdict on the charge of leaving the scene after knowing a person had been struck by the vehicle he was operating, but a Guilty verdict on the charge of second degree manslaughter. He was sentenced to serve three to five years in jail, and the presiding judge complemented me on my excellent work on the case.

The next case proved to be delicate in both subject matter and how I chose to handle it. It took place in early March, and my role was to defend a father in an assault case against a 14-year-old babysitter.

We were able to secure a verdict of NOT GUILTY and my client was so grateful that he came to my office with his wife and his parents the next morning. He paid the balance of the legal fee, but he also took me to Portland, Maine where he purchased me a 21-inch television that he had me select and when we got back, he installed it in my office above the bookcases. There are so many nice people in the world.

The one common thread between these cases is that each and every one of them drove home the point that I always wanted to strive to be the best lawyer that I could be. To this point, I felt great about my professional performance, but I always knew that I could do better. That I could always work harder and be a better lawyer.

Forgetting this fact. Forgetting that you should always be working on yourself and on your own knowledge base, is what causes lawyers to become sloppy.

I can promise you one thing. I was never sloppy.
My next big case started up on March 18th when I got a federal case. Now, the important thing about this case was that the defendant was accused of being one of the nation's ten most wanted criminals of the time.

The case was brought to me because the defendant was married to a local girl who knew me by reputation. She wanted me to take the case and to quite literally save her husband.

The first time I went to visit him at the Charles St. Jail in Boston I had Attorney Jackson Holtz join me in his defense. My first impression was that I found this man to be a gentle person and we fought to oppose extradition. We argued extradition in April.

We lost.

This was one of those cases that was going to drag on for quite some time.

In August, 1953, Carolyn, and I went to North Carolina to visit the defendant at the prison. We also consulted with his North Carolina lawyer, Judge Harold Bennett. At the time, he was originally sentenced without a lawyer and this was allegedly his first offense. He was given 20 years in prison.

Why do I tell you this?

Because I feel that it was a great victory. By late April, the defendant was paroled in North Carolina and was able to go home.

On September 16th, I worked an all day jury trial on the case of State vs. Edmund Price. Price was charged with operating a motor vehicle while intoxicated.

Here was what I was up against.

The defendant was faced with four separate police officers who would each be testifying that they had witnessed his intoxication. My wife even told me later that a local police officer made the comment to her of, "What can Fred do with four police officers who will all be testifying he was drunk?"

What could I do indeed!

I worked on the case all evening. This trial continued the following day. Some 100 people had gathered to use the Strafford County Superior Courtroom for some meeting that night when the jury returned a verdict of NOT GUILTY at 8:30 p.m.

When everything was over, Judge Robert Griffith called me into chambers and congratulated me. He said, "I have to give credit where credit is due. Catalfo, you did a splendid professional job and you made the Court and the Bar proud. You conducted the case masterly". He continued to say that he truthfully did not think the defendant had any kind of a chance, but my performance even convinced him that the defendant might just, might just, be innocent. The Judge then said it was a day like this that made him feel that it was worth going to law school.

By the time 1954 rolled around it was election season again, and I was ready to fight right down to the finish line.

The election shaped up like this.

The Republican incumbent, current County Solicitor John Brant, was opposed by Republican Attorney Glenn Davis while myself an my former law school roommate John McCarthey fought for the Democratic nomination.

The campaign was brutal, and it was non-stop from day one.

My wife and I personally visited every single Democratic ward chairman in Dover, Somersworth and Rochester as well as every town in Strafford County. We had my entire family working for my nomination. My law office located at 440 Central Avenue served as both a law center and my political headquarters.

I had my three sisters, a friend and my wife working on addressing political literature.

The one thing that I remember from this campaign was that I was constantly bursting with energy.

James Nadeau was my chairman in Dover. He and I visited many of his friends together and I campaigned in Dover meeting some 50 people at their homes. In Rollinsford, I had George Economos as my chairman. He campaigned hard for me. Noel Chasse was my chairman in Somersworth. My wife and I campaigned in Middleton, Farmington, Rochester, Rollinsford, Dover, Somersworth, Lee, Madbury, New Durham and Strafford.

On primary day, John McCarthy had workers in a number of wards in Dover and elsewhere. I heard several days later that Maurice Murphy (former mayor of Dover) went around these wards, paid these workers for their day's work and sent them home so that by late morning, John's political army had abandoned their posts.

My organization was not only more numerous, but they worked free of charge and were too dedicated to abandon me. They were fired up for the campaign and all felt they had a stake in the outcome.

Truly I was blessed with great support, and that day I won the Democratic primary.

The celebration was legendary! All of our friends and family gathered at our home to enjoy this victory and to surround us with their joy and their love. The following afternoon and evening I went around the County with Carolyn to thank each of my supporters personally.

But winning the primary is only the first step, and it is often interesting how things have a tendency to turn out.

A few days later the two officers who were involved in the Dover Children's Home Case, William Bigger and john

Wormell, showed up in my office and wanted to talk. It turns out that the two of them were not at all settled as to how that case had turned out and they had new information they wanted to share. We spoke at length and between the three of us came up with the follow ad to run in all Stafford County newspapers. All said and done, this ad was viewed by an estimated 30,000 people through circulation of the paper.

CATALFO WAS RIGHT

We, John Wormell and William Bigger, former Police officers of the City of Dover, were the Original investigating officers of the so-called

DOVER CHILDREN'S HOME CASE

We were summoned to the Home on March 22, 1950 at 3:00 A.M.. We found a little child beaten and locked in a dark, cold and unfinished attic. The door leading to the attic was secured by a chair braced against the door so she could not get out.

WE WERE ADVISED NOT TO COOPERATE WITH CATALFO, WHO WAS COUNTY SOLICITOR AT THE TIME, AND NOT TO MAKE ANY STATEMENTS TO HIM ABOUT THESE FACTS.

We Urge You To Vote For Catalfo – Who Tried To Do An Honest Job

By Monday, October 17th, 1954, the political campaign was in full swing. I visited every person I could, I attended rallies, I gave speeches. Literally I did everything that I could to get my message out to the people and to help further my campaign.

Election Day rolled around and I don't think that I sat still for one full minute. I was busy every single moment, plus my gracious staff was on hand at my law office, driving cars through every city ward and present at all town-voting places.

I know that we did everything that we could, and that evening when the polls closed we finally shut things down. We closed the office and headed back home to wait for the results to start rolling in.

I can promise you that things were quite crowded! I was so grateful for every person there and for all the support and love that they had shown to my wife and I during the campaign.

When the results came in we found out that I had won! I had beaten out the Republican candidate and good friend of mine Glenn Davis, and once again I would be the County Solicitor.

My first adventure as County Solicitor? I moved!

My wife and I decided that it was time for a change. So, in December of 1954 we moved out of our little apartment into a larger duplex. We now had three bedrooms. We now had a washroom. Quite simply, we now had room!

One of the trials that I have had to face for most of my life are the lingering injuries that I suffered as a result of my plane crash. Specifically I have had serious problems with chronic pain in my lower back.

In early February of 1955 the pain became so severe that I could do nothing more than come home, fall into a chair and cry like a baby. I had shooting pains for my lower back to my toes and numbness in both of my feet. I was upset, not just about the pain, but that the pain was getting worse. I knew that if it continued to get worse soon I wouldn't be able to walk at all.

That was my fear.

It was more than my fear, it was my horror. I was terrified that the doctors would look at my back and tell me that I was facing the reality of living my life in a wheelchair.

My wife was concerned, but there just wasn't much that she could do. She kept me warm and comfortable, but ultimately we both knew that I needed to go back to the doctor.

I was examined a number of times by Dr. Bernard Manning, who provided me pain pills but decided that I needed to make the effort to see a specialist. So, within a week my wife and I were on our way to the Lahey Clinic in Boston.

They had some good news and some bad news for us.

The good news was that they did not think that I would lose the ability to walk. The bad news was that they could not completely relieve the pain. It was something that would simply become a part of my life, and something that I have been forced to learn to live with.

I was okay with that. I was okay with everything they said after "we do not believe that you will cripple.

Personally I find a great deal of pride in the fact that very few people know about this constant pain and no one has ever heard me complain about it. My sight has been impaired since my cornea was cut in the plane crash. My left arm is 4 inches shorter than my right and has severe radial nerve damage. I have very little feeling in my hand, and my arm is often completely useless.

My goal was to live my life in spite of the pain. I did whatever I wanted to do and went wherever I wanted to go. I even played in a softball league with several of my fellow lawyers. They never knew. They never knew about the constant pain I felt on a daily basis and I never wanted them to.

On March 1, 1955, I had the honor of lecturing to a pre-law class at the University of New Hampshire. I spoke to them for an hour and told them in part the following:

"To you future lawyers, judges, legislators, the well-being of your people and the security of society are, in large part, entrusted. You will engage in a profession, not a trade. While you will find means of a livelihood in the law, that will not be your principal concern. You will be of service to your fellow man, with an eye on his benefit and aid and not primarily to your benefit and profit. For this is what the profession demands. Those who follow the profession are men and women who are dedicated to the service of mankind. The personal interests of the attorney are secondary and subordinate to the good that they can do. They are the repositories of other's secrets, the recipients of confidence, the custodian of other's goods. The goods, often the reputation and the very lives of others are entrusted in their care with full trustfulness and complete confidence. They are expected to be men and women of high ideals, sound principles and complete integrity. No other group does the safety and the welfare of society so depend. In joining the number of those who follow the law, a man makes large promises of unselfish devotion and of service and assumes real and heavy responsibilities."

That summer my closest friend, Dr. Eddie O'Rourke, a public health officer with N.A.T.O. stationed at Salzburg, Austria, and his wife, "Torkey", were encouraging Carolyn and I to spend a few months with them in Europe.

We had never been to Europe, but it was someplace that we both wanted to go. After discussing it, the answer was quite simple.

We would love to!

But, before we could go, there were a few logistical issues to take care of. For one thing, I had decided to move my law office. I would still be in the same building, but now I would have eleven rooms to work with instead of the two that I currently occupied.

For another, my wife had to finish out the school year!

We did everything that we could to tie up loose ends, and on June 12th we were ready to head out. Several of our friends gave us a bon voyage dinner at the Daris Tea Room. They presented my wife, Carolyn, with two-dozen long-stem red roses while I was given a movie camera.

The presentation was made by Daniel McCooey, M.D., John Rogers Penn served as toastmaster and Mayor John Shaw of Rochester served as principal speaker. During his talk, he gave me a glowing tribute for my "championing the common man and for my friendliness, courageousness and energy in the public office". There were nearly 150 people present. The room was overcrowded.

By Saturday, June 18th, 1955, we were packed for a trip to Europe. We said good-bye to members of our family here in Dover, New Hampshire and I called my brother, Joseph, in California. We spent the night with Carolyn's father and mother in Watertown, Massachusetts.

The next morning Carolyn and I started our trip by going to St. Luke's Catholic Church for Mass. Then Carolyn and I went to the Logan International Airport in Boston and boarded a four-propeller Trans Atlantic plane on Trans World Airlines (T.W.A.). The plane refueled in Canada and flew on for eleven straight hours.

We finally landed at Shannon Airport in Ireland at 9:00 a.m. Ireland was beautiful, but the best thing to see was our dear friends, Doctor Eddie and Torkey O'Rourke waiting for us as we walked off the plane.

From there we dove head first into a full 60-day trip on a lifetime. It was a whirlwind, but every moment was packed and rich and so full of life that I wouldn't and couldn't want it any other way. We went to the Blarney Castle and kissed the Blarney Stone then jumped over to England where we picked up my friend Eddie's new Ford and the four of us drove straight through to Scotland.

That night our room was in a drafty old castle outside Edinburgh, one where suits of armor stood guard over each and every door. It was the kind of place where your imagination could easily get the best of you and one we were eager to leave before our heads even touched the pillow! As we walked past the silent sentries towards our room for the night, we started to hear loud, continuous screams that made my hair try to crawl its way up the back of my neck.

I can tell you today that we made it through the night, but it was a close call. As soon as the sun peeked its first ray over the horizon we jumped back in Eddie's Ford and hit the road. Looking back we managed to have a good laugh, but from there on out we had a firm, yet unspoken rule. Hotels and motels when traveling....no castles!

During our trip we were able to visit Holland, Belgium, Spain and France before circling around and heading back to Italy. The Italian Rivera to be exact, as well as Milan and Florence.

By the 10th of July it was time for Eddie and Torkey to head home. They took the train back to Salzburg, Austria and we hated to see them go. They did however leave their Ford with us, allowing us to continue our trip and head on to new adventures.

For me, my time in Italy was by far the highlight of the trip. Carolyn and I traveled to Rome and Naples, taking in the sites before heading to Sicily to see my family. The trip took four full days but finally we reached Biancavilla.

I had been in this village when I was just 5 years old, but I had never seen it as an adult. We visited my father's brother, Anthony Catalfo, as well as his sister, Francesca Catalfo. The village was like something out of a movie. Tiny little streets, paved with stones seemed to crawl through narrow alleys and wind around beautiful old buildings. There were very few cars in Biancavilla at this time, and our Ford definitely stood out wherever we went!

The houses were amazing. Once you went inside, the rooms felt tiny; very little furniture, small windows and no lawns or flowers to speak of. There was no industry in this town. If you wanted to survive, you farmed. It was as simple as that, and it was not until this trip that I fully grasped what my parents had given to me by coming to America when they did. I saw what my life would have looked like and I was humbled.

Don't get me wrong, I loved my family, but I did not want to be forced to live the way that they did.

I am so grateful that my parents were able to leave Italy. In Italy I would never have had the chance to go to college. I would not have become a lawyer and may not have ever even made it off of the farm. I am so grateful to have been born in the United States. Grateful for the freedom it offered me and for the opportunity it presented. It allowed me to become the man I am today and to live the amazing life I have enjoyed.

On Sunday, July 24, 1955, we attended Mass at Santa Maria dell Elemosina Catholic Church in Biancavilla. It was the very church my parents worshiped in and were married in on June 28, 1912. What a remarkable moment. To be sitting in the same church where my parents not only met, but spent so much of their youth. I was so in awe of the history contained in that building that it was hard to concentrate on anything the priest was saying.

From Biancavilla we traveled to Riese, Sicily. The village where my mother-in-law, Giovanina (Bartoli) Mosca, was born.

On July 26, 1955, I was in Palermo, Sicily with Carolyn, on vacation. We finally got transportation by ship to Naples. We took the Ford that belonged to Dr. Eddie O'Rourke on board and in the middle of the afternoon, the ship finally sailed.

On July 27th, we took a train from Rome to Abruzzi in Pescara. The next morning we took an old, banged-up bus from Pescara to the interior of the mountainous area and an hour later arrived in the village of Carpineto della Nora. The bus driver was drinking from a gallon of wine while driving and served as a mailman as well. He also sang while driving.

It was a death trap, but we made it! And we had a fantastic story to tell when we got home.

Carolyn's uncle, Carlo Mosca, was waiting for us with several of his children and a mule. We then climbed and climbed by foot for several miles before reaching their home called "rocca russo." After a nice Italian dinner and enjoyable time, we walked down the mountain to the bus and to Pescara. Let me be honest here and tell you that these people, our family, had nothing. They were happy, but Carolyn and I wanted to be able to offer them something. We didn't have extra money, but I did give away my watch. It wasn't much, but it was admired by many and it was something we could leave behind.

At this point it was finally time for Carolyn and I to head back to Austria and return the O'Rourke's car to our dear friends and their six children. Our final day with Eddie and Torkey was spent in Salzburg, a beautiful city, rich in history and music as well as the home of Mozart.

We took the train to Rome from Salzburg, Austria. Eddie and Torkey took us to the railroad station and it was hard to tell them good-bye. At that point, we honestly did not know when we would get the chance to see them again.

The final stop on little world tour was Lisbon, Portugal. We took more sightseeing tours and finally on Saturday, August 20, 1955, we boarded a four-engine propellered T.W.A. plane and traveled all night, back across the ocean to Newfoundland, Canada to refuel. From there it was on to Logan International Airport in Boston and then home.

Carolyn and I were pleased to see her parents, Thomas and Giovanina Mosca, my mother, Vincenza Catalfo, my sister, Mary, and her husband, Roland Oates, and my brother, Joseph, waiting for us at the airport. We all went to Carolyn's parents' home for a nice dinner. Carolyn and I stayed with them overnight.

The next day we returned to our apartment at 54 Silver Street, Dover, New Hampshire. It was hard to get back to the real world after such an amazing adventure, but I soon resumed my duties as Strafford County Solicitor and my private law practice.

In early June, 1956, the Executive Committee of the New Hampshire Democratic Party met to select an interim state chairman to replace the late John Hodgdon. The Committee selected Attorney Robert Branch of Concord. He got nine votes and I got five.

In the meantime, I was not only Senior Vice Commander of the Department of New Hampshire Disabled American Veterans, but also Chairman of the D.A.V. Convention Committee. The Convention was a three-day affair held here in Dover beginning on Friday, June 15th, 1956. We published a convention yearbook and the City was bedecked with flags. I had help from members of various chapters and auxiliary to help with the convention and I was grateful for their help.

On Saturday morning, June 16, 1956, we had memorial services in front of the City Hall, including raising of our American flag, a firing squad and the playing of taps and the National Anthem by the Dover High School Band. We held our 8th Annual Department Convention and the Auxiliary had their 5th Annual Convention. Over 500 disabled American veterans participated. We had a morning and afternoon business session at the City Hall and I was elected Commander of the Department of New Hampshire Disabled American Veterans for 1956-57.

That night we had a banquet at the municipal auditorium. It was a sellout! Dr. Daniel McCooey, a member of Chapter #5, served as toastmaster and among the guests were Thomas

Keenan and Governor Lane Dwinell. We held installations of newly elected department and auxiliary officers.

On Sunday afternoon, we held a two-hour street parade on Central Avenue in Dover. It included military units from the U.S. Army, the U.S. Navy and the U.S. Marines, some ten drum and bugle corps, several marching bands as well as two bagpipe bands. It was a very patriotic display, and I felt so proud to be a part of it.

The Democratic National Convention assembled in Chicago the week of August 12, 1956. I was not a delegate, but friends of mine, such as Francis Dostillo of Keene and Felix Daniel of Manchester, called me and invited me to join them. They were all delegates for U.S. Senator Estes Kefauver of Tennessee. My wife, Carolyn, packed up our bags and we left for Chicago the evening of Tuesday, August 14th. We took turns driving and we pulled over during the night to sleep in the vehicle for a couple of hours.

We had a nice time at the convention and I supported Governor Adlai Stevenson of Illinois. He won the nomination over Estes Kefauver with ease.

The next morning, Friday, August 17th, there was a political struggle between Estes Kefauver and my friend, U.S. Senator John F. Kennedy of Massachusetts, for Vice President. I moved among delegates to solicit support for Kennedy, but when the vote was tallied he was short by just one vote. Kennedy took to the podium and withdrew his name, moving in favor of Kefauver.

I enjoyed the convention. I still retained my friendship with the New Hampshire delegates and I enjoyed being with "Jack" Kennedy and helping him out.

From Chicago, my wife, Carolyn, and I drove to San Antonio, Texas to attend the Disabled American Veterans National Convention the following week. Since I was Department Commander for New Hampshire, I had a duty to be there and felt that it was worth the additional time away from my office.

During the national campaign in the fall, we had the pleasure of being visited by U.S. Senator John F. Kennedy here in Strafford County. It occurs to me that the time I spent with Kennedy was both a blessing and a curse. I was given the opportunity to *know* the man that most only saw as a symbol. But I was also forced to later endure the loss of a friend as well as the shock of losing a leader.

What was Kennedy like? He was interested in people. He always wanted to know the story behind a person and find out the details that made their life unique. I can remember how every time we would stop, he would want to know about who we were about to meet. Who were they? What was their situation? And, most importantly to him, what could he do to make it better?

This was John F. Kennedy. The man dedicated his life to improving the lives of those around him, and this is the man that our country lost.

On Saturday, September 29th, 1956, Carolyn, and I and many friends that wanted me to be the New Hampshire Democratic State Chairman attended the Democratic State Convention. The convention was held at the Carpenter Hotel in Manchester. We had a heated, boisterous convention. I had favorable delegates from all parts of the State and nearly everyone, including gubernatorial candidate, Mayor John Shaw of Rochester, James P. Nadeau, Nick Shaheen of Dover and many others from Strafford County.

The Democratic Executive Committee first brought in the name of Joseph Scott, but with it was a minority report with my name for Chairman. It was obvious that the majority of the delegates preferred me over Joseph Scott and the convention delegates were ready to vote for the minority report and Alfred Catalfo, Jr. as the new chairman. I spoke highly of Joseph Scott of Manchester. I proposed that whoever was elected chairman would remain in that office until after the election and then we would call for a new election for the chairman.

Unexpectedly, Joseph Scott withdrew his name in favor of Alfred Catalfo, Jr. It was put to the convention and in a resounding voice vote, I was named Democratic State Chairman. I had every intention of winning, but it was late. The election was only five weeks away!

I worked hard for the next five weeks. We had headquarters in every city and in large towns. We had developed teams for nearly every ward to get the Democrats and Independents to vote our way. I traveled nearly every day to different parts of the State. Many times I accompanied our governor candidate, John Shaw, on some of these trips. This job did not pay a salary or even expenses.

However, the election on November 6, 1956, resulted in a landslide for U.S. President Dwight Eisenhower over Governor Adlai Stevenson.

Shortly after the election, some effort was made by a few Democrats to oust me as Chairman. We had an Executive Committee meeting in Manchester on
November 13,1956 and several of the members, headed by Attorney Tom McIntyre of Laconia, wanted to replace me as Chairman. I would not resign and I refused to recognize the motion, which was out of order. The majority agreed with me.

I had called for the resumption of the Democratic State Convention for December 8, 1956 to help reorganize the party and resolve this issue of the Democratic State Chairman once and for all.

On Saturday, December 8, 1956, we reconvened the Democratic Party Convention at the Carpenter Hotel in Manchester, New Hampshire where we adopted a new Constitution and By-Laws. The affair was well attended and there was a feeling of high hope for the Democratic Party among all of the roughly 350 delegates in attendance.

About two-thirds of the delegates were close acquaintances of mine so I was prepared to fight for my position if forced.

However the opposition that I had anticipated failed to materialize. The Executive Committee retired and about 15 minutes later returned to the full convention and gave me a unanimous vote of confidence. It was a harmonious convention. We had food, music, soft drinks and it was a very friendly affair.

Chapter 12:

A New Generation

You would think that with all I had going on that I would have put all the milestones of adulthood behind me. After all, I was happily married, a successful politician, a well-known lawyer, and had traveled the world just to name a few.

But there were still a few hurdles left for me to cross.

The first of these, and one that I was more than ready to tackle, was to own my own home. Rental proprieties are great, and they had helped us to get started in our marriage, but I was ready to move on. I was ready to find the house of my dreams and to move in with my beautiful wife.

Plus, I wanted us to be settled in our new home by the time we started a family.

Finding the house was the easy part!

On January 3, 1957 Carolyn and I purchased a palatial home located at 20 Arch Street in Dover, New Hampshire under the G.I. Bill. The house was amazing and simply packed with potential, but it had been badly abused and vandalized on and off over the years.

But we could see past that. We could see past the neglect and the disrepair to the beauty that lay hidden beneath the surface. Our goal was to restore this beautiful home to its original splendor.

The house its self had everything we could ever ask for. It came equipped with 3 ½ baths, seven upstairs bedrooms, a foyer with a circular stairway, a large kitchen, washroom, pantry, a back first-floor toy room, a large living room, a large dining room, a law library and three porches, two on the first floor and one upstairs porch overlooking the back gardens. The ceiling in the library was gold leaf. The downstairs floors were parquet. We had five fireplaces, a slate roof, copper gutters and a four-car garage. We had a circular fountain, two wall fountains in the back gardens and five sunken gardens.

Can you see why we fell in love with it?

This was much more than just a house. It was an estate, one where we would make our home and start our family.

Attorney Lucius Varney, a successful patent lawyer in New York City, built the home in 1914. Varney was a confirmed bachelor who built the home for his mother and his aunt.

When we first closed on the property, the building was in shambles. But over time we brought back the radiance room by room. We started with a full new electrical system, outside spotlights and crystal chandeliers in every room.

Then we repaired the oil furnace that provided heat throughout the home to help balance conditions throughout the property. Originally we had thought that my father-in-law would be able to do this repair for us. He was a maintenance man for one of the local school and felt that he could fix the original furnace rather buying a new one. This didn't turn out to be the case so he lent me the money to have the work done. I paid him back immediately, just as soon as I was able to recoup my finances from purchasing the house.

Then we moved on to the next project, and the next one after that and the next one after that!

It took some time, but slowly we brought the old place back to life.

After we had lived there for some time we learned that Franklin D. Roosevelt had stayed there overnight in both 1932 and 1936 while campaigning for President. For me it was like a sign. Like this was the right place at the right time and I was exactly where I was supposed to be.

During this time, Carolyn and I were trying to start a family. We had our careers. We had our home. We had everything that we needed to welcome and care for a child of our own. What we didn't know at the time was that we were already well on our way!

Two weeks after we purchased the house, on January the 14th, my wife gave me some of the best news yet. We were going to have a baby! Our first child was officially on the way and we were going to be parents in just a few short months!

Carolyn and I were inundated with happiness! It seemed as if all of the pieces of our life were falling into place, making all my hard work worth it. Every minute of struggle, every hurdle I fought to cross was more than worth it the moment I found out that I was going to be a father.

With the baby on the way, it was time for a few things to change. The first of which was that on March 29th my wife took a leave of absence from Woodman Park School, where she taught the 7th grade. She wanted to spend the next few months preparing for the baby to arrive and taking care of her health.

I was fully on board with this plan and supported any decision that she might make.

But, as I had learned time and time again, no matter what is going on in your personal life, time moves on. For me this meant fulfilling my obligations as a lawyer and to my family.

One such event took place on Saturday evening, June 1st, 1957, I was honored by the Bellamy Chapter #5 of Dover at a banquet held at the Rainbow Gardens in Somersworth, New Hampshire. I was awarded the Disabled American Veterans National Citation for Outstanding Service as Department of New Hampshire Commander 1956-57. In attendance were my wife, Carolyn, my mother, Vincenza Catalfo, my three sisters, all members of the D.A.V. Auxiliary, and many friends. Over 200 people were present. Judge David Williams of Massachusetts, National Junior Vice Commander, was the principal speaker and Past Department Commander and friend, Emerson Follotte, served as toastmaster.

Next, my wife, Carolyn and I attended the Department of New Hampshire Disabled American Veterans Convention held in Laconia on June 14th, 15th and 16th, 1957. As Commander, I was in charge of the entire convention, but was fortunate enough to have some very talented and dedicated people on my team.

The center point of the whole event was a large parade held on Sunday afternoon. It was a huge event, one that was attended by thousands and lasted nearly two full hours.

By the time my next engagement rolled around towards the end of the month, my wife was too far along in her pregnancy to go with me. I was needed in Washington D.C. as the Democratic Chairman of the state of New Hampshire and I was worried that the trip would be too hard on Carolyn. On

Sunday June 28th, I drove her to her parents house so that she might spend the time with them while I was away in Washington.

The next day I spent about four hours at the Democratic National Headquarters and several hours with U.S. Senator Estes Kefauver of Tennessee. I was there as the New Hampshire Democratic Chairman.

And this was how our life progressed. I traveled from engagement to engagement, taking Carolyn with me when we felt it was safe for her and the baby, and traveling on my own when it would be too hard on her.

Several days before my wife was due to deliver, she decided to take a few days to go and visit her mother. Her doctor was in Boston, and she was due to deliver at The Richardson House of the Lying In Hospital, now known as the Brigham and Women's Hospital in Boston. My in-laws lived much closer to the hospital then we did, and Carolyn and I felt more comfortable with her staying nearby.

And, as with many pregnancies, we had our share of false alarms! Carolyn made the trip to the hospital two or three different times, thinking she was in labor, only to be sent back home. During the last trip I spent the entire day and most of the night with my wife as they told her she was in false labor once again. I only left and went home in the middle of the night because I was due in court early the next morning!

Throughout the day I would contact the hospital, checking on Carolyn, only to be told that she was doing fine and resting comfortably. I honestly didn't realize that during all this time my wife, Carolyn, was at the Richardson House of the Boston Lying Inn Hospital giving birth to our first child. My son entered our world at 4:45 p.m., but I did not find out until 7:15 p.m.!

Not a single person tried to call me!

I finished my cases, stopped by the Police Station, stopped by to visit some friends and had other friends stop by to see our new home. It wasn't until my sister Ida called me that evening screaming "It's a boy! It's a boy!" that I even knew what was going on!

The dads are always the last to know!

I instantly hung up the phone, called the hospital and was told that both mother and child were doing well.

That was all I needed to hear!

Within just a few short minutes I changed clothes, picked a box of cigars and was on the road to Boston. With every mile of the trip happiness was literally exploding out of my body! I couldn't wait to get to my wife and to meet my new son for the very first time.

My first stop was to go straight to my wife's private room and check on her. She looked a little pale, but was so happy. Back then they didn't keep the babies in the rooms with their mothers; instead they went to the nursery. That is why I, like so many other fathers of the time, saw my new son for the first time through the large window in front of the nursery. I was not allowed to hold him, just stare through the window at the little boy that was my son.

He was so handsome. He had a beautiful Italian face and a thick crop of dark brown hair. In that moment I was so overcome with emotion that all I could think to say was, "That's my boy!"

My sweet wife, Carolyn, remained at the hospital after our son was born for about a week. It may seem like a long stretch, but that was the custom at that time.

I wanted her to stay as long as she needed to get the best possible care. Of course this meant that I was making the commute to and from Boston each day, but that was fine with me. I would stop by and pick up my mother or anyone else who wanted to see the baby and we would hit the road.

My son's first rite of passage took place when he was less than 6 weeks old. What could possibly happen at such a tender age? We had him baptized at St. Joseph's Catholic Church. In that moment, throughout that day in fact, my little family was surrounded by love. We held a christening reception at our new home that was attended by some 400 friends and relatives! There was live music, plenty of food and overflowing fellowship.

From there it was back to business as usual. Or, in my case, politics as usual! As Chairman of the Democratic State Committee, I worked constantly throughout the fall to help with various municipal elections. Truly it seemed as if one campaign flowed into another until I was caught up in a constant cycle of meetings and voting.

I loved it!

Some of the events were pretty run of the mill, but some of them had more meaning than I can portray to you on a simple printed page. They say that a picture is worth a thousand words? Well, then some of these experiences were worth a million!

One of these events was held on Saturday November 16th. On that night my beautiful wife and I traveled to Boston as guests at a testimonial dinner for U.S. Senator John F. Kennedy and Congressman John W. McCormack held at the Commonwealth Armory. It was a black tie event, and my wife wore a light blue evening gown and an orchid and I wore a tuxedo.

The Armory was packed with over 5,000 people and Carolyn and I were fortunate enough to be head table guests.
I was invited as the New Hampshire Democratic State Chairman. Every Democratic State Chairman in the New England States was present.

The affair was to launch my friend, "Jack" Kennedy, for President of the United States. The world would have to look far and wide to find a more qualified candidate. He loved people, he loved politics, he was very intelligent and he was philosophically sound. He was a veteran of World War II, a personal friend and he loved our great country. He was a Disabled American Veteran and a member of the Cambridge Chapter.

The next morning, after attending Mass, I issued a statement supporting John F. Kennedy for President of the United States. It was my pleasure to issue that statement.

On December 3rd, 1957, we held a fund-raising dinner for six candidates at the municipal auditorium in Dover, New Hampshire. The event was put on by the Democratic State Committee and it was a sellout with over 400 guests in attendance.

John Shaw served as toastmaster. He had been Mayor of Rochester on three occasions and a Democratic candidate for

Governor in 1954 and 1956. The principal speaker was Paul M. Butler, Chairman of the Democratic National Committee.

Following the successful affair, my wife and I held a private reception at our own home. We had music, food and drinks for some 200 present, which involved newspaper, radio and television personnel. Honorable Paul M. Butler spoke to the media at an in house news conference. The event was a success and we had a wonderful time.

Believe it or not, with all of this going on, I still found the time to practice law!

One case that stands out from this time period was a jury trial in which I defended, a local man accused of aggravated assault on a 37 year-old woman. The trial took place in the Rockingham County Superior Court in Exeter from Monday, December 3rd, to Tuesday, December 10th, 1957 and was prosecuted by County Attorney Linsay Brigham.

During the first week, the State put witnesses on, such as a doctor, Exeter Hospital records, a neighbor, a state trooper, two children of the victim, and the victim herself. I did extensive cross-examination on each of the witnesses and there were inconsistencies in their stores. I also extracted some exculpatory evidence from several of the witnesses. During the trial, I took numerous objections and exceptions and Judge George Grant, Jr. held conferences, both at the bench and in chambers.

The following week, the defendant testified on his behalf. The jury was out nine hours ended up deadlocked and were finally dismissed. The judge ruled it a hung jury. A second jury trial took place two months later from January 28th to 30th, 1958 and the defendant was found NOT GUILTY.

This trial proves the difference that a good lawyer can make. Not just anyone could have won the Not Guilty verdict for my client, and I was proud to offer him a strong defense and a positive outcome.

As 1958 moved into my life, I was blessed with a family that I loved. Not to mention that I enjoyed my law work and the challenges I faced as Democratic State Chairman. Keep in mind that the position of Chairman paid no salary and did not even pay costs for secretarial assistance or paper or stamps or travel expenses. Everything was gratuitous and came out of my own pocket. Nevertheless, I was dedicated to turning New Hampshire into a Democratic fortress.

This goal was not without some opposition and friction within my own party, but most of the opposition came from Republican newspapers who fired hostile print at me.

It was obvious that I was being targeted by the competition, and it should have been just as obvious that I would not take that kind of assault lightly.

My aim was to answer back those hostile newspapers and to get those few members who opposed me within our party to postpone their goals and join me. My fondest hopes were that our Democratic party would succeed in the 1958 state and congregational elections.

In the meantime, I was able to go home during the day from time to time for short periods to enjoy my baby boy. My talented mother, Vincenza Catalfo, did most of the babysitting at our home at the time and we were fortunate to have her. The schedule worked out perfectly for us.

My mother would come each morning before my wife and I left for work. Then, she would stay until Carolyn was home from school at about 3:00 in the afternoon to relieve her. Then either my wife or I would drive my mother home, or she would take a taxi.

By March 30th, 1958, the Democrats of this State were determined to win New Hampshire. We had adopted a platform and were attempting to find candidates for every elective office on the ticket. We were committed to become significant as a party this year and take the presidency in 1960 with Kennedy.

In the meantime, I represented a defendant, in a two-day jury trial. He was charged with contributing to the delinquency of a minor by aiding and abetting in the concealment of stolen property. On April 15th, he was found to be Not Guilty.

On April 17th, 1958, Enoch Shenton, City Editor of the Concord Monitor and a political columnist for various newspapers across the State went a bit too far in his quest to discredit me as a political force. His article was rejected for print by all newspapers across the State, except the Rochester Courier. The article under the column titled, "The State House Courier" stated that the reason why some Democrats want to replace Catalfo as Chairman of the State Democratic Party was to "remove the pig in the parlor element from the party and replace him with lace curtain Democrats."

Those were fighting words!

I contacted one of my closest friends and former roommate in law school, Attorney Thomas Flynn, and I showed him the article. All I wanted was A Retraction, but Mr. Shenton refused. So, we did the only thing that we could, we filed a lawsuit in the Strafford County Superior Court. This also happened to be something that both Thomas and I were very very good at!

At first, a judge ruled that this was a political privilege and dismissed the case.

Bull!

The New Hampshire Supreme Court overruled the judge and stated that if I could show that the article was written with malice, I could recover.

You bet I could show malice and a personal attack!

Shortly before the case went to trial, in late April, 1961, it was settled. I got the retraction I originally wanted, along with an $8,000.00 settlement, which represented over $60,000.00 today.

On June 7th, 1958 we held one of the most inspiring events of my political career. It was a highly anticipated Jefferson-Jackson Day Dinner at the State Armory in Manchester, New Hampshire. The principal speaker before over 1,200 roaring Democrats was U.S. Senator, John F. Kennedy.

Perhaps you've heard of him?

Kennedy was fantastic. He was great, impressive and loved by all of us. His beautiful wife, Jacqueline Kennedy, was with him. As Democratic State Chairman, I had compiled an eight-page program booklet to go along with the event as a whole.

Also as Democratic State Chairman I was required to give a speech at the event. The following denote part of the remarks I gave that evening:

"It is a pleasure to extend to all of you a cordial welcome on behalf of the New Hampshire Democratic State

Committee. This 103rd annual Jefferson-Jackson Day Dinner is a significant milestone in the annals of our party's history.

We have with us tonight the United States Senator of Massachusetts as our principal speaker. The Country is fortunate to have Senator Jack Kennedy available to lead this country as our President! America is so lucky to have him!

This dinner also launches officially the 1958 Democratic campaign which will result in victory in November.

We have made great strides toward cracking this supposedly impregnable G.O.P. stronghold in New Hampshire. In a normal election year only 10,000 votes divide the parties. In December of 1956 we adopted a constitution and by-laws to govern our affairs. Since that time the Democratic State Committee has met on numerous occasions to determine policy, which will express the philosophy of our great party.

Thanks to your generosity and cooperation we are gradually succeeding in accumulating the necessary funds for a successful campaign. As many of you know, two years ago we had only $22.00 in the party treasury six weeks away from a state and national election. This problem is being corrected. This afternoon we have concluded our unprecedented pre-primary platform convention and our platform this year will express more fully and vividly the philosophy of our party and the issues of this campaign. We are also engaged in broad plans to fill the entire Democratic slate of officers from top to bottom to prevent what took place in 1956 when we lost 200 of the 399 seats in the house and 10 of the 24 seats in the senate by default.

In the months just passed, for the first time in many years, a Democrat was elected to the office of Mayor in the City of Concord, which is considered the prime stronghold of the opposition party because it is there that 67% of the state employees live. The Democrats have regained the mayoralty seats also in the cities of Keene and Nashua and have maintained mayoralties in Manchester, Somersworth, Rochester, Laconia, Franklin and Berlin. All indications tend to show that the Democratic Party in New Hampshire has become strong enough to win in 1958.

As Chairman of the Democratic State Committee, I assure you that the drive to organize even the smallest communities in New Hampshire will continue. There will be no let-up until the State of New Hampshire has voted a Democratic administration, which all of our people deserve and have so long waited. I wish to thank each of you for your part in making all of our accomplishments possible."

Our National Committeeman, Bernard Boutin, introduced Unites States Senator John F. Kennedy as our principal speaker in a more formal way in a short while, but I lauded Jack Kennedy for his greatness and told the membership how fortunate all Americans would be with Jack Kennedy as President of the United States. That evening, U.S. Senator Jack Kennedy, his wife, Jacqueline, and my wife, Carolyn and I had a special photograph taken together. I had the photograph enlarged to 42" by 36," oil painted and placed in a large wooden gold painted frame that it has remained on one of my law office walls all these years.

On September 26th and 27th, 1958, we held our New Hampshire Democratic Party's State Convention. We published a booklet for the affair, which included, among other things, letters from Mrs. Franklin D. Roosevelt, President Harry S. Truman, U.S. Senator Estes Kefauver of

230

Tennessee, former Governor of Illinois, Adlai Stevenson, U.S. Senator John F. Kennedy, our Democratic candidate for Governor, Mayor Bernard Boutin, Governor of Massachusetts, Foster Furcolo, Governor of Maine, Edward Muskie, Governor of Connecticut, Abraham Ribicoff and Governor of Rhode Island, Dennis Roberts.

It was a colorful, noisy Democratic State Convention held at the Carpenter Hotel in Manchester, New Hampshire. The Convention had all the color, enthusiasm, and thrills of a national convention in miniature scale.

The Convention opened on Friday evening with a tremendous Drum and Bugle Corps display inside the convention hall. It was terrific. All the noise, the yelling and screaming, the signs and flags all over the place, and the demonstrations were great. Following the National Anthem, speech after speech was given and each one was devoted to the Democratic chances of sweeping New Hampshire this year.

The best speech of the evening on Friday night was that which I gave about our chances, what we have done, what we expect to do, and what a tremendous amount of harmony and unity we have and will continue to have even after the convention is over. The platform was probably one of the most academically sound jobs done by either political party.

On Saturday at noon we had to cancel the Drum and Bugle Corps parade of 14 units because of a heavy downpour of rain, but we had one of the Drum and Bugle Corps units come into the convention hall and they escorted the future Governor and the future first lady, Mayor and Mrs. Boutin, to the rostrum.

After the festivities, such as the National Anthem, saluting of the colors and prayer, I gave out a bombastic speech for unity and at that time the surprise was sprung when I stated, "that it is fitting and proper and in the best tradition of the Democratic party that the gubernatorial nominee should select the Democratic State Chairman and other state officers, and that the other 32 men and women who are on the Executive Committee should comply with his wishes." When I made that statement, after a lengthy speech about party unity and harmony, the convention went wild because it reached a climax and a sign of relief since there was a tremendous split in the ranks as to who should be the State Chairman and about 60% of the delegates were standing pat for Fred Catalfo to be re-elected State Chairman.

Attorney J. Murray Devine was named Democratic State Chairman and I was appointed Chairman of the Democratic Special Activities Committee and a member of the Executive Committee as well.

On Tuesday, November 4, 1958, our Democratic candidate for governor, Bernie Boutin, lost to Republican Wesley Power by 6,625 in an off-year election. A total of 206,000 votes were cast. It was disappointing to me, but in retrospect, Mayor Boutin gave a good account of himself.

With all that had gone on during the election, by the time Thanksgiving rolled around, my wife and I knew that it was time for a break. We hated to leave our young son, even for a day, but we decided to spend a long weekend in New York City just the two of us.

It was hard to be away, but he was getting along just fine with his grandparents and they loved having him.

How did we know this?

Well, because we called several times a day to check on him!

The time away was good for us and we returned home refreshed and ready to jump back into the daily grind that life had to offer. Plus when we got home we had a huge surprise waiting on us. Our son had learned to walk!

I knew right then that life was never going to be the same, and I couldn't wait!

234

Chapter 13:

Life, Politics
&
JFK

For me the year 1959 was one to remember. My life was filled with joy and to me each day was brighter and more vibrant than the one before.

Why you ask?

Because each and every day I was given the chance to spend time with my family, work at a career that I loved and watch my young son grow and thrive. Freddie was beautiful and vivacious in a way that enamored both my wife and I.

Since both of us worked during the day, we had a babysitter at home while Carolyn was teaching. But we were also fortunate enough to have both grandmothers also babysitting when needed and sometimes even when not needed! It was lovely to watch them fall in love with their grandson and have the opportunity to shower him with affection and joy.

Even though I was very busy at my law office and often in court, I always made time to visit my son at home. But even then I knew that our relationship had to be my top priority. So I made it a point to take him with me to work as often as I could. You would think that a law office would be no place for a small child, but he loved it. And why wouldn't he? Every time we walked in the door he had all four of my secretaries jumping to entertain him!

I even took him to court with me!

There were often days when I had only minor matters to attend to in court. Those were the perfect days to take him with me and let him be a big part of my day. No one minded his presence, and I loved having the chance to show him off. Besides, he was so well behaved, even at such a young age, that it was hard to notice him sitting near the front of the courtroom.

This was our life, and we loved it. We treasured the simple moments. Things like my father-in-law having the chance to take his 1½-year-old grandson to the duck pond on Easter Sunday, moments that you hold on to because they are both precious and fleeting.

One moment that I would have liked to forget was the night of March 19th, when my law offices were ransacked by a group of thieves. The police received the call at 3:45 a.m. and immediately notified me so that I could join them on the scene.

My entire office was completely trashed, with desk drawers, files and other items thrown everywhere. It was complete chaos. Luckily nothing was taken, but the mess they left behind was significant.

As the police were searching through the building, they heard a noise coming from my own office. It seems that the thieves has used a back fire escape to gain entrance to the building and had chosen that route to escape as well.

At the end of the day I was only glad that no one was injured and that nothing was done that could not be undone. In my line of work I knew all to well what could happen when a simple robbery went terribly wrong.

On a professional front I faced two significant trials in 1959 that did their best to test my skill as an attorney.

The first of which was a Manslaughter Trial.

My client was arrested and charged with manslaughter for killing a peeping tom outside his home in Hillsboro, New Hampshire. There was no doubt in the prosecution's mind that the defendant fired his rifle and killed the victim yet it was my job to plant the seed of doubt into the mind of the jury.

My job was more than cut out for me.

The trial started Tuesday, May 19th, 1959 with an all male jury in the Hillsboro County Superior Court in Manchester with Judge Robert Griffin presiding.

What happened several weeks prior to March 10th, 1959 was that some person in the wee hours of the morning walked toward the large kitchen window overlooking the Contoocook River to watch the defendant's wife give herself a sponge bath in her kitchen sink as she prepared to go to work. Suddenly, she looked up to see an unknown male looking into her window.

She screamed.

Her husband and their two boys jumped out of bed. The defendant described what she had seen. The Hillsboro Police were called and they provided surveillance for the next few mornings. Unfortunately, the peeping Tom never returned and the police were forced to forgo their protection detail after a few days.

In the meantime, her husband, Reginald Gerbert, put his hunting rifle nearby, loaded, and the rifle did have attached a telescopic lens. He had every intention of capturing this "peeping Tom" on his own and holding him at gunpoint until the Hillsboro Police arrived.

This brings us to the morning of March 10th, 1959.

On that day at roughly 6:30 a.m. the peeping tom crept towards the kitchen window of the defendant's home where the defendant's wife was once again taking a sponge bath before work. Now, it is important to note that the victim operated a bread truck. However, he left the truck some distance away on Route 202 then walked to the defendant's home on foot.

When the defendant's wife saw the intruder some 15 feet from the window, she screamed out. Her husband raced out of his bedroom with his rifle and yelled at the peeping Tom.

"Stop, I have you covered!"

Suddenly as the defendant reached to open the screen door, the gun went off, striking the peeping tom in the back of the head and killing him instantly.

Only that single shot was fired.

It was going to be a close case. The reason is that the police got there first and developed the theory of how the crime was committed. I blamed the Hillsboro
Police for this. Had they done their job, there would have been an arrest of the deceased for criminal trespass and we would not be here for this trial.

When the defendant heard his wife's scream, he thought the intruder had entered their home and his wife was in danger. He took the loaded gun to the defense of his wife. The gun barrel struck the screen door and went off accidentally.

I had Charles Ouellette, a local carpenter from Rochester, go to the scene and reconstruct the door area as demonstrative evidence. From there it was easy for our experts to show what happened. When the gun was fired, the State tried to show that the peeping tom was 103 feet away because of blood in the snow. However, they failed to account for the fact that the snow and the blood had been disturbed following a snowstorm by a snowplow.

One of our experts, George Benjamin, a consultant engineer, said to the jury that if we were to accept the State's theory of peeping tom's location at the moment the gun was fired, then his body would have had to be located in the middle of the Contoocook River.

Elmer Eldridge, a sergeant in the U.S. Army and a gun expert with 20 years of military service told the jury that the Gerbert gun had a trigger that was defective. This meant that the trigger was extremely sensitive and lacked the necessary four-pound pressure as a safety factor. He also testified that the telescope bolted to the barrel could not have been used in the darkness of the early morning hour.

All of this testimony backed up my own argument that the gun had gone off accidentally and that the death of the peeping tom was an act of God. When the verdict came back, the defendant was found NOT GUILTY. He and his family sold their home to pay the balance of my legal fees and costs.

As a result of this case I received many compliments both personally and through the mail. One of the most meaningful came in the form of a written note from Attorney Jackson Holtz of Boston (former U.S. Attorney) which enclosed a news article that appeared in the Boston Globe on May 16, 1959. He said, "Dear Fred - The enclosed clipping from the Boston Globe of May 26th - your fame reaches our city - Regards, Sincerely, Jack".

Another letter came from Mayor Joseph Benoit of Manchester, New Hampshire, who said, among other things in a letter dated June 5, 1959, "and congratulations for your Clarence Darrow victory in your recent case".

On June 12th, 1959, I tried an interesting case in the Dover Municipal Court. I represented a rugged six-foot ex-Marine who was charged with assaulting a police officer in a brawl on the night of June 8th. The officer pulled a service revolver and ordered the ex-Marine not to move or he would shoot. Judge Ovila Gregoire found my client NOT GUILTY of the charge of assaulting the police officer and also NOT GUILTY of resisting arrest. A third charge of being intoxicated was voluntarily dismissed by the State halfway through the trial.

My client had been a passenger in a vehicle operated by a friend. Both testified that the police officer stopped the vehicle for no reason and that the officer struck the first blow on the defendant with his club.

In the fall of 1959, my friend, Patrick Greene, ran for Mayor of the City of Dover as a Democrat against the incumbent Mayor Republican Melvin Morrison. On November 2, 1959, Mr. Patrick Greene was elected. To round out the victory, the Democrats also won seven of the nine councilmen seats.

After we counted the paper ballots in my Ward III, we all went home, but not for long. The Republican officials of Ward III were apparently not happy with the results. They decided to

240

return to Ward III with the ballots and recount them without the Democratic officials present.

They made this decision without telling any member of the Democratic party, and it was only due to the fact that I drove past the Ward house that I even realized what was going on in the first place.

I was on my way to another area when I noticed that the lights were on in the Ward house. I stopped to see what was going on, but was shocked by what I found when I entered the building. The long tables were packed with officials who sat, counting ballots with pencils scattered everywhere. I immediately put a stop to the operations, demanding to know what was going on.

They had no answer.

Mayor Morrison asked for a recount later because it had been a close election, but after the official recount was well underway with no significant changes, the mayor terminated the recount and Patrick Greene was officially proclaimed the mayor of the City of Dover.

Even with so much going on in my professional life, my family was still my top priority. My wife and I always made a point to spend time, not only with each other and with our son, but with our extended family as well. This could be something as simple as going to spend Thanksgiving weekend with my wife's parents at their home.

Then we took some time for ourselves.

We left our son with Carolyn's parents and went to spend a few days in New York. It has been said, "A happy wife results in a happy life." I fully agree with this statement!

My wife and I loved having time to ourselves, but we still missed our son. We knew that he was safe and sound with his grandparents, but that didn't stop us from calling to check on him several times a day! We went shopping and saw several shows and on Saturday afternoon, November 28th, 1959, we went to see the Army-Navy football game at the Municipal Stadium in Philadelphia, Pennsylvania.

It was a very colorful affair watching the cadets of the U.S. Military Academy and the midshipmen of the U.S. Naval Academy march into the over-crowded stadium to the blast of the marching bands. The game was great too. We had a fantastic time cheering the Navy to a 43-12 win over the Army.

By late December, 1959, I announced that I would seek a seat as a delegate for the Democratic National Convention. My goal was to support my good friend, U.S. Senator John F. Kennedy, in his quest for President of the United States.

On January 8th, 1960, the New Hampshire Democratic State Committee filed a slate of delegates pledged to support U.S. Senator John F. Kennedy at the Democratic National Convention. I was a delegate in the First Congressional District. Our goal was to win in the March primary to fulfill our wishes and Senator Kennedy's name was filed for the New Hampshire First in the Nation March Primary.

I'm not sure, even today, that the American people realize how fortunate they were to have a man such as John F. Kennedy want to run for President of this country. He was completely dedicated to serving his country and to doing everything that he could to improve the quality of life of the American people. I, for one, am proud to have called him my friend.

And, I know that I did my part to help him secure his nomination and his Presidential seat. After only a short meeting, the Strafford County Democratic Committee endorsed Kennedy 19 to 2, while the City Committees of Dover, Rochester and Somersworth also voted to back U.S. Senator John F. Kennedy for President.

On March 1st, 1960, the Strafford County Young Democrats put on a banquet at the Municipal Auditorium in Dover to honor Mayor Patrick Greene and the elected members of the Dover City Council, Dan Richard, Robert Herlihy, Raymond Stackpole, Andrew Courteau, Attorney John D. McCarthy, Arthur Grimes, John Maglaras (all Democrats) and Irving Webb and Paul Karkavelas, Republicans. I served as toastmaster and we had Edward "Ted" Kennedy, younger brother of U.S. Senator John F. Kennedy as the principal speaker.

Now, even though the Young Democrats held this event, it was at its heart a purely Democratic affair. And, with over 350 individuals in attendance, Ted Kennedy took full advantage of the opportunity to speak highly of his brother and ask that the people of Strafford County pledge their support.

When you look at the election process from the stance of a member of the general public, it may seem like a glamorous series of events. This could not be further from the truth!

In reality, winning an election is grueling. It is a series of thankless tasks that arrive one right after another with each night bringing a new sea of faces that it is your job to win over.

But it is a process that I love. I love it because I believe in the Democratic process and in the greatness of the American people.

I tell you this because I want you to understand that I was more than happy to do everything that I could to help my friend John F. Kennedy win his bid for President. I didn't care how many events I had to attend or how many people I had to meet, I was willing to do whatever it took.

U.S. Senator John F. Kennedy came to New Hampshire again the day before the First in the Nation Primary, on Monday, March 8th, 1960. Originally, the evening reception was scheduled to be at my personal home, but as the interest in Kennedy grew, so did the number of prospective attendees! It soon became apparent that even my home was not large enough to handle the large crowd that we were expecting.

After looking at the size of the event as a whole, we decided to move the reception to the Dover Municipal Auditorium. We were fortunate that the Patrick Greene, the mayor at the time, was able to make the auditorium available to us under such short notice.

Now, when I tell you that this was a large event, I'm not exaggerating. Honestly I'm not sure how to put it into words, but let me see if I can paint an accurate picture.

The event started off with a large parade, featuring both the Graniteer Drum and Bugle Corps as well as the Granite State Highlanders, a local kilted bagpipers band. They marched proudly down the street leading the way for the Senator and his wife, Jacqueline.

In the beginning, my job was to assist a local deputy as he fired the flares and provided them to passengers on each side of each vehicle. The flares were a little extra touch that gave the parade a little "pop" of excitement and fun. But, I didn't get very far into my assigned task before I was notified that Senator Kennedy wanted me to join him.

244

My friend, Nick, got someone else to replace me and I joined the Senator and his wife in their vehicle for the ride to City Hall where over 1,000 enthusiastic supporters were waiting for him. Once there I was given the honor of joining the future President of the United States on stage for his speech.

The First in the Nation Primary election gave U.S. Senator John F. Kennedy a total of 45,568 votes. I and all of the other pledged delegates for Kennedy were elected.

From Strafford County there were three of us that ran as pledged delegates for Kennedy. Of those on the slate in Strafford County, I had earned the most votes with 2,837; Mayor Robert Filion came in second with 2,796 and Attorney John D. McCarthy came in third with 2,626 votes.

I received 9,948 votes in our district.

The primary exploded in the last two days of the campaign when Governor Wes Powell, Republican from New Hampshire got involved and accused the Senator of being soft on Communism. This not only brought a sharp blast from Senator Kennedy, but U.S. Vice President Richard Nixon came to the defense of Senator Kennedy and reprimanded his State Chairman in New Hampshire, Governor Powell.

California, here we come!

Before I could head out though, there were still a few matters of the law to take care of. One of these was the defense of 26 year-old defendant in the murder of his wife. I had originally though that the case would be over much sooner, but it was necessary to continue due to the death of the defense expert psychiatrist. Because of his passing we were forced to find a new doctor and have a new set of evaluations completed. This process takes time and it added significantly to the overall length of the trial.

Here is the back story.

On September 8th, 1959, my client was indicted for the murder of his wife, as well as the attempted murder of his mother-in-law and a separate male victim. These crimes allegedly took place in Somersworth on April 16th, 1959.

The police claim stated that he entered his mother-in-law's apartment at 12 Franklin Street in the early morning hours and killed his estranged wife, after first shooting down his mother-in-law. Police said Rankin also shot the man before leaving the apartment and giving himself up to police.

Both older victims were described in critical condition after the shooting, but both recovered from chest wounds. The defendant was given mental tests and was found to be competent to stand trial.

By Friday, March 18th, 1960, Attorney Thomas E. Flynn and I were defending for both the murder and the attempted murder charges. In four days, we had only drawn nine jurors. We eventually got a negotiated plea to the three charges. On the murder case, he was sentenced to 20 to 35 years so under the present rules, he would be eligible for parole after about 13 years. On the other cases of attempted murder, he was sentenced to 8 to 10 years on each, but to be served concurrently with the penalty on murder.

The penalty was significant, but so were the charges. At the end of the day Tom and I felt that we had done everything that we could to minimize the charges and, in doing so, impact the amount of time served. Sometimes that is all you can ask for.

My next big case involved the defense of W.M., 19, on the charge of murder.

The story given to us by the prosecution was as follows. The defendant escaped from the Hillsborough County Valley Street Jail, Manchester, and, in the process, was alleged to have killed a guard, age 58, by striking him on the head with a cribbage board. After the escape Louis Wyman, New Hampshire Attorney General, was quoted in the Boston Traveler, as saying if the defendant was arrested he "will go for hanging." The police added to the frenzy by stating that the victim was slugged to death with a cribbage board.

By April 1st, 1960, the defendant was arrested at gunpoint in a friend's apartment in Manchester.

Now that you have the basics, let me tell you what I was able to find during my own investigation.

The defendant was originally in jail awaiting trial for automobile theft. It was during this time that he made his escape attempt and struck the victim with the cribbage board. After spending some time looking into the victim, I found that he suffered from a chronic heart condition. When this factor was taken into account, it became apparent that the victim had most likely died from complications related to his heart disease rather than the blow from the cribbage board.

On Wednesday, June 8th, 1960, the defendant, who had undergone a psychiatric examination by the State at their New Hampshire Hospital, was found to be of sound mind to stand trial. I prepared to defend him for murder.

After the presentation of several key points I was able to have the defendant's first-degree murder charge reduced to manslaughter in a negotiated plea with Attorney General

Louis Wyman. The victim, a guard at the Valley Street Jail in Manchester, had a bad heart and he died of heart failure. The blows with the cribbage board did not necessarily kill him. Nevertheless, the defendant committed the crime of escaping and aggravated assault on the officer. The murder charge was reduced to first-degree manslaughter.

I told the court in addition to the above information that not only was the defendant age 20, but the escape was provoked because his girlfriend got into trouble with the Manchester Police. This upset him and he wanted to get out. During his escape attempt, he ran into the victim, who cut him pretty badly in his attempt to apprehend him. The cribbage board was a weapon of self-defense rather than a method of offense. The defendant pled guilty to manslaughter and received 25 to 30 years. In those days, he was obligated to serve 2/3rd's of the minimum sentence, so he would be serving about 16 ½ years on good behavior.

In April, 1960, I tried a four-day jury trial in the U.S. District Court in Concord, New Hampshire on the case of U.S. v. J.F. He and two others were accused of swindling the life's earnings of an elderly couple. This case ended in a hung jury. In the second trial, he was found guilty. His two companions both had pled guilty before the J.F. trial and had to wait for sentencing until the J.F. case concluded. They should have waited! J.F. got five years and his two companions each got 20 years.

On May 17th, 1960, I went to the defense of City Prosecutor, Attorney Philip Keefe. The police were putting pressure on him in relation to cases he was prosecuting. I went to the several radio stations and our local paper to try and help the general public understand the role of the City Prosecutor.

It is the duty of prosecuting attorneys not only to prosecute the guilty, but also to protect the innocent. It is for him to determine how each case should be disposed with circumspect discretion. The police criticism of our City Prosecutor was an inequitable interference of his duty and a bad reflection on law enforcement.

As Chairman of the Democratic Platform Committee on Labor, we had a meeting at my law office and provided 25 resolution proposals for our convention. This included minimum wages, medical coverage for all those who receive Social Security and matters concerning working people who, as a whole, are helpless without the protection of the Democratic Party.

We held our 12th Annual Disabled American Veterans Convention in Dover, June 9th through 12th, 1960. The City was bedecked with flags. I served as Chairman and we collected money by sponsors and yearbook advertisements to pay for this affair.

On Thursday evening, June 9th, we held a convention social. At the time, we were veterans of World War II so most of us and our wives were still able to dance and enjoy ourselves. Refreshments, drinks and music were in abundant supply and everyone seemed to have a fantastic time.

On Friday, June 10th, we held a social function and entertainment at the Veterans Building. The affair was well attended by some 400 of us. We had a very active, energetic auxiliary who took over all of the duties assigned to them. On Saturday morning we held a memorial service in front of the City Hall. It included the Dover High School Band playing the National Anthem and the firing squad and the raising of the American Flag and prayers for the departed comrades. The auxiliary took part in this impressive affair. The Department and the auxiliary met in a morning and afternoon session and elected officers for the year. Then we held our convention banquet at the Simpson Pavilion. Our Past Department Commander Emerson Follette served as toastmaster and we had United States Senator Styles Bridges as the principal speaker.

The convention concluded Sunday afternoon with a patriotic eight-division parade, which lasted two hours and was attended by over 50,000 people. This parade included three bands and fifteen drum and bugle corps along with military units, veterans and fraternal organizations. Donald MacLeod, Past Commander of Dover Post #8, American Legion, served as parade coordinator.

Later that month I had the honor of serving as co-chairman of the "kick-off" dinner for Mayor Bernard Boutin held at the Carpenter Motor Hotel in Manchester, New Hampshire on Saturday, June 18th, 1960. We were all ready and waiting for Robert Kennedy to show up as the principal speaker.

Boy were we in for a surprise!

Imagine how we felt when instead of Robert, his brother, U.S. Senator John F. Kennedy arrived in his place. When it was his turn to speak, he had us all in boisterous laughter by saying, "My brother, Bobby, was too busy to come down himself, so he sent me to take his place tonight." My wife, Carolyn, and I and many of our friends were in attendance.

Now it was finally time to head off to sunny California!

I was thrilled that the Convention was held during a time that my wife was on summer break so that she could travel with me to Los Angeles. I was elected a pledged delegate to nominate my friend, John F. Kennedy, U.S. Senator from Massachusetts, for President of the United States.

On June 22nd, 1960, we packed our 1959 Pontiac Star Chiefton four-door sedan with a roof rack for our suitcases so we could leave more room inside the vehicle. After saying our goodbyes to my family, we traveled to Watertown, Massachusetts to spend the night with my in-laws.

From there the plan was simple!

My wife, son, mother-in-law and I would all leave the following day to drive to California. My father-in-law would fly out to join us in a few days. It would be a long drive, but we were all looking forward to the trip as a whole. Besides, we were going to make the most of our travels and the things that we would see along the way! We arrived in California July, 7th 1960.

Some believed that Jack Kennedy was not electable because he was Catholic. These negative prognosticators based this opinion because New York Governor Al Smith was Irish-Italian Catholic in the 1928 election and lost to Herbert Hoover in that year.

I did not buy this.

I thought Senator John F. Kennedy was the best qualified person to lead this great country of ours. He arrived in Los Angeles, California that day.

On Sunday, July 10th, 1960 we drove to the International Airport and picked up my father-in-law, Thomas Mosca. He flew from Boston with some of the New Hampshire delegates. Carolyn's father, Tom, would travel with us the rest of this trip. That afternoon, my wife, Carolyn, and I attended a huge reception at the Biltmore Hotel for Jack Kennedy and his pledged delegates. We met with him personally at this affair.

The next day we attended the first day of the Democratic National Convention at the Los Angeles memorial Sports Arena.

It was packed!

The second day of the Democratic National Convention commenced with breakfast of the New Hampshire delegates with Attorney Robert Kennedy as our guest at the Biltmore Hotel, then a meeting of the entire New England delegation with U.S. Senator John F. Kennedy as guest. My wife, Carolyn, was with me. We also were in attendance at the late afternoon and evening convention. The nomination was between U.S. Senator "Jack" Kennedy and U.S. Senate President Lyndon Johnson of Texas.

On Wednesday, July 13th, 1960, Carolyn and I attended the third all-day Democratic National Convention at the Los Angeles Memorial Sports Arena. In the evening, John F. Kennedy was nominated Democratic candidate for U.S. President on the first ballot. I was pleased and it was one of the greatest political moments in my life.

Kennedy was nominated and I had helped to make it happen!!

So what is one suppose to do after one of the greatest victories of their life? Why I went to Disneyland of course!

And it got even better, because that night I was able to get extra tickets so that we could attend the final evening of the convention. Attending were my wife, Carolyn, our son and I, as well as my brother, Joseph, and my in-laws, to watch the final evening of this convention.

We stayed in Los Angeles Friday, July 15th, 1960, sightseeing in our car and visiting Knott's Berry Farm.

Then it was time to start the long trip home.

On Friday, July 29th we finally arrived back in Watertown at the home of Carolyn's parents and after having lunch there and calling my mother, Vincenza, we drove on to our own home.

Overall this was an amazing trip. My family and I were able to see some of the most amazing sites in America and I loved every moment of it. Round trip we covered over 10,500 miles all packed into our 1959 Pontiac Chieftan station wagon!

On August 2nd, 1960, at 8:00 p.m. I attended a New England Election Strategy Committee meeting at the Parker House, Boston, at the invitation of Attorney Robert Kennedy. It was an exclusive group of about 50 persons where we exchanged ideas and prepared for the election of U.S. Senator John F. Kennedy for U.S. President. I attended with Democratic State Chairman, Attorney J. Murray Devine of Manchester.

On August 15th, 1960, I defended a woman for serving alcoholic beverages to a minor while working as a waitress at the Kimball Hotel in Dover. I cross-examined the alleged minor if he had exhibited age identification to anyone and he admitted he had a false birth certificate that he disclosed to the assistant manager showing he was over 21 years of age. The Dover Municipal Court Judge Ovila J. Gregoire found her NOT GUILTY.

Even as I sit here writing this to you my dear friends, I feel like I am putting forth a rapid fire chain of events, but you have to realize that is how my life was. I was never still! It felt like every moment had three things scheduled over top of it and I was just enjoying every minute of the daily grind.

I admit that I worked a lot, but I am blessed to have been able to work at something that I loved and had a passion for. To me working long hours was not a hardship. A hardship would have been working those same hours, stuck back in the Mill, if I had never taken control of my life and pressed forward towards my dreams.

Dreams my take work my friends, but I can promise you they are worth it in the end.

Next on my own list of things to do was to file as a candidate for the State Senate for the 21st District. I appointed my good friend Robert Herlihy as my campaign manager, but I must admit that my own campaign was not my primary focus at the time.

My goal in 1960 was to support the entire Democratic ticket and to help Kennedy get elected for President of the United States.

Our 21st Senate District was Republican, but I thought I could break into it with my organizational skills and political knowledge.

I was wrong.

Attorney Tom Dunnington won 6,791 votes to my 5,540.

I may have lost the battle, but I can promise you that we won the war!

It ended up being a close election, but in the end our own "Jack" Kennedy was elected President of the United States over Vice President Richard Nixon.

We won! JFK was officially President and, to me, the country was in the best possible hands.

Two hundred sixty-nine electoral votes were needed to be elected President of the United States. Senator John F. Kennedy got 303 electoral votes. Vice President Richard Nixon got 219 electoral votes. Senator Harry Byrd, a Democrat from Virginia, got 15 electoral votes.

Once the election was over, it was back to the real world. And, for my family and me, that meant facing one of the most frightening experiences of ours lives.

On the night in questions, Friday December 16th, my wife and I put our beautiful 3-year-old son to bed and then I headed back to my law office to get some much needed work done. My goal was to tie up loose ends so that Carolyn and I would be free to drive to Watertown the next day and spend the weekend with her parents. That way they could spend some time with my family and I would have the opportunity to do some Christmas shopping in Boston.

Just as I was finishing up, shortly before 1:00 a.m., the phone rang. It was my wife and she was absolutely terrified!

She was whispering so softly that it was hard to make out her words, but I could tell that she was scared. She told me that there was a burglar in the house and for me not to come home without the police because she was scared that he would hurt me. She did not know if he was armed or not, but her first thought was of my safety.

I can promise you that was not my own first thought.

As soon as she hung up I snatched up the phone again to call the police. I let them know what was going on, but more than that, I wanted to give them a warning. They had better get there first, because if I did, then I was going for blood!

I put on my coat, picked up a large sharp pair of scissors and raced out of the law office and raced home at high speeds, jumped out of my car, raced to the front door of our mansion, turned on the lights and screamed for my wife, Carolyn. It took a few minutes for the police to arrive, but by that time I had already run to my wife and then raced to my son's bedroom. Fortunately he was unharmed and unaware of what had taken place this night.

My wife was terrified. It took everything in me to console her as we allowed the police to search the house from top to bottom.

They found nothing.

My wife was terribly affected by this horrible experience. She was nearsighted and did not have her glasses available when she was apprehended by this son of a bitch! She could not describe him because she did not have the opportunity to identify him. It was dark and she was without her glasses. She gave him all the money she had in her pocketbook located in the bedroom, about $300.00.

The Dover Police never solved the case and their interest quickly faded away.

Mine did not.

Following that night I can promise you that I made some major changes around my home.

For starters, my wife was never left alone again in the evening. If, for some reason, I had to go out at night, then we made sure that someone was with her while I was gone.

Secondly I had a state of the art security system installed throughout the entire home. Every single room was covered, including the entire cellar and the entire attic and with controls on both the first and second floors connected directly with the local law enforcement.

To take things one step further, I also purchased three handguns and got police permits so I could carry one of them loaded in my car. I left a loaded gun at my home and another at my law office. These guns were always loaded and hidden. I am grateful I never had to use any of them, but I will never forget the fear that surrounded that night.

Chapter 14:

Changes

On Tuesday, January 17th, 1961, my wife, Carolyn, and I traveled to Washington, D.C. to attend the presidential inauguration of President Elect John F. Kennedy. Even though we made the trip by car, the miles seemed to fly by.

I was so excited!

After all the hard work, this was the moment we had all been waiting for. Finally my friend, John Kennedy would be sworn in as President of the United States of America. This, my friends, was a victory on many, many fronts. Most of you reading this book only know Kennedy through what you have heard on the news.

I knew the man himself.

His vision was unmatched. His patriotism was unwavering. If there was one man in all the country that was uniquely suited to be President of the United States, in was none other than Kennedy. I'm trying now to put it into words, and in truth, it's next to impossible. All I can tell you is that on that day I felt better for the future of our county than ever before.

Once we arrived in Washington it was one grand event after another. First we were invited to attend a cocktail party held at our own hotel. The party was put on specifically for those individuals attending the inauguration from New Hampshire.

What none of us could have predicated was that the entire city of Washington D.C. was brought to a screeching halt thanks to our dear friend Mother Nature. For two days the city was pelted with record amounts of snow that made all of us fear that the inauguration would not be able to be held on time.

I am very happy to say that our fears were in vain! Well, not entirely in vain. As it turns out, the only reason the inauguration could be held on schedule was that some 10,000 soldiers descended on D.C. with trucks and other types of snow removal equipment. They worked all through the night on Thursday and even into the day on Friday. I'm sure that it was a never ending and thankless job, but I for one am very grateful for all of their hard work!

On Friday, January 20th, 1961 John F. Kennedy was sworn in as president of the United States of America. What a wonderful day! We started out attending the inauguration then moved on to watch then inaugural parade.

I still remember it like it was yesterday.

I remember how Pennsylvania Ave. was covered with American Flags no matter where you looked. I also remember how youthful and vigorous Kennedy was as he and his beautiful wife Jacqueline, rode and later walked along the parade route. Over a million admiring spectators refused to let the snow and cold temperatures discourage them in any way.

I should know, I was one of them! My wife and I were lucky enough to have reserved bleacher seating directly across from the presidential reviewing stand.

Many of you may not know this, but it isn't until after the parade that the real party gets started!

I am talking about none other than the Inaugural Ball.

My wife and I were able to once again count ourselves among the fortunate as we were invited to attend the ball as the personal guests of our good friend, and the new President of the United States, John F. Kennedy and his wife Jackie. The ball was held at the National Guard Armory and it was a wonderful evening all the way around. I can remember now as I walked through the room how Kennedy's powerful words from earlier kept ringing through my ears. "And so my fellow Americans. Ask not what your country can do for you, but what you can do for your country!"

Even now that speech still has power, but to hear it live sent chills down my spine.

Another thing that I remember from that night was how beautiful my wife looked. She wore a lovely light blue evening gown with a fresh orchid clipped to her shoulder. I wore a tux. It was just one of those fairy tale nights when everything goes right.

We had a grand time enjoying being with each other and friends and having the chance to briefly say hello to our President and his wife, Jacqueline. The day and the evening and the night became melted into one glorious memory.

By the time we made it back to the "real world" it felt like the whole week had been some kind of elaborate dream from which we never wanted to wake.

The next few months flew by as my life was so filled with joy at each and every turn. It seemed like one good thing was happening right after another.

For one thing on April 23rd I was honored with a national citation at a Disabled American Veterans dinner. For another, on April 20th, my dear friend and former law school roommate, Thomas E. Flynn, was appointed Judge of the Portsmouth District Court. I can tell you this. Tom was a great lawyer and this was a position that he more than deserved.

One interesting fact about Tom was that he was the one who established the practice of wearing a black robe in his court. Prior to his being named, judges in our municipal courts simply dressed as they would any other day. Tom felt that the position deserved a more dignified look, and, once he put the procedure in place, all of the lower courts followed a short while later.

One of the more interesting cases that I took on during this time pertained to a group of students who protested the Civil Defense Law that was passed by the New Hampshire legislature and supported by Governor Wesley Powell. The law stated that in the case of a nuclear or atomic attack, we were to take refuge in a nearby store, behind a door or behind an available window.

The point being that there were no realistic shelters in place.

Now, the first thing that you should know about this case is that there was at that time, there was mass hysteria around this issue. Therefore, the first thing that I did was to file a motion requesting that Judge Bradford McIntire disqualify himself from the case and grant a continuance for three to six months down the road. I also asked that my three clients be tried separately from each other and from the other defendants.

I did this for a few reasons.

First, I felt that the judge in question did not have the appropriate credentials to preside over a court of law. He operated a clothing store and had no law school education. Second, I wanted time for the hysteria around the issue to die down. And, third, I felt that the defendants were entrapped when the police allowed them to proceed instead of stopping their actions before the proceedings got started.

My motions were denied and Judge McIntire eventually found every defendant guilty.

Later, Admiral C.A. Brinkman, the State of New Hampshire Civil Defense Director, stated that a civil defense shelter would be worthless because the City of Durham was in close proximity to the Pease Air Force base in Newington and the Portsmouth Naval Shipyard. If an atomic bomb was detonated there, the temperatures would boil, destroying all life and property. There would be 100% destruction, 100% deaths and no chance whatsoever of saving one life.

I maintained that if we would have sufficient notice and if we had adequate high speed roads, just maybe, we might be able to escape. That is if we could move the population prior to an atomic explosion some 100 miles away. This would require organization, advanced preparation and God on our side. Certainly removing people off the street is not going to do it.

The reality was that this law was not to test our patriotism. It was a law to test our desperation and our stupidity.

On May 29th, 1961 my wife and I were invited to attend the Jefferson-Jackson Dinner held at the Commonwealth Armory in Boston. And, while this may sound like just another event, I can promise you that it was much more than that. For that night, with some 6,000 people in attendance, Carolyn and I were the personal guests of President Kennedy, the principal speaker of the event.

We were also invited to attend a Kennedy birthday party at the Carpenter Motor Hotel in Manchester, New Hampshire on Friday, June 2, 1961. We had about 1,000 present and Edward Kennedy, the President's brother, was the principal speaker. I served on the Banquet Committee.

I cannot stress to you enough how joyful my life was at this point. It was as if everything were finally coming together. My wife and I so enjoyed our vivacious, beautiful son. He was the light of our lives and a constant source of joy. So much so that Carolyn and I mutually agreed that in the spring of 1961 she would resign as a schoolteacher and devote herself to being a full time mother. Not only to our son, but also to any future children we might have.

The decision, for us, was an easy one. I was making good money as a lawyer so we no longer needed my wife's salary to make ends meet. In fact, we would not even need to adjust our lifestyle.

Plus, for me, this was like reaching a milestone in my own life. Carolyn was a wonderful mother. She was loving and kind in every possible way imaginable. So, for me to be able to allow my children to enjoy her full time was a reward in and of its self.

My next case is one that I will never forget. Not due so much to the content of the case, but more to the unusual chain of events that took place. It all started on August 6th, when I was paid a retainer for the defense of four men.

Pretty normal so far...right?

Well, a few days later when I was in the Cheshire County Superior Court I was informed that my clients were asking to speak with me. They were being kept in a guarded conference room in the building and, in all honesty, this was not a strange occurrence.

Then, shortly after I entered the room, one of the defendants started asking me questions. As I answered him I suddenly saw two of the other defendants disappear from a nearby window some 30 feet off of the ground.

I wanted no part of this.

Instantly I yelled for the guard and got out of the room. The guards gave chase and one man was caught near the Courthouse with severe damage to one of his ankles. Another was caught a few days later. He managed to navigate the fall okay, but developed an infection from cuts he received while jumping over a barbed wire fence.

A few minutes later the judge called me into his office demanding to know what had happened. Truly I did not know what to tell him! So, I suggested he speak to the officers on guard duty at the time.

That wasn't good enough.

The judge wanted to know, from me, exactly what had taken place while I was in the room. As I stood there, facing the judge in his own chambers, it struck me how odd it was for the two of us to be alone together. I mean, it was not uncommon for any given judge to request a meeting, but usually there was a court officer present as well as other attorneys.

As I said, this particular meeting was a bit unusual.

Well, before I could really figure out what to make of the situation, the judge opened the top drawer of his desk, pulled out a handgun and pointed it at my head. He said, "Cataflo, I have the urge of pulling the trigger."

Can you imagine?!?!?! Crazy? Scared? I wasn't sure what was going on, I just knew that I needed to get out of that room as soon as possible.

I told the judge to please put the gun away as I was backing slowly towards the door in an effort to go for help. Luckily I made it out, but then soon found that I couldn't do much more than fall into a chair smack in the middle of the courtroom. May seem an odd place to most people, but I felt at home in the courtroom. Plus, the room was full of people and it offered me a safe place to stop for a moment and gather my thoughts.

A few short minutes later I was approached by a court officer who informed me that the judge would like to speak to me in chambers for a second time. I thought for a moment, then agreed on the condition that several court officers as well as a public stenographer would be present as witnesses.

He agreed. And why would he not? After all, he had no idea what had taken place and would not think there was anything out of the ordinary about my request.

I walked back into chambers and took a seat. The stenographer was there to capture every word and there were two uniformed officers lined up against the back wall. For a moment, the judge and I stared at each other, each wondering what the other would say, but I jumped first.

Quickly, so he would not have the chance to interrupt me, I said, "My name is Alfred Cataflo Jr. I am a member of the New Hampshire Bar and an officer of this court. A short while back today the judge and I were in this very room alone and he pulled a gun out of his desk and pointed it at me in a threatening manner."

I then turned to the judge and demanded that he admit what I said was true as well as produce the gun since there was no way he had time to dispose of it.

Total silence.

I waited another beat or two, then stood up and announced to the room that I had other matters to attend to. I thanked them for their time, asked to be excused and left the room.

Somehow I managed to play it off like this entire incident didn't shake me in the least, but that couldn't be further from the truth. It was a truly traumatic moment and one that has haunted me to this day.

For my next case I represented a defendant on the charge of arson. He was indicted on charges of feloniously, willfully and maliciously setting fire to a house located on Governor's Road.

Here was the meat of the case. My client rented the house on the day of the fire in question. His landlord, maintained that the defendant set fire to the house, thus the charge of arson. Our defense was that the stove was defective.

And it was a strong defense.

I was able to use two expert witnesses to prove that the stove was defective and, therefore, the defendant had nothing to do with the fire. The jury was out for two hours, then returned with a verdict of NOT GUILTY!

As a professional, my life was soaring. As a husband and father? It just couldn't get any better!

Why you ask?

Well, in August of 1962 my wife and I were blessed by the birth of our 2nd child, a daughter! She, like her older brother, was born in Boston at the Richardson House of the Lying Inn Hospital, and she was absolutely beautiful. Both mother and baby came through the delivery with flying colors and on that day our little family grew by one.

Let me tell you something friends, that little girl had me fully and completely trained from the very first minute that we met. As soon as I laid eyes on her, she owned my heart, plain and simple.

In the summer of 1962 I made a very important decision. I decided to run for the United States Senate, opposing the Republican incumbent of 14 years, Norris Cotton.

Now, keep in mind that this was not a decision that I made lightly. In fact, before the final decision was made, I had a private conversation with my wife to make sure that I had her full support of the issue. After all, this would be a full-time campaign unlike anything we had tackled before. I would be out on the trail night and day for the next 3½ months and I would not be able to practice law during this time.

It was also going to be very expensive.

After looking at all of our options and possibilities, we agreed that if I had no opposition in the Democratic primary, then it was a go.

I had no opposition in the primary!

268

Running for the Senate may seem to be a very straightforward undertaking, but I can promise you that it is not. For not only do you have to consider your own ticket, but you have to take into account every other member of your party as a whole that is up for election in your district.

For me that meant looking at how Attorney John King of Manchester was running for Governor. How Attorney Tom McIntyre of Laconia was running for the four-year United States Senate seat to fill out the position left by the late Republican United States Senator Style Bridges. Also Two term Mayor Olie Huot of Laconia was running for U.S. Congress in our First District and Attorney Gene Daniel of Franklin was the Democratic candidate for the U.S. Congress in the Second District.

When you are a member of a party, you run as a team. We took this stance to heart, and we all went out of our way to support one another.

In the primary election on Tuesday, September 11th, 1962, the Republican Governor Wesley Powell was up-ended by Republican challenger John Philbrick. This was a major upset. But the even bigger upset came on October 18th when the Republican Governor Wesley Powell hit the headlines everywhere in the State when he announced that he would throw his support to Attorney John King, Democratic candidate for Governor, against the Republican candidate, John Philbrick.

During his television program, Governor Powell said that citizens were fed up with the Republican Party's old guard. He called on his supporters to vote for John W. King in the November election.

As a result of this unexpected support, the New Hampshire Democrats looked forward to the election of their first governor in 39 years. The votes came in and Attorney John W. King was elected by a 39,694 majority vote! Fantastic!

In terms of the September primary, the Republicans had a four-way contest to replace the late U.S. Senator Style Bridges. Congressman Perkins Bass ended up defeating Doloris Bridges, wife of the late Senator. She charged Congressman Perkins Bass of violating election laws and took him to the New Hampshire Supreme Court to disqualify him. She was eventually turned down, but Attorney Thomas J. McIntyre of Laconia was elected as the United States Senator.

Other G.O.P. candidates in the Senate primary race were former Republican Congressman Chester Merrow and incumbent Maurice Murphy, who was appointed by Governor Wesley Power to fill the vacancy caused by the death of U.S. Senator Style Bridges. Mr. Merrow supported our Democratic candidate, Tom McIntyre, in the November election. Later, Chester Merrow changed political parties and joined the Democratic party.

My own quest for the Senate floor was a different battle entirely. I was not running a race to fill an open spot. No, I was running against incumbent Republican Norris Cotton. Cotton had held his position for 14 years and was very popular throughout the state. My campaign was well thought out and thorough, but in the end I failed to score an upset.

By September 8th, 1962, I was on the attack. I questioned the contributions Cotton received at a fund-raising dinner held in the fall of 1961 in Washington, D.C. The reason for the dinner was to raise funds for Cotton's upcoming re-election campaign. I claimed that the list of contributors to Cotton's campaign may have included representatives of businesses that had dealings with the Senate Commerce Committee, which Cotton was the Chairman of.

Plus, since about one-third of these contributors were from out of state, why would they have an interest in Senator Norris Cotton's re-election? They were obviously paying indirectly for future favors. For the icing of the cake, fourteen of these contributors listed Post Office boxes in lieu of addresses.

I asked the New Hampshire Attorney General, William Maynard, to investigate the financial report of Senator Cotton, who reported that more than half of his contributors came from outside the state of New Hampshire. I listed his out-of-state contributors and released their names and amounts to Attorney General Maynard on September 12th, 1962.

The "smoking gun" so to speak was that Mr. Cotton had not reported any of the contributions. I found out about them from other sources who had first hand knowledge of the situation as a whole.

On September 13th, 1962, I left for Washington, D.C. and the following day I met with United States President John F. Kennedy. We had a nice chat at the White House and I took photos and a video with him that was used as part of my campaign.

In my platform I urged for the passage of the Medicare Bill, which the Republicans, including ultra conservative Norris Cotton, were opposing.

By September 25th, 1962, I was urging that our Supreme Court remove U.S. Senator Norris Cotton from the ballot for the November election. Attorney Joseph Millimet of the law firm of Devine and Millimet of Manchester volunteered to represent me in the New Hampshire Supreme Court. A great person and excellent lawyer, he was also President of the New Hampshire Bar Association at the time.

At this point I was campaigning seven days a week, for what felt like 24 hours a day. I traveled from one end of the state to another without let-up in my quest for the senate. I knew what was going on in the courts, but I was responsible for what was going on in the streets.

As expected, our Republican Attorney General, William Maynard, decided to do nothing about the contributions to Cotton as reported. The Supreme Court scheduled a hearing for October 5th and William Maynard refused to produce records to support my allegation. He filed a motion to quash my demands, but the Supreme Court ordered the records to be produced.

On the day of the trial, the Supreme Court was crowded as the five judges listened to the case. It took the better part of a day, and in the end all we could do was wait. In the end it was a battle fought in vain. The New Hampshire Supreme Court decided to dismiss my petition.

I was not going to be discouraged.

For my next attack I blasted my opponent for his use of the American Legion Hall in Derry for his campaign headquarters.

Why you ask?

Well, first of all this was in direct violation of the American Legion Constitution and By-Laws. It was also contrary to the intended use of a town hall by the taxpayers of the state of New Hampshire.

Additionally, Mr. Cotton was not a veteran and I was able to prove, through the use of the congressional record, that he had continually voted against veterans in cases such as the Emergency Housing Bill, the 1959 Veterans Benefit Bill and the 1962 Veterans Pension Act. He voted against veterans to convert National Insurance life insurance to a modified pension payment plan, the 1962 Veterans Administration Bill and voted to cut millions from the V.A. budget. The Senator was also one of the key people responsible for killing the World War I Veterans' Pension Act.

If you think that this was just another political battle, let me assure you it was not. Our country, at this point, was facing a crisis. On October 23rd, 1962 President Kennedy informed the American public that the Soviet Union had established missile bases in Cuba. This act of aggression left him no alternative but to order a naval blockade of Cuba as a whole.

Times were tense and tensions were running high.

That is why it was so important for the American people to see the kind of people they were voting into office. Now more than ever we needed people who were willing to stand against the coming storm and fight for this great country.

I was willing to be one of those people.

I did everything that I could to show the people of my state the Cotton did not have the best interest of New Hampshire at heart. I showed how his vote on the appropriate bill amendment was in direct contrast to what he was telling the people of his state. In fact, I charged that there was a rider on the bill that gave 35% of ship overhaul and repair to private yards and that the Nautilus, originally scheduled to be overhauled at the Portsmouth Naval Shipyard, was reassigned to the Electric Boat Division of General Dynamics at Groton,

Connecticut. Meaning that the work would be sub-let by Electric Boat company and taken out of the State of New Hampshire entirely.

As a U.S. Senator, Mr. Cotton was not interested in the people of New Hampshire!

I worked long and hard, but could not win. I was grateful that I had so many people who supported me and grateful to my wife, Carolyn, and members of my family. During the campaign, I would on occasions take my son, Freddie, age five, with me. My wife, Carolyn, campaigned for me almost on a daily basis with Mrs. John King, Mrs. Myrtle McIntyre and Mrs. Olie Huot, but on most evenings, we would meet at a campaign gathering here or there in one part of the state or another.

After the campaign drew to a close I was offered a position with the U.S. Department of Labor in the legal division, but in truth that did not interest me in the slightest. If I was going to be a lawyer, then I would rather be my own boss!

From there I guess you could say that life returned to normal.

In the spring I served as Chariman of the 1963 Disabled Veterans Convention, which was held in Dover. This meant that I over saw the creation of the convention yearbook, secured speakers such as Senator Tom McIntyre, Governor John King and Judge Thomas Flynn and scheduled the various events our members would attended.

One such event was a Convention dance held at the Municipal Auditorium. We were all young then and most of our members danced to the music of a live orchestra. Then, on Friday, June 14th, the Trench Rats and Alley Cats put on a street parade with four divisions and four bands. That evening, after the 6:00 p.m. parade, we had a social and entertainment at the Veterans Building. It was a well attended affair and there was plenty of food and drinks.

By the time August rolled around my wife and I were more than ready to take a vacation. After all of the work we had put in this year, we were ready to head off with our little family and find some time to just enjoy ourselves and each other. So, we decided to pack up our two young children and head out to Ottawa Canada and Lake George, NY.

The trip went by so quickly that it seemed like as soon as we got there, it was already time to come home. I hated to leave, but I loved every minute of time spent with my family and it was amazing how just those few days could help to recharge my batteries and make me ready to jump back into the daily grind.

Little did I know what was coming and that there was no way I could ever be ready for it.

November 22nd, 1963.

Recognize the day? Yeah, most people do.

For me it started out just like any other day. I was sitting in my law office getting some work done when suddenly a young man that I did not know burst into the room screaming, "Someone just killed President Kennedy!"

I was stunned.

For a moment I couldn't even move as my mind refused to accept this horrible news. And not just me, everyone. We were all shocked that something like this could have happened, and on American soil no less.

As soon as I was able to move, I jumped up to run over and turn on the television in my office, my entire staff joining me in mourning the devastating news.

I had to search for a moment, but then suddenly all channels were carrying the story as America was held captive. John F. Kennedy, our hope for the future, our bright and energetic young president, my friend, was dead.

He was assassinated by a rifle shot while riding in an open motor vehicle in Dallas, TX. The President suffered a bullet wound to his skull and was pronounced dead shortly after he arrived at the hospital. The shooter, a communist bastard by the name of Lee Harvey Oswald who once defected to the Soviet Union and was chairmen for a committee known as "Fair Play for Cuba Committee", was apprehended in a nearby theater.

Not knowing what else to do, I closed the office and remained closed for the next 4 days. My wife and I sat glued to the television as we watched one of our own worst nightmares unfold before our eyes. It was one of those times when you hold your children close because you fear for the future and what it might hold.

I was literally stunned by this horrible event and so was our Nation.

As I said, Oswald was arrested for murder in a nearby theater shortly after the assassination. He had killed a police officer while attempting to flee the scene of his crime. Two days later he himself was killed by a Dallas nightclub owner, Jack Ruby, during a jail transfer.

The whole event changed the course of American history forever. Now we will never know what Kennedy would have become, and we will never know what America would have become under his leadership. His was a life cut far too short, and a loss that we all continue to suffer to this day.

Throughout the entire ordeal my heart, and the heart of my wife went out to the President's wife, Jacquline. She had been riding with her husband when he was shot, but fortunately was unharmed.

Physically that is.

Mentally I'm sure it was another story.

Let me take just a moment to paint a very vivid picture for you my friends. Just one and one half hours after Kennedy was pronounced dead, Lyndon B. Johnson was sworn in as President of the United States. Vice President Johnson had been riding in the third car behind the Kennedy vehicle and escaped unharmed.

By his side as he took the oath of office, standing with her head held high was Jackie Kennedy.

Of all of the memories that people claim of that day let me tell you what stands out the most to me. The image of the beautiful and poised Jacqueline Kennedy standing next to Lyndon B. Johnson as he took the oath of office. She was strong, quiet and composed as she faced the American people.

Why does this image stand out to me?

Because at a mere 1½ hours after President Kennedy was pronounced dead, Jackie stood to face us all still wearing clothes stained with her husband's blood.

Chapter 15:

Gone

Those that do not work within the law community usually view it as a bit of a stagnant and boring job to hold. I can assure it is not. Every morning I would get up, kiss my family good-bye and head out into a day that was completely unpredictable. I have tried to include some of the better stories here to share with you in this book, but there was far more than I could ever hope to put into words.

For example!

One Saturday morning in late March of 1964 I was called up to defend a Mr. R. M. on an assault charge. I presented the evidence, and just as I finished, the defendant's ex-wife, charged to the front of the court room and began beating me about the head and face with her fists. Not wanting to hurt her, I tried to defend myself, but her attach was so vicious that it ended up knocking me back into my chair.

The judge instantly order her removed from the courtroom, but in truth the damage had already been done. R. M. was found guilty and given a 30 day suspended sentence while his ex-wife was arrested for assault. Charges that I later had dropped.

Now, after all of that, you would think that she would have had a good reason to lose her mind, right? Well it turned out that the defendant was on trial for assaulting the current roommate of his ex-wife. She was angry that my defense would be too good and that he would end up getting off the hook.

So, she was mad at me for doing my job rather than her ex-husband for assaulting her roommate!

Didn't make sense to me either, but what can you do?

It was around this same time that my wife and I welcomed our third child into the world. In late Spring, 1964 my second daughter was born at the Richardson House of the Lying-Inn Hospital in Boston. This was the same hospital where all of my children were born and it has a very special place in my heart.

Her birth was something special. Not just because she was the baby, but because by that time my son Freddie was old enough to realize what was happening. He was excited about the baby and about getting a new baby sister. He was proud to hold her and to show her off when people came to visit. I loved the way that my family was growing and watching my children begin to form the bonds that I shared with my own siblings.

After the birth of my youngest, we all stayed in Boston and remained there for a few days, spending time at the home of Carolyn's parents.

By June 22nd, 1964, life had fallen back into its standard routine, and I was called upon to be the attorney for A. H., age 21. The defendant was charged with murder while perpetrating arson. A the victim, 67 had died from burns suffered during a fire that destroyed most of the downtown business district in Lebanon, New Hampshire and caused upwards of three million in damages.

This case was different in that it was not negotiated in any form. My client chose to enter pleas on all four indictments and they were as follows:

1. Arson - a dwelling house of W. L. at Mill Street
2. Arson - the Mayflower Real Estate storage shed at 13 Mill Street
3. Manslaughter - of H. L.
4. Manslaughter - of G. L.

He was sentenced to 13 to 25 years on the arson of the L. dwelling. Judge Martin Loughlin continued the other three indictments indefinitely. On good behavior, he would serve about eight years. This shows a strong departure from the time served statistics that you hear about today. In those days, a defendant was required to serve two-third's of the minimum sentence before being eligible for parole. Now in many states, the defendant is required to serve a minimum of 20% of their time before they become eligible for parole.

On Tuesday, November 4, 1964, President Lyndon Johnson defeated Senator Barry Goldwater by a large majority and helped take over both Houses of Congress for the Democrats. Governor John King was re-elected and Olie Huot won the congressional seat in the First District here in New Hampshire.

My wife, and I attended the Inaugural Ball for Governor and Mrs. John W. King. It was a formal affair and enjoyable at the Carousel Ballroom in Bedford, New Hampshire on Friday, January 16, 1965. Later we traveled to Washington, D.C. to attend the formal Inaugural Ball and meet President Lyndon Johnson and his wife, "Lady Bird".

While in D.C. we also had the pleasure of attending the President's Club Dinner held at the Sheraton Park Hotel. The

President's Club was made up of people who had contributed $1,000 or more to the recent presidential campaign. My wife and I were a part of that club and we greatly enjoyed our time at the event.

We also enjoyed having the chance to attend the Presidential Inaugural Ball at the Statler Hotel. My wife looked beautiful, as always, and we had a wonderful evening with many of our New Hampshire friends.

The next day we were able to watch the swearing in ceremony and inaugural parade with seats directly across form the President's reviewing stand. I felt a sense of pride in watching President Johnson address the crowd and in the Democratic party as a whole.

All in all it was a wonderful trip, but there was one last thing that we had to do before we could leave D.C. We had to stop by and visit the grave of my good friend, President John F. Kennedy. Staring at that slab of marble I remembered Jack and how he always had a smile on his face.

That is how I want to remember him. I don't want to remember the parade in Dallas, I want to remember the great man who I both respected and admired.

It was difficult to stand at the foot of that tomb, difficult to face who was buried within and to know exactly what our country had lost.

When I returned home I learned that Governor John King had appointed me to his military staff with the rank of Naval Lieutenant Commander. This was a great honor and one that I enjoyed. I was fitted with new uniforms for the occasion and felt a strong sense of pride when wearing them.

The next trial that I would like to share with you was held on March 26th, 1965. I defended a Lieutenant, age 48, of Pease Air Force Base on a charge of operating a motor vehicle while under the influence of intoxicating liquor. The trial was in the Durham District Court and the State had Officer Ronald Brunelle and Police Captain Daniel Murray testifying. The defendant testified, along with his wife, a bartender, and two witnesses who stated he was not drinking before he drove the car and was fit to drive. He was found Not Guilty.

On April 19th, 1965, the Disabled American Veterans Bellamy Chapter #5 held a Chapter banquet and awarded me a national citation, the highest honor by the National Disabled American Veterans.

That summer it was all about the kids. We took two vacations with them, and could not have enjoyed the time more. I am glad that we took those trips. Glad for every moment that we spent with our children and all of the joy that was held within our family. Because I did not know what was waiting for me just around the corner.

On November 8th, 1965 my sweet wife had a Doctor's appointment. She had not been feeling well and thought that it was time to get checked out. We expected something, but we did not expect to hear the word Cancer.

When I went to speak to the Doctor on my own he did not paint a pretty picture. He informed me that my wife was in grave condition and that she probably would not live another two years.

I was in shock.

How could this be happening? How could this be fair?

It wasn't fair! It wasn't fair to her, wasn't fair to me wasn't fair to our children! Damned!! I was terrified and devastated all at the same time.

Carolyn was the rock of our family. The glue that held all of us together and showed us what it meant to love. How would we survive without her? How were my children suppose to grow up without their mother? Our children! How was I suppose to tell them what was coming? We loved her, and even more than that, we needed her.

My wonderful wife was only 41. She spent the next 19 days at the Hospital for Women in Brookline and I sat by her bed every single day. The rest of the time I felt like a juggler who was doomed to fail as I tried to be with our children during this time of need while also practicing law.

When she came home from the hospital I immediately had a bed installed in my home office so that she would not have to face climbing the stairs. We did everything that we could to make things as easy as possible on her, wanting her to rest and heal as she fought the disease that ravaged her body.

Her parents would come every weekend with her mother staying with us every other week. My own mother came every day. All of us had the same goal; to keep Carolyn comfortable and to help her spend time with the children.

On February 4th, 1966 my wife and I attended the Governor's Ball. She wanted to go and I wanted to give her the world.

I still remember how beautiful she looked wearing a bright red top over a white evening gown. I wore my navy blue Lt. Commander uniform. We spent the evening with the Governor and his wife as well as our good friends, Senator Thomas McIntyre and his wife. Everyone was so kind and they went out of their way to make Carolyn feel both welcome and special. Even sitting here now it fills me with warmth to think about it.

It made me determined to keep that smile on her face.

So, just a few short weeks later I loaded up my wife, her parents and our three beautiful children and flew to Miami, FL for an entire week. Miami was warm, and inviting. It offered a break from the harsh northern winter, and it was exactly what we needed at the time.

And we had fun!

It was as if being in Florida made all of us forget about the Cancer and the constant cloud that it hung over our heads. When we were there we could just have fun and be a family.

But then we had to go home. And then it all came crashing back with stark, cold clarity.

In April, 1966 my beautiful wife had critical surgery at the Hospital for Women in Brookline. She was in the hospital for a full week and I do not think that I ever left her bedside during that time. I would go to my wife's parent's home each evening to see our children then return to her as quickly as possible.

Coming home brought more changes to our family. Now the bed in the law office was for far more than just convenience and ease, it was necessity. My wife now slept in that bed each night as stairs had gone from tiring to impossible. The circular staircase that led from the foyer to the master bedroom might as well be a mountain, and the long trek up more than she could face.

We tried to keep life normal, to make it look and feel as though nothing had happened. We said this was for the children's sake, but it was for our own mental peace as well.

When our anniversary came I bought my wife a car, a beautiful new 1966 Mercury Comet in a bright cobalt blue.

And I worked.

In February of 1967 my wife and I decided once again to take our children to Florida for a week of fun in the sun. It was a wonderful trip. The kids loved the swimming pool and seeing everything that Florida had to offer. My wife and I loved seeing the joy on their faces at every new adventure. To this day it is one of my favorite vacations that I have ever taken.

When we got home, it was time to start planning for a couple very special events, the birthdays of my wife and my precious little daughter. We decided, after careful consideration, that we would celebrate both events together and held the party in June 1967. My wonderful wife turned 43 and sweet daughter turned 3.

We had two birthday cakes at the party and it seemed like everyone was there. A huge Italian family affair! Crazy from the word go, but I wouldn't have it any other way. By the end of the night none of us could keep from smiling.

The birthday party had gone so well that I decided that I wanted to surprise my wife and take our family on another vacation. So, the first week of July, we all headed out for Montreal, Canada. The trip was a blast! To me it was just wonderful to see my wife and children enjoying themselves and each other.

My next case was one that is definitely worth mentioning. It involved the Mayor of Concord, New Hampshire, J. Herbert Quinn (who I represented) against the Board of Aldermen. This case was huge and it eventually hit the front pages of all of our State newspapers for over a month straight.

On Wednesday, July 19th, 1967, the Board of Aldermen suspended the elected Mayor in a 12-minute meeting. They claimed misconduct in office. The only misconduct he could have been charged with was that he was a Democrat. He did not attend the 12-minute meeting. By Friday, July 21st, 1967, I filed a Petition to Reinstate the Mayor. I got Orders of Notice and had the sheriff serve them on each of the 14 Aldermen and on the Chief of Police of Concord.

The whole "misconduct" used by the Aldermen was that Mayor Quinn reported that one James Langley, the editor of the newspaper, "The Concord Monitor," had spent time at the Brick Tower Motel drinking and reported to the police that Langley might be driving while under the influence of intoxicating liquor. He was attempting to protect the public! The Mayor allegedly ordered a member of the Concord Police to make a false report. Mr. Quinn denied that he ordered a police officer to make any false report or arrest.

Momentarily, the issue was that Mayor Quinn was suspended and such an action was invalid and illegal. I argued before Judge Hugh Bownes of the Merrimack County Superior Court that New Hampshire had no cases on point and if the power to suspend was treated lightly, we could anticipate chaotic conditions in Concord and elsewhere in the State. This man had committed no misconduct as Mayor. He stole no money and committed no crime and the City Charter gave the Aldermen no authority without first providing a formal removal action.

The Concord Police Chief, Walter Carlson, charged that Mayor Quinn ordered one of his police officers to wait for editor James Langley outside the Brick Tower Motel and arrest him (if he drove his vehicle). The officer reported that Mr. Langley was not there.

The City was represented by two lawyers in this matter; Fred Upton, who represented Chief of Police Walter Carlson, and William Maynard, a former Attorney General, represented the City of Concord.

Judge Hugh Bownes ruled that the Aldermen and the City of Concord did not have the power to suspend Mayor Quinn and declared such an action invalid and illegal and Mayor Quinn was entitled to a formal hearing. He was reinstated.

We were involved in a three day hearing August 2-4, 1967 at the Concord City Hall and the Aldermen voted 13 to 1 to ouster Mayor Quinn. A large crowd was present during the hearing and some of this crowd was hostile. The Aldermen were removed from the City Hall with police protection and taken home in paddy wagons.

I brought a Petition for Certiorari to reinstate the Mayor in the Merrimack County Superior Court on August 4, 1967. A hearing took place on Tuesday, August 15th. I represented Herbert Quinn and Arthur Bean, Attorney Stanton Tefft and City Solicitor Charles Keeley represented the City of Concord. I called the necessary witnesses and Judge Hugh Bownes on Friday, August 18, 1967, re-installed Mayor J. Herbert Quinn to his elective office for the second time.

The judge in his ruling, among other things, stated that none of the 14 members of the Board of Aldermen were disqualified on grounds of prejudice, participating in the conspiracy or pre-judging of the charge and some may not have had the right to sit on the impeachment panel. He also stated that careful consideration and analysis of the facts did not constitute such misconduct in office so as to legally justify the removal of Mayor Quinn from office.

This case was appealed to the New Hampshire Supreme Court, who upheld the ruling of the Board of Alderman. On September 20, 1967, the Court unanimously upheld the ouster of Mayor J. Herbert Quinn by the Board of Alderman.

This was not the outcome we had hoped for, but it was a hard fought battle and there was nothing else that we could have done.

In February of 1968 my personal friend, Governor John King, appointed me to the Governor's military staff for the third time. My sweet wife, Carolyn, and I attended the Governor's Ball on February 2nd, 1968 in Manchester, New Hampshire. As we left the house that night I remember how proud and excited our children were. They loved my uniform and the beautiful gown worn by their mother.

It was a wonderful evening, full of fun, friends and food, one that brings a smile to my face even now.

On November 11th I served as 1967 Veterans Day Parade Marshal leading the annual parade In Dover. It was a four-division parade with some 1,500 involved in the parade and watched by an estimated crowd of 20,000.

This was right before I began work on the J.S. case. In this case I was called to represent a 22-year-old Newmarket man, J.S., for murder committed early February last year. On January 29, 1968, the defendant entered a plea to second-degree murder and got life from Judge Thomas J. Morris.

In those days, this usually meant he would be paroled after 16 years.

An eyewitness to the murder was Newmarket Police Officer Sgt. Howcroft, who saw the defendant holding the victim, age 16, with a gun in a wooded area when he arrived. When the officer ordered St. Pierre to let go of the girl's arm, St. Pierre fired two shots into the girl. When the officer fired at him, Jimmy St. Pierre fired another shot at the girl, who was lying wounded on the ground. I used a psychiatrist, Dr. Harry Kozol of Boston. The doctor was good and he helped reduce the first-degree murder charge to second degree. Attorney Wayne Mullavey, who later became a Superior Court Judge, served as co-counsel.

I tried a jury trial on February 1st and 2nd, 1968 in the Rockingham County Superior Court in Exeter. My client, age 28, had been indicted for reckless driving of a motor vehicle with death resulting. The jury found him guilty. The County Attorney, Glen Graper, asked he be sent to State Prison one to three years. I won the argument with Judge Thomas Morris. He received one year in the County House of Corrections, all suspended, and went home.

At this point Carolyn, had been suffering with cancer for over two years. She and I had been blessed with three beautiful children and they were the light of our lives. We loved spending time with them and watching them grow and change. We loved watching each of them develop their own personalities as well as likes and dislikes. Most of all, we just loved being a family.

That February we decided to take what had become our yearly trip to Miami. It was great to have a break from the harsh northern winter and soak up some sun before spring made it to the great white north. We enjoyed the 13-day vacation and visited a number of places with our children.

We did not realize it then, but this was to be our last vacation as a family.

On March 26th, 1968, I defended a male, age 22, for rape before a jury in the Strafford County Superior Court. He was found Not Guilty by the jury on the rape charge, but was found guilty of simple assault. He was sentenced to six months at the House of Corrections, all suspended, and he went home. The trial lasted three days.

By Easter it was apparent that my wife's health was taking a turn for the worst. That Sunday, with our children all dressed in their new outfits, my wife was simply too ill to accompany us to Mass. I took the children by myself, but spent the entire time praying for my wife. I think that I knew then that our time together was limited.

Less than two weeks later on Monday April 29th, I started my day just as I would any other. My family and I had breakfast together before all heading our separate ways.

My day was full, with a busy morning at the law office followed by an afternoon in court in Massachusetts. I defended a young lady charged with accessory to larceny. The case was tried and she was found NOT GUILTY. I was paid $500.00. I felt buoyant as I drove to my law office at 450 Central Avenue.

It was a good day.

After I arrived back at my office late afternoon, I called my home to speak to my wife, but was surprised when my mother answered the phone.

She was crying.

In those moments it was as if time stopped and the world quit turning on its axis. Through her tears my mother told me that my dear wife had been taken to the hospital in Boston by my brother-in-law late that morning. They wanted to call, but they also wanted to protect me. To give me just a few extra moments of peace before the bottom dropped out of my world.

I cried.

I was emotionally devastated. One of my secretaries took me home after I spoke to my mother-in-law by telephone. Mrs. Mosca told me that Carolyn was at the Hospital for Women in Boston and her father, Tom Mosca, was there with her. My sweet wife had always tried to protect me. She didn't want them to bother me. Can you imagine?

When I arrived to my home at my mother was there in charge of my children. They looked so small that day and I remember thinking "How will they be able to handle this?" For even then I think I knew what was coming.

I called the Hospital for Women every few minutes. I was informed each time that she was resting comfortably, but they were still unable to provide her with a private room. None were momentarily available.

I was going out of my mind, unable to eat, unable to stop pacing even for a moment. I was so wound up that my family called Dr. Bernard Manning, who came to our home and injected a sedative to calm me down. They knew that I had to be able to hold it together, for my children's sake if not my own.

My brother-in-law along with my brother Sam, drove me to Boston. When I arrived at the Hospital for Women in Brookline, it was wait - wait - wait. I was told that the doctors were trying to save her life and that she had been moved to a private room.

That was all.

They would not tell me anything else and they would not let me see her.

It was now Tuesday, April 30th, 1968, after midnight. As I sat there in the hospital with Carolyn's father I didn't know how I would face what was to come. How would I get out of bed each morning? How would I hold my children and tell them that everything would be okay when I wasn't sure that was the truth? How would I go on without my wife?

I didn't know what to do, what to say. I just existed as the clock ticked one minute into the next. At some point I inquired if my wife had been given the final rites of the Catholic Church and I was told she had about 4:00 p.m. yesterday.

This should have offered comfort, but it did not.

At about 12:45 a.m., I was finally permitted to see Carolyn. I walked in the room and there was my beautiful, radiant wife propped up against the stark white of the hospital bed. She looked beautiful and I told her so, I told her how much I loved her. She appeared happy to see me and was more concerned with our children than her own grave condition. She wanted to know how their day had been.

We were together for about ten minutes. She was passing her fingers through my hair and spoke to me for a moment or two, and before I could respond, her hand dropped.

She was gone. That quick. In the span of a single second, my life was forever changed, and it would never be the same.

Within seconds I was pulled away from her bedside as doctors and nurses swarmed the room. They told me she had a fighting chance.

They were wrong.

At 2:10 a.m. my wife left this world. She took one last deep breath and expired.

I was being tortured by this moment. One that I knew that I would face but could never be fully prepared for its horrible reality.

I wish that it had been me instead of her. It was the end of the world for me. The end of a dream come true.

At some point I was allowed to see her lifeless body along with my father-in-law. Standing there watching tears rolled down the face of a man that I had never known to cry was a whole new level of pain. She was my wife. She was his child. She was our world.

We left the hospital and went to Watertown to his home in the early morning and when we broke the news to Carolyn's mother. What a tragic moment for all of us.

My sister came for me and drove me back from Watertown to Dover. I got home just after 8:30 a.m. My mother was at home with my little daughter.

I called two secretaries to my home and they helped me and my sister, prepare for a funeral. We selected a beautiful blue dress that was one of my wife's favorites. My brother, Joseph, selected a mahogany casket. We selected Wiggins Funeral Home because it was the largest funeral home in Dover and with the understanding that no others would share the building with my wife during her wake. I selected the pallbearers and my secretaries contacted them with my personal address book, which included relatives, friends of Carolyn, as well as mine.

Later that same morning the moment came that I had dreaded. I had to tell my children what had happened. I broke the news to my children. It was a terrible duty. I explained to them that their mother was very sick and God did not want her to suffer any longer, so God had taken her to heaven. We cried together, their presence my only comfort.

On the night of my wife's wake the funeral home was packed. My entire family was there to support me as well as relatives from Massachusetts and many, many other people.

While it was nice to see how loved my wife had been, the entire event was torture. I was bleeding inside. No matter who I talked to, or where I turned the reality was that my wife, the woman I loved with every breath laid in a casket.

There was no escaping that. I tried to sleep, but could not. Tried to get drunk but could not. My reality was unacceptable and I could not change it. This was too much to face, three motherless children and the death of my wife.

I don't know what I did on May 1st and 2nd, 1968. I was at my wife's wake all afternoon and evening both days with my sweet children, my family, Carolyn's parents, relatives and many,

many friends, including schoolteachers, lawyers, judges, police and court officers. Their faces were all blurred by the pain.

On Friday morning, May 3rd, 1968, my wife's body was taken to St. Joseph's Catholic Church in Dover for a Solemn High Requiem Mass. The church was packed. The funeral procession included Governor and Mrs. John King, U.S. Senator and Mrs. Tom McIntyre, six vehicles of flowers and a procession of some 75 motor vehicles. All schools were closed for the day. My three children and I followed her casket out of the church, tears flowing down my face the entire day.

This is what the end of the world must feel like. Even now I haven't recovered from this moment. Time has passed and the pain has dulled, but it will never fully fade.

In the next five weeks, my sister took a leave of absence from work to take care of my children. She and her husband lived at our home with us. In addition, my mother, was at our home every day, including overnight stays. We also had a full-time housekeeper and I was with my sweet children every possible moment I could. I tried to surround my children because I never wanted them to feel alone. I knew the pain that they felt, and I never wanted them to feel as if the rest of their family, including their father, had left them along with their mother.

In what felt like a continuing assault on my sanity, U.S. Senator Robert Francis Kennedy of New York state, who was campaigning for U.S. President, was shot in the head by an assassin's bullet at the Hotel Ambassador in Los Angeles, California on June 4th, 1968. He was a younger brother of President John F. Kennedy and I knew him personally. It was an emotional shock to all of us. It is a shame to destroy such good and talented people.

My wife's death shook me to my very core. In the days that followed it was difficult simply to force myself out of bed each morning, and if not for my children, I might have failed in even that simple task. But as much as I hated the fact, life continued to move forward.

I could not give up my law practice when I had a young family to raise, and I could not expect my family to put their own lives on hold indefinitely. So, I hired a young woman, a 24-year-old college graduate, as a live-in nanny. My sister and her husband stayed for a few more weeks to help with the transition and my mother continued to come every day.

She was provided with a car to take my children wherever they needed to go. She would be my right hand when it came to them, and I need someone who I could depend on.

On June 21st, 1968, my four-year-old daughter graduated from Mrs. Carberry's kindergarten class. We were so proud of her and it was nice to have something positive to celebrate. I felt that it was important to try and make life feel normal to my children, to give them the routine that they were used to and to keep living as a family.

So that is what we did.

In June of 1968 we took a vacation to Lake George. The Nanny stayed in one room with my two daughters, while my son and I stayed in another. In August we went to Quebec, again accompanied by the Nanny. Slowly the children began to smile again and then they began to live, to enjoy their days and their surroundings.

That is what my wife would have wanted for them.

One of the more interesting cases from this time was a D.T., 35. T. was accused of murder in the shooting death of L.C., 54. The victim, a merchant seamen who maintained a camp in the Lord Hill section of Effingham, was shot in the back.

Despite my best efforts, we could not negotiate so the case went to a jury trial commencing June 4th and ending June 11th, 1968. We claimed that the shooting was accidental because this was one of several shots fired by the defendant to signal the victim. Because they had no telephones in the camp, this was a way to signal each other. The jury didn't buy it. Instead they found him guilty of first-degree manslaughter and he was sentenced to three to five years in prison. On good behavior, in those days, he would have to serve two years before being eligible for parole.

My life was always busy. I was a busy trial lawyer with a thriving practice, but my children were my top priority. They had to be. Always.

My heart was shredded, but my life had to continue.

So, I worked.

In late October, I tried a jury trial in the Strafford County Superior Court in the matter of State v. W. C., who was indicted for rape. After a four-day trial, he was found NOT GUILTY on October 22, 1968.

Next I started a jury trial in the Strafford County Superior Court on Tuesday, November 12th, 1968. The case of State vs. P., a man charged with armed robbery.

By this time, the Nanny had left the position of housekeeper and of taking care of my children. An older woman replaced her. Things were going fine until Wednesday, November 13th,

1968. That morning, during the middle of the second day of trial, one of my secretaries came to the courtroom to tell me that they received a call from the new Nanny. Apparently she had left her job and was calling from Maine. This meant that in just a few short hours my four-year-old daughter, would be dropped in front of our home by her nursery school teacher in heavy drifts of snow, with the house locked and no one home.

I imagined a potential disaster!

My other two children, would be coming home during the noon hour by taxi, again with no one home and arriving to a locked house. The judge stopped the trial and I raced home with one of my four secretaries to serve as a babysitter. I immediately called my mother, who came to my house to be with the children while I could figure out what was going on.

I searched through the house and quickly figured out that while the Nanny had left no note to explain her actions, it was clear that she had no intention of returning. All her clothing and personal belongings were gone along with the petty cash of over $100.00. Also, she had taken the time to clear all of the liquor out of the cabinet.

A true model of what a human being should strive for.

In the meantime, I returned to the Strafford County Superior Court to continue with the trial of State v. P. My father-in-law and mother-in-law joined us in filling in for the care of my children for the next several weeks until I was able to replace the Nanny.

The case of State v. P. was negotiated on the third day and he changed his plea and was sentenced to two to five years.

On January 29th, 1969, as President of the Strafford County Bar Association, we gave Judge Robert Carignan a banquet, which I had organized. Some 400 persons attended the affair to honor him at the Elks Lodge in Rochester. T. Casey Moher, the Strafford County Attorney, introduced me to award our judge a plaque. He informed the audience that I was not only the former Strafford County Attorney and now President of the Strafford Bar Association, but by far the youngest looking lawyer because of my hairdo, which drew thunderous laughter.

On Saturday, February 20th, 1969, I drove my three children to New York City. We stayed there for four days with my good friend Dr. Eddie O'Rourke and his family. Eddie was the Public Health Commissioner of New York City at the time and it was nice to have his family living close by once again.

On one early evening, I took my children to Radio City Music Hall to watch the Rockettes on stage. Dr. O'Rourke had his chauffeur drive my children and me in his public health limousine from the Bronx to lower Manhattan to do some sightseeing. We were all delighted with this experience. We were dropped off at Macy's Department Store where I purchased Easter outfits for my three children and other clothing and gifts. After we ate at a nearby restaurant, we took a taxi back to the O'Rourke residence. That evening, I took my children to Times Square to see the movie, "2001 Space Odyssey."

This kind of time with my children is what I lived for during those days. I loved having the four of us together and I never felt closer to Carolyn than when I held my children close.

My time as a lawyer, while satisfying, couldn't even come close but it was interesting.

Like the time that I was invited by good friend and fellow attorney, Arthur Reinhart of Portsmouth, to join him in the defense of C. W., age 47. The defendant was indicted for first-degree murder in the slaying of his wife. She was at the time eight months pregnant with a third child and had been physically assaulted.

The defendant's story was pretty straightforward. He denied the assault on his wife and he took the stand stating he had been out that night drinking and came home at about 1:00 a.m. and found his wife lifeless. He then ran to check the two young children in their bedroom to see if they too had been assaulted but they were sound asleep. He did not call the police for fear that they would blame him for killing her.

He then decided to take his own life.

He told the jury that he went upstairs, locked himself in the bedroom and laid down to "die" next to his dead wife and unborn child. He took a number of sleeping pills after he wrote a note to his stepson asking not to be disturbed. He said, "She was my world."

The note he wrote to his stepson was found attached to the front door of the home. Friends who had come to play cards discovered the defendant and his wife's pregnant body in their locked bedroom at about 8:00 p.m. the next day, March 30th. The first-degree murder charge had been reduced before the trial began to second-degree murder. The jury trial took place in the Rockingham County Superior Court in Exeter and lasted eight days. I served as attorney-in-chief. We introduced nine witnesses who testified that C. W. and his wife lived a harmonious happy life together and none observed that there was any friction between them.

The jury found him guilty of second-degree murder on May 15th and Judge George Grant, Jr. sentenced him to life. In those days, he would probably be eligible for parole in 16 years or so.

On Wednesday, October 22nd, 1969, I started a jury trial defending State v. R. L. in the Strafford County Superior Court on an indictment of accessory to a bad check. On the second day of jury trial he was found NOT GUILTY.

On Thursday, October 30th, 1969, I took three of the four secretaries with me to go to Hawthorne College at Antrim, New Hampshire, where I was guest speaker in the Sociology class on the subject of criminal law. After the lecture, my secretaries and I had lunch with Jere Chase, President of the college. He was my former football coach and Science teacher at Berwick Academy in 1936-37.

On November 10th, 1969, I purchased a green 1970 Pontiac Bonneville four-door sedan. The next day we had a four-division veterans parade here in Dover, New Hampshire at 6:30 p.m. I not only organized the affair with a good committee, but I also served as Grand Marshal. I was in my Disabled American Veterans uniform and my children enjoyed watching the affair.

These were the peaceful days. I wish that all days could be peaceful.

On Sunday, December 7th, 1969, right after I had finished dinner with my three children, my mother, my mother-in-law and father-in-law, all hell broke loose to interrupt our tranquil day. I was asked to defend K.H., age 19, wanted for manslaughter for killing one of his own friends in his apartment. After numerous telephone calls with his parents and the Rochester Police, I drove to Haverhill, Massachusetts to meet the defendant. He agreed to surrender himself and I drove him to the Rochester Police Station. He was also wanted by the U.S. Marines for leave without authority for the past four months.

I defended him for manslaughter for the fatal shooting of L.M., age 16. It appeared that the defendant had invited a number of friends to his apartment for a party and shortly after midnight, they were eating pizza and drinking beer. The police alleged that the defendant pulled out a 22-caliber rifle and pointed it at the victim, who was sitting on a bed. The victim said, "I hope it isn't loaded." The defendant pulled the trigger and the bullet hit the victim in the face.

However, five young women, between the ages of 14 and 18, were my witnesses to the shooting and they all gave evidence as follows: the victim picked up the rifle and checked it to see if it was loaded. He pulled the trigger several times to check out the gun. Nothing happened. He then handed the gun over to the defendant and told him the gun was not loaded. Then the defendant pulled the bolt of the gun back and pulled the trigger himself a couple of times and nothing happened. He then pointed the gun at the victim's head and said "Don't worry, it isn't loaded" and pulled the trigger and the gun exploded and the victim fell to the floor.

Finally, after he waited in the Strafford County Jail for trial, the case was nol prossed by the Attorney General's Office on April 1, 1970. He was turned over to the U.S. Marines and taken back to California.

In December 1969, my seven-year-old daughter, got to take her first trip to the Portsmouth Hospital. She was scheduled to have her adenoids removed the following day and she was very nervous about what was to come. My in-laws, came with us and we all tried to make the experience as easy as possible for my little girl.

I stayed at the hospital most of the day and I assigned the extra care to a friend a registered nurse. The operation was on December 9th and when I was allowed to see her, she looked so small and tired. Trust me when I say that this is not a sight that any father wants to see, even when you know that the child is fine. Your heart and your head will tell you two very different things. My other children came to the hospital to join me. I stayed at the hospital until 9:00 p.m. The following day it was my pleasure to go to Portsmouth to drive her home. She had been so brave, sweet and beautiful.

At this point I had a very difficult decision to make. Up until now, much of my time and energy had been spent running for and participating in public service. And, even now several friends were asking me when and if I planned on running again.

The answer was no. Another dream was forced to die. I loved politics, and I hoped to run again some day, but now was not the time.

I loved my time in public office, but at this point, my main duty was to take care of my three children. I maintained a great interest in politics and the Democratic Party, but I could not abandon my responsibility of caring for my children. Running for statewide public office required campaigning seven days a week from early morning to late at night.

Practicing law gave me a means to support them and was a source of great personal joy.

For my next case I defended J.M., age 18, on a charge of first-degree murder in the shooting of A.B., 48. Allegedly, the victim drew a knife and inflicted a wound on the defendant. Then, later that day, the defendant purchased ammunition and met the victim by the railroad tracks near a familiar fishing place known to both men. As soon as he saw the victim he fired one shot into his head and then unloaded the rest of the ammunition into the fallen body. I claimed that the police procured a confession from the defendant illegally. By January 23rd, 1970, I was back in the Rockingham County Superior Court. The doctors classified the defendant insane, and they ruled that he must have been insane at the time of the incident. The defendant was committed to the New Hampshire State Hospital and the murder charge was withdrawn.

I enjoyed the law practice and I was lucky to find myself inundated with work. For example, on Monday, January 26th, 1970, I went to the Auburn District Court on a case which was continued. Then I went to the Superior Court in Exeter for 1:00 p.m. on a motion hearing in the case of State v. P.L. From there it was back to the office where the reception area was crowded with ten separate clients - rush - rush - rush and then home to be with my children. We were together from 5:30 p.m. to 10:00 p.m. I permitted them to stay up an extra hour. My mother, who was doing the babysitting at the time, disagreed with me. They are my children and if I want to spoil them a bit, it was my pleasure. Plus, I liked having the time with them.

On January 27th and 28th, 1970, I tried a jury trial in the York County Superior Court, Alfred, Maine, State v. R.B. At about 5:15 p.m. on the second day, the jury returned a verdict of NOT GUILTY. After being with my sweet children briefly, I was at my law office from 7:00 to 10:00 p.m. with three of my four secretaries, at which time I had consultations with 12 different clients. My law office on occasion worked a second shift and many nights I was called on to try cases in night court.

On March 6th, 1970, M.M., a girl, age 21, from Trinidad, West Indies, arrived at the airport in Boston. She was Catholic and she would serve as a live-in housekeeper and babysitter to my children. I drove her to my father-in-law's and mother-in-law's home on James Street, Watertown, Massachusetts to meet everyone.

The following day my mother-in-law, Giovanina Mosca, came home to Dover with her to acquaint her to our home and to show her what her duties were as a live-in babysitter. The next morning the Nanny came to St. Joseph's Catholic Church with me and my three children.

On Friday evening, April 3rd, 1970, I attended the annual fund-raising dinner held at the Sheraton-Wayfarer Hotel in Manchester, New Hampshire. About 1,000 noisy Democrats attended. I and some six others were honored as past Democratic State Chairmen. I enjoyed the moment and it was nice to be recognized in this fashion.

On May 18th, 1970, I tried a jury trial in the Rockingham County Superior Court with Judge George Grant, Jr. presiding. B.B., Jr., 29, was charged with assault with intent to commit murder. He had been at the Ship Ahoy Café in Portsmouth, New Hampshire on February 11th, 1970 and shot the victim in the chest.

The victim survived.

The defendant pled guilty to a lesser- included offense of aggravated assault before the trial was concluded and he was sentenced to not less than one and not more than three years in the State Prison. My friend and then law associate,

Attorney Richard Krans, assisted me. He is a very intelligent and talented lawyer.

The Disabled American Veterans Convention took place in Dover that year. I was the Chairman of the affair and the 1970 Convention Yearbook was dedicated to my wonderful late wife, Carolyn Joanne Catalfo. The headquarters were at the Ramada Inn and the City of Dover was bedecked with flags. I personally enjoy this patriotic conclave.

I served as Parade Marshal and I loved every minute of it.

I agreed to defend a young man and his father in the Superior Court in Clarksville, Arkansas. They were charged with larceny of firearms. I hated to leave my children, but the case appeared challenging and exciting and it excited my professional ego. I had an Arkansas lawyer join me. By 7:15 p.m. on Friday I had the Court dismiss the cases.

I will admit to you that I led a very interesting life even for a lawyer. On Monday, October 5th, 1970, I tried a jury trial all day in the matter of State v. J.H. in the Strafford County Superior Court. On Tuesday, October 6th, 1970, the jury found the defendant guilty and while the jury was deliberating, I started a second jury trial in the case of State v. C. After 5:00 p.m. H. was sentenced to two to five years in the State Prison. On Wednesday, October 7, 1970, I first went to the Rochester District Court for a case scheduled as #1 so I could get back to the Superior Court on time. My client was acquitted for operating while under the influence of intoxicating liquor. Then I went to the Superior Court all day for the second day of jury trial. The next day, Thursday, October 8th, 1970, the C. case went to the jury at about 12:00 noon. I started another jury trial at 1:30 p.m. in the matter of State v. M.M. for armed robbery. In the middle of the afternoon the jury returned a NOT GUILTY verdict on the State v. C. case. On Friday,

October 9th, I tried the case of State v. M.M. most of the day. The case was continued until Tuesday, October 13, 1970, because of Columbus Day on Monday. On Friday during the noon hour, I settled the case of Estate of C. v. Traveler's Insurance Company for $52,000.00. Then, on Tuesday, October 15, 1970, the jury returned a NOT GUILTY verdict on State v. M.M. Not bad!

I love to practice law and enjoy the heat of battle. Additionally, on Saturday from 8:30 a.m. to 12:00 noon, I had consultations with over 30 clients at my law office nonstop.

We ran out of chairs.

Chapter 16:

Love Returns

Not long after the loss of my wife, I was approached by a lawyer friend of mine who had suffered a similar tragedy in his life. His wife had passed suddenly leaving him with small children to both raise and provide for. He gave me some very sound advice that I am grateful for to this day.

He told me to date.

To make a point and take time for myself even when it would feel wrong to do so. He even admitted to me that his own biggest mistake had been to lock himself away in the role of provider and ignore his own need for companionship.

I'll admit that it wasn't the easiest advice to take. Especially at first. But nights are long when they are spent all alone, and eventually I began to creep my way back out into the dating world.

The dates I went on at that point were just for fun, for companionship. I was trying to ease my own pain and there was no way I was even thinking about looking for a wife or any type of long-term commitment. My commitment was to my children.

I remember hearing the song *Help Me Make It Through the Night* and listening to it over and over again for no other reason that it explained so clearly how I felt.

But even with all this rolling through my head and going on in my life I was soon forced to ask myself a very important question.

Do you think that it is possible to find love twice in your life?

I didn't. Perhaps I wasn't open to loving again because the pain of loss was so sharp and raw in my heart. I knew the reward, but I also knew the sharp cost that waited for me was too steep of a price to pay.

That all changed three years later in the Spring of 1971 when I met a girl named Gail Varney. Gail had stopped by to visit her mother, a lady who worked in my office building, and I couldn't help but notice her. From the moment I saw her I was mesmerized. She was 22, an only child and was studying to be a teacher at the University of New Hampshire.

I asked her out. Can you blame me? It was like a compulsion I simply couldn't ignore. But she wouldn't hear of it and I couldn't really blame her. We were an unlikely pair after all. Me with three children and her still working on her own degree, just starting out in life.

Three weeks later I saw her again. Again at her mother's office and again she drew me to her like a magnet. This time when I asked her out to lunch she agreed.

I don't know what came over me, but I literally forgot about a criminal case scheduled in the Durham District Court at 1 o'clock that very same day. Luckily my law associate, Dick Krans, was onsite and able to take over the case for me. Not only did he take it over, but he also won, so two strokes of luck for me in the very same day!

When I returned to the office at 4:00 p.m. my four secretaries were giggling and teasing me unmercifully. It was the only time in my entire career that I forgot to go to court!

Love flew into my life in the span of a single afternoon and I could spend another 300 pages telling you how much Gail has meant to my life.

Do I love Carolyn any less? Not at all.

Have I forgotten her? Not even a little.

But my time with her was destined to end. Not through our own doing or decisions, but through things that were far beyond our control. The 22 years we were blessed with on this earth were and are precious to me.

She was there when I started my career and together we built the family that I still love.

But then she was gone and that chapter was closed against my will.

Gail came into my life at a different stage. I was 52 years old and well established with a family to care for and a career. She was raised in a different generation. She had the love, patience and attitude that fit into my life as it was when we met.

And I am pleased to share with you that as I write this now we are sharing our 41st year together.

Gail did become a teacher for 12 years and later obtained her Master's in Education from UNH. She then left teaching and went to law school in Boston. In 1988 we married, she graduated from and passed the New Hampshire Bar followed by the Massachusetts Bar in February of 1989.

We are partners in life and in work because we click. We have the same sense of humor, we laugh, we share sorrow, we have seen each other through all the ups and downs that life has had to offer. We are each other's biggest fans and we are inseparable....a team in every sense of the word.

We have seen our share of victories and heartaches but we help each other along the way through all of life's celebrations and trials.

I never expected to get old...or should I say *infirmed*. I'm 94 as I write this and quite happy about that fact. Especially when you consider the alternative!

I think Gail was waiting for me to gracefully retire, but when at 90 I was still pulling a 60-hour workweek, it was time for us to have *the talk*!

I still have the passion for the law and for trial work, but physically my back and legs were slowing me down. I had to face that frailty of life, but I wasn't sure I could let it all go. Together we decided to close the office, sell the house and move our life to Gatlinburg, TN.

Quite a jump isn't it?

Why Gatlinburg? Because it is a wonderful and captivating place!

Gail and I have traveled extensively. We have been fortunate enough to see the world by land, air and sea, but no other place has captivated us quite like this little county tourist town tucked away in the Smoky Mountains. To put it in perspective, Gatlinburg has 3,700 residents, but 10 million visitors!

For us it offer the 4 seasons we had grown to love in New England but with a much milder winter and a whole host of interesting sites and activities.

When I started as a young lawyer I wanted to establish my practice in Miami, but Carolyn did not want to leave her parents. I loved the energy of the cites, life and action. We have that here in Gatlinburg. Even if I can't do everything I would like, its an environment that is always moving and changing.

Gail and I were both admitted to the TN bar. I was admitted at age 91 upon the recommendation of judges I was still practicing in front of. Our good friend, Attorney William Shaheen, who seems to know everyone everywhere, got us our Tennessee sponsors. Today we are still active members of the New Hampshire and Tennessee bars. Gail is still active in Massachusetts and inactive in D.C..

What do we do to keep busy?

Well, I am writing this book! And Gail, she does occasional pro bono work. I am still amazed that I was finally able to let it all go, but what a blessing that has been.

I love this time with Gail. It is a luxury to have time with my wife without the pressures of a career pressing in from every side. I stay involved with the law, politics and current events, but they no longer determine my day-to-day life. Instead we take the time to explore the area, enjoy new friends and enjoy our time with each other.

Gail has been by my side thru all the expected and unexpected times of my life as I have been in hers.

There are still times when I think back to that summer of my youth when I allowed a gypsy to read my palm on a dare. Two loves, she told me, two happy and successful marriages that each blessed me in their own way. I laughed at her then, but she was right. There is a happily ever after and I have found it with Gail.

As for my children, they grew up and have families of their own now. Two are lawyers, like me, and the third is a college professor. I have two grandsons, and two granddaughters with two of the four already in college.

Looking at them now I can say that I am proud of myself and of my parents. If they had not pushed out of their comfort zone none of this would have happened. They had the strength to push for a better life, not only for their children, but for mine as well. For my grandchildren and the generations to come.

The other option would be for me to have grown up a poor farmer in Italy like so many of my relatives who live there still to this day. Let me clarify that by saying I would have ended up as a very *bad* very *poor* farmer in Italy.

I have no talent for farming!

As to me, if I had not have pushed out of my comfort zone and dared to challenge convention by first going to high school, second going to college and third going to law school, I would have remained a factory worker for the rest of my natural life.

It's even likely that my children would have done the same. They wouldn't have been able to be educated in private schools or attended the college of their choice. And who knows what their lives would have held for them.

By coming to America my parents gave the next generation a chance. A chance to find their own dreams and a chance to go so much further than we would have been able to go in Italy.

I for one am glad they took that chance.

Chapter 17:

My Philosophy

I've been asked many times in my life a version of the following questions:

- "How did you succeed where so many others have failed?"
- "How did you overcome these obstacles?"
- "What is your secret?"

or perhaps better put

- "What is your philosophy?"

The truth is that I didn't have one. At least, not at first. I just instinctively move forward, live my life and problem solve.

Well, it probably won't surprise you that the answer is usually satisfactory to those asking the questions. So I decided to organize my thoughts into a list of sorts. And, since everything these days seems to be broken down into a "Top 10," I've also decided that I'm going to give you my very own "Top 10."

As in **Fred's Top 10 Philosophies for Life!**

1. **God**

I would have to put God first in all things. I do believe in him and I do believe that he has had a hand in my life right from the very beginning. There were times in my life that all I had was faith and trust in the Lord above.

No one gets a perfect life. Remember that.

And, it's not what happens to you that defines, you but rather how you react to it that matters. How you are able to cope, deal and overcome the highs and lows that life has to offer. I was raised in the church. I respect the church and I believe religion can help you in your darkest hour no matter what trial that may be. Trust in God above all else my friends, it will take you far.

2. Self Pity

Self Pity just isn't for me. I have had plenty of reasons to indulge in that particular past time during my life, but what would have been the point? What would it solve? What would it prove?

The answer? Nothing. Absolutely nothing.

And the reality is that no wants to hang around a whiner!

Remember, everyone has their issues to deal with and chances are good that yours aren't the worst in the room.

Yes, I have lived in poverty, had a plane crash, and lost my wife, but that does not make me some special wounded person that gets a pass when it comes to being a decent human being. There are, in fact, other people besides me on the planet. Getting wrapped up in your tragedy will eventually have you looking back on a life that hasn't been lived but one that has simply been suffered through.

That is where regret comes from my friends.

Personally I believe in opportunities rather than regrets!

I have dealt with the low points of my life in the best way that I knew how. Yet I never felt sorry for myself. Even when my wife died I felt worse for my children's loss than my own.

3. Critics

By now you must realize that the world is full of critics. The more prominent you get in life the more critics will come out of the wood work to bite at you.

Just remember this. Everyone has something to say and opinions are worth what you pay for them.

Personally I break criticism into two categories, constructive and destructive. If criticism is constructive, then instead of being offended, I take it as an opportunity to learn. Even if I don't agree with what I'm told, there may still be a lesson to pull from the moment. After all, if someone thought enough of me to try and help me then the least I can do is listen to what they have to say.

Destructive criticism I've built a resistance to. I view this as the critic's lack of character and nothing more. It's their problem, not mine. It makes them feel more important to take me down and by definition that is simply a form of bullying.

Here's the truth of the matter. If someone makes a habit of going around spouting off destructive criticism, then odds are good that they are nothing more than a loser with more faults than the last three people they put down.

4. Fear

Fear is a useless emotion unless you are standing on the railroad tracks watching a runaway train bear down on you. Fear can paralyze you. Most of the time it is baseless as the things you obsess about will never come to pass.

The best way to deal with fear? Ignore it. If you ignore it and push past it then eventually it will cease to exist all together.

I could have stayed in New Hampshire after graduating from high school and gone to UNH. It wouldn't have been much of a change and I would have been comfortable. I could even have lived at home.

I chose instead to go to the University of Alabama where I did not know a single soul. A northern in a southern university at a time when location mattered. I went to Alabama, I learned, I grew and I gained much in that single year, a year that would not have happened if I let fear rule my life.

Get out of your comfort zone, face your fears and face change. One thing I guarantee, change will fine you whether you want it to or not. And I've always found that it's far better to be proactive and live life to the fullest rather than waiting around for things to happen.

We get one shot at life my friends....there is no second chance.

5. Fate

I have always had an internal sense of knowledge about myself. I knew my present circumstances did not have to dictate my fate or my future. I also had the fortitude to push past the present toward the future that I wanted. I figured out what I needed to do, one step at a time, and then I pushed forward until I conquered it.

Fate is not about circumstance.

People often get wrapped up in one detail or another and create roadblocks to moving forward. Well, let me tell you this. You can either make the changes that you need, or you will find yourself one day older, one year old, one decade older, and still standing in the same spot.

Tell me this. Do you still want to be making the same old complaints about life 5 years from now? I thought not. So...do something about it! Get up, put one foot in front of the other and figure out what you need to do to change your life.

Break it down if you have to. Tackle one section at a time and don't even think about giving in, or giving up. Soon you'll be looking back at who you were in awe as you look ahead to a better life.

6. Forgiveness

I forgive offenses aimed at me. It's that simple. After all, the only person who suffers in lack of forgiveness is you. If I have known a person for years and know them to have my best interest at heart, then most of the time I assume that the offense was out of character, spawned from anger, frustration or some other emotional problem the person might have.

If someone is a repeat offender with little to no redeeming factors then move on. Put it in the past and leave there while you move forward to live your life. Trust me when I say that life is too short to allow people to torment you on a whim.

But no matter what it is always best to forgive.

7. Failure

Fear and failure, or fear of failure, is the biggest obstacle to success. I guess I should be grateful for it because if it didn't exist, then there probably would have been many more applicants fighting for my seat in law school!

No one wants to fail. But how many people never start, never even try, because they fear what might happen? Failure is a problem solving technique. Whatever you tried that didn't work is a lesson learned. Don't accept it as the end of the road, look at it like a chapter in the middle of the book and enjoy the journey.

Analyze what happened and find another way to approach the problem. After all, other people overcame the roadblock; just ask anyone who is successful. I promise they didn't get that way without a few bumps in the road.

Remember, don't give up and don't give in.

8. Entitlement

I hate to be the one to break it to you, but you aren't entitled to anything in this life. Sorry to disappoint, but that's the truth of the matter. If you want something, then you need to earn it, plain and simple.

If you want a promotion then do something to stand out from the crowd. Don't think that you have earned one simply by holding the crown of tenure. Sitting in the same seat for years on end does not a leader make!

So earn it! Improve yourself every chance you get. Take the time to learn a new skill, ask for more responsibility, help out a co-worker, do something constructive. Really it doesn't matter what you do.....just do something positive!

No thing is ever yours unless you have earned it.

9. Career

Find something you love and work at it. Try to constantly improve your skill set and be the absolute best that you can be at what you do.

Why?

Because when you do, others will notice.

If you feel weak in an aspect of your career, then seek out the answer. Take a course, ask for help, practice on your own time, the options for self-improvement are endless these days. Another good option is to learn from the elders in your field and find a mentor to guide you on your journey.

And remember that all careers will have their ups and their downs. But by taking the initiative and going the extra mile then you have the power to improve your standing no matter what situation you find yourself standing in.

Drive equals success. Complacency equals stagnation.

10.   Confidence vs. Ego

First off let me say that you will need a healthy dose of both to succeed in this world and sometimes you will have to fake it.

Like in a job interview. That is the perfect time for sweaty palms and nervous stutters, but it's your only chance to sell yourself. And you'd better be good at it because I promise that no one else will do it for you.

I have a lot of confidence and some would even say a big ego. But I also recognize that ego is often not on my side. The ego feeds its self even if it's not in your best interest.

Yes, I feel that I'm a great lawyer, but this idea does not come from ego. It comes from a lifetime of hard work, study and dedication to the career that I have chosen. Those facts give me the confidence to say that I'm a great lawyer because I have put in the time to be just that.

There is a difference between thinking you are wonderful and actually doing the work to be wonderful.

Confidence comes with competence and then ego should follow...not lead.

If you have made it to this point in the book, then you have read my story. You know the trials of my life and that there were plenty of opportunities for me to hold a grudge.

But to what end?

I could have held my father's words and actions against him until his dying day, but what would that have changed or helped? Maybe I would have felt some kind of vindication, but it would have been empty. And I would have missed out on so many wonderful moments with both my father and my family as a whole.

It is about letting go of the past and believing with all of your heart that you do not have enemies. Don't get me wrong, its not that I just forget about all of the negative things that have happened. I just choose to leave them in the past rather than carry them with me into the future.

I acknowledge that humans are imperfect. Even me! I know that there are times when I do or say things that are wrong. But I like to think that my good moments outweigh my bad ones.

Growing up, when I was made fun of or criticized, I made it a habit to look at the reason for the criticism rather than focus on the offense against me. If it was something that needed to be changed, such as the broken English of my youth, then I changed it. I did the work and changed my behavior for the positive.

After all, *my* actions are the only ones within my control. They are the only ones that sit on my conscious. The actions of others are their problems!

Today I look back on my life and I feel that I have done the best that I could do. I provided justice for my clients and ensured that each one was granted a fair trial. I treated those around me with respect even if I was not granted the same courtesy.

I will end with this. Like every good Catholic boy, I am very familiar and even comforted by the Lord's Prayer. It is the one prayer sent to us by God and it's simple words show us how we are to live ours lives each and every day.

In short, he sums it up nicely.

"And forgive us our trespasses,
As we forgive those who have trespassed against us."

Here is the question that I leave you with. At the end of this life we will all stand in front of our Lord, begging him for both his forgiveness and his mercy. If He were to turn the question and ask you, "what forgiveness and mercy did *you* give to others during your lifetime?"

Would you be prepared to answer?

ACKNOWLEDGEMENTS
to those that helped in preparing
my life history:

To Carrie Woods, a talented editor from Oolewah, TN who spent many hours editing this manuscript from a voluminous 1000 pages plus to its current form. (cbwoods907@gmail.com)

Patricia (DiCicco) Gower, my secretary from Dover, NH, for typing the first draft.

Kathy Vale, my secretary in Sevierville, TN.

Fred "Fritz" Wetherbee, writer and television host of "New Hampshire Chronicles".

Mrs. Jeannette (Wentworth) Varney for her reading of the draft and making various corrections.

Made in the USA
Lexington, KY
17 April 2016